8695

FATIMA TODAY

Rev. Robert J. Fox

Front and back cover illustrations by Patrick Diemer

CHRISTENDOM PUBLICATIONS
Crossroads Books
Route 3, Box 87
Front Royal, Virginia 22630

ISBN: 0-931888-11-5

This book has been read and approved by P. José Galamba de Oliveira, Canon of Sacred Theology, and Diocesan President of the Commission for the Causes of Jacinta and Francisco Marto, Leiria, Portugal.

Fr. Fox dedicates this book to the Immaculate Heart of Mary, whose son he wishes always to be in Jesus Christ. May this book serve to establish more fully devotion to the Immaculate Heart of Mary, the Mother of God and the Mother of us all.

Fr. Robert Fox, nationally known newspaper columnist and best-selling author, is the founder and director of the apostolic community of young men who aspire to the priesthood, known as the Sons of the Immaculate Heart of Mary. The SIHM are dedicated to serving Christ through the media.

CONTENTS

Foreword

This book aims to be much more than the story of Fatima. It seeks to penetrate the memoirs and official documents of Fatima and interpret them for our own times. The value of the book was happily recognized by the Rev. José Galamba de Oliveira, known in Portugal as Canon Galamba, who wrote its preface. To have a man of the distinction of Canon Galamba call this "an original book about Fatima" is an honor for which I am grateful, and recommendation enough. This priest theologian has played a great part in the Fatima events for many years, and has served as President Judge of the Commission for the Cause of Jacinta and Francisco.

Many books have been written about Fatima. Many of them simply repeat the same story in different words. In preparing this volume, I have not only studied documents on Fatima but also interviewed priest-theologians and Fatima scholars in Europe. This book was written upon the premise that Our Lady of Fatima brings a message from heaven for modern times; it is a message for the *world*, and one to which we must respond.

This is not a book simply to entertain. It brings a stimulating message, a call to action, challenging all to live the Gospels. It is not a story simply to edify the pious. It is a book to make uncomfortable the comfortable and to bring renewed hope, faith and love to those truly seeking Jesus Christ and His Church.

The story of Fatima has often been written, read, and even offered for entertainment by the secular media. Such stories have moved few to action and have bothered few consciences because they did not probe the depths of the message. Few have actually heard the call of heaven behind the story; few have realized that Fatima was a reaffirmation of the word of God, and therefore few have acted upon it. In my work as Director of the Fatima youth apostole in the U.S.A. called the Cadets of Our Lady of Fatima, I have seen thousands of youth in the United States and other countries meet in cells for prayer, study, and action according to the message of Our Lady of Fatima. In this book, I hope to probe the different aspects of Fatima chapter by chapter, showing how it affected the lives of the children and how the Church reacted, and reflecting upon the events of the world in the decades since God's Mother appeared on that mountaintop in central Portugal. One might say that this book attempts to explain Lucia's famous *Memoirs*.

In this book about Fatima, I hope many will discover for the first time the meaning behind the story. May they be open to God's graces so as to accept the challenge and *live* the message. If they discover the Good News which is Fatima, they will want to share this book with others.

Grateful acknowledgement is given to the Sanctuary of Fatima for permission to reproduce some of its pictures. I also thank Father Louis Kondor, S.V.D., Diocesan Postulator and presently International Vice Postulator for the Cause of Jacinta and Francisco, for providing us with rare and special pictures.

Father Fox

Preface

It is an honor for me to write a preface for this wonderful book; however, I have hesitated to do so because of my lack of expertise in the English language and because of the value of the book itself.

I must congratulate the author for the precious gift this book offers to all who will read it. It is not easy to write a book about Fatima without repeating what so many writers have written before, in the different countries and in several languages.

When reading this book we notice its value by the original way of writing about Fatima as history, and about Jacinta's life. Such a work could not have been done without deep meditation and without a serious study of the Fatima documents. The author reveals a great admiration for the lovely character of Jacinta; therefore he is able to give us a special, true and perfect "esquisse" of Jacinta that will be very useful for the apostolate among the young people. The knowledge of Jacinta's heart makes us better by her spiritual influence.

We must be convinced that the future of the Church and of the whole world is in the new generation's hands. The world will be tomorrow what the youth of today will make it. So, everything we could do in behalf of them will become a benefit for humanity tomorrow. I say to you: "Perhaps some oppositions and misunderstandings will come up with your way of living and apostolic work. Don't stop! Go ahead! If you keep on confidently, God will be with you and some others will join you very soon.''

I appreciate also the chapters on Communism or Marxism and the life and doctrine of Marx, Hegel and their friends. It appears to me to be an original work so that everybody can have a correct explanation of the nature of Marxism. In all, I thank God and our Heavenly Mother for the inspiration the author received from Heaven to do this work. May this book bring its readers to a deep devotion to little Jacinta in order to obtain from Heaven the miracles we need for her beatification and canonization.

P. José Galamba de Oliveira
Canon of Sacred Theology
Diocesan President of the Commission for the Causes
of Jacinta and Francisco Marto
Leiria, Portugal

Introduction

As the Introduction to this book, I quote D. Alberto Cosme do Amaral, the current Bishop of Leiria-Fatima, from a speech he gave in the Cova da Iria:

"The entire excellence of the Eucharistic Sacrifice comes from the Sacrifice of the Cross. Present in our midst, the Jesus of Calvary is the priest and the victim of the new altar. On Calvary He Himself offered Himself to the Father, while on the altar He uses His ministers. There His immolation was accomplished through the shedding of His Blood, where here it is sacramental, in virtue of the double consecration. This interior oblation, ever living in the Heart of Christ, even after His Ascension is, as it were, the soul of the Eucharistic Sacrifice.

"Let us call to mind the Servants of God, Francisco and Jacinta, who lived fully and in an exemplary manner this oblation of reparation. . . . The little shepherds identified themselves in such a striking manner with the Mystery of Christ, Priest and Victim. They captured and lived in a remarkable manner, if we remember that they were children, the necessity of reparation for personal sins and the sins of the world. If reparation does not constitute the kernel of the Message of Fatima, it is, nevertheless, one of its most salient aspects.

"Sin is an offense against God. Through it, man constitutes an end in himself; he seeks a particular or relative good instead of seeking the Supreme

11

Good which is God; he deviates from his ultimate goal; he closes himself to love; he upsets the order of the universe, which was originally created for the glory of God; he repels the friendship of Christ and wounds His Mystical Body which is the Church.

"Sin, which deprives God of His glory, which is the cause of suffering to Jesus and Mary, which introduces social disorders into the world, such as wars and crimes, requires reparation. 'What did she say?' someone asked Lucia. 'She said we must amend our lives, and not offend the Lord Our God any more, because He is already so much offended; that we are to pray the Rosary and ask forgiveness of our sins . . .' (Visconde de Montelo).

"The Fatima message identifies with the appeal to interior conversion, to change our lives, to return to the ways of love with a love ever greater, a total love, a contemplative and crucified love. The love of children is tender and compassionate. Jacinta said: 'Why don't you tell me to go and kiss Our Lord over there?' and 'Why is Our Lord nailed to a cross like that?'

"When Jacinta heard the story of Jesus' sufferings, she was moved to tears. 'Our poor dear Lord! I'll never sin again! I don't want Our Lord to suffer any more!' (*Memoirs*) Francisco preferred to pray alone, 'to think and console Our Lord, who is so sad.' When Lucia went to school he remained in the church with the hidden Jesus. When he fell ill, he would send his love to the hidden Jesus, and when he felt poorly he gladly suffered to console Our Lord. When his head ached, he offered it first of all to console Our Lord and Our Lady. He ardently desired to go to Heaven, there to console Our Lord and Our Lady very much (see *Memoirs*).

The lives of the Servants of God, Francisco and Jacinta, are unmistakably theocentric, like that of Francis of Assisi who roused the people of Umbria, its hills and valleys, with his cries: 'My God and My All! Love is not loved!' Why are our souls not filled with the fervor of love like these children of the Serra de Aire? Why are we so half-hearted and calculating in our giving of ourselves? Why do we continue to keep aloof in our living the radical demands of the Gospel? If we do not do as they did, we shall not become citizens of the Kingdom of Heaven. . . .

"We can see that the spirituality of the Servants of God, Francisco and Jacinta, is profoundly Trinitarian, rooted in the mystery of all mysteries— the Mystery of the Most Holy Trinity, reaffirmed by the Angel in 1916. It is, at the same time Christological. For them as for Christians of all time, Mary is the way which leads to Jesus, in the most direct and efficacious manner. In their love for Our Lady they learned to love Christ, in the Mystery of His Redemption and in the mystery of His Eucharistic presence. The Christ of the Cross, the Christ of the Host, polarized their hearts, their whole capacity of loving. Their spirituality is ecclesiological. The seers prayed and mortified themselves for the Holy Father.

"Jacinta never forgot that vision of the Vicar of Christ, in a very big house, kneeling by a table, with his head buried in his hands, weeping. Outside the house there were many people, throwing stones, cursing him and using bad language. One day I met Pope Paul VI, in an hour of great suffering, and he, clasping my hands in his, begged me with tears: 'Yes, yes, pray much for me.' Then I understood that the prophetic vision of Jacinta was being fulfilled to the letter in the person of that Pontiff who one day came as a Fatima pilgrim, just as little Jacinta so much desired. I understood, too, her loving and generous response to the call from heaven: 'Poor Holy Father, we must pray very much for him!' 'O Jesus, it is for the love of You . . . and for the Holy Father.'

"It is hardly necessary to say that the spirituality of the Servants of God, Francisco and Jacinta, is ardently Mariological. It was the vision of the Lady brighter than the sun—'Oh, what a beautiful Lady!'—that gave to the lives of the little shepherds the impulse towards the great transformations carried out in their simple and candid souls, and launched them definitively on the ways of self-giving, which denounce and condemn our tepidity and mediocrity.

"The spirituality of the seers, Francisco and Jacinta, bears the mark and signs of authenticity—it is Trinitarian, Christological, contemplative and apostolic. In it are admirably expressed the Mystery of Christ, the Mystery of the Church, the Mystery of Mary, illumined by the Mystery of the Trinity, the source of all mysteries. It carries out, in favor of humanity, the trajectory of the Church, the community of salvation, from God to God, bearing with it the universe redeemed by the Blood of the Lord.

"Let us thank the Blessed Trinity for the treasure granted to the Church and to humanity in the persons of these Their Servants, Francisco and Jacinta. Let us ask God that they may be glorified with the glory of His saints, inspiring the Holy Father to beatify them, a moment so anxiously awaited by the faithful of the whole world. In the midst of a society that is corrupt and corrupting, which makes no effort in safeguarding its best treasure— the candor and the smile of the child—the beatification of Francisco and Jacinta would raise the standard of Redemption and the beacon of hope for humanity which has lost faith in itself because it has lost faith in God.

"May the Blessed Virgin Mary be our Mediatrix in this cause—she who revealed herself before the delighted eyes of the three children. And may she help us also to become like the innocent and little ones of the Gospel, to whom the Lord gives wisdom to understand the hidden mysteries of the kingdom."

1.
The Story and the Message of Fatima

The town of Fatima lies atop a mountain of the Serra de Aire, at almost the exact center of Portugal. It was there that the Mother of God gave a message to three little shepherd children, a message for the entire world. We shall begin by introducing the children.

The oldest of the three was Lucia de Jesus Santos, the youngest child of Antonio and Maria Rosa Santos. She was born March 22, 1907, and baptized on March 30. Francisco and Jacinta de Jesus Marto were brother and sister, and first cousins of Lucia. The two families lived near each other in the village of Aljustrel, which is located in the parish of St. Anthony.

Francisco and Jacinta were the youngest children of Manuel and Olimpia Marto. Francisco and Jacinta's mother had remarried after the death of her first husband, who was a brother of Lucia's mother. Olimpia had two children from her first marriage, and by her second husband she had seven children. Francisco was born on June 11, 1908, and baptized on the 29th of that month. His youngest sister, Jacinta, was born March 11, 1910, and was baptized on the Feast of St. Joseph, March 19. The parents of both families were strict in the guidance of their children. Each family owned a little land which they cultivated for their living.

Before the apparitions, the children were quite ordinary. They were normal, healthy, and of happy disposition. They herded their parents' sheep in the countryside, and exposure to the sun and open air gave them a robust health. While they were good children, they had typical childhood failings.

Lucia was ten years old when Our Lady appeared to the three. She was much loved as the youngest in her family, but was by no means considered a beautiful child. She was plain-looking with brown hair, prominent teeth, and a large mouth. She was plump by nature. Her sparkling dark brown eyes reflected her magnetic personality which drew other children to her and won the love even of adults. Lucia had a lively spirit and was very much a leader.

Francisco, the next oldest of the three seers, was but nine at the time of the apparitions of Our Lady. He was handsome and was easily recognized as a brother of Jacinta. He had fair hair, dark brown eyes, and a gentle expression. Francisco was not a leader by temperament. He often lacked zeal in games and seemed indifferent whether he won or lost. He was passive but friendly, and easily obeyed the girls with whom he herded sheep.

Despite his gentle temperament, Francisco had many manly characteristics. The darkness of night in no way frightened him. He handled lizards and snakes fearlessly, winding them around a stick and even feeding them sheep's milk. He loved birds and would feed them crumbs from his lunch. His compassion for animals was shown in his protests to other boys who caught birds and robbed their nests. He once paid a boy to free a bird, and as it flew away, he instructed the little creature not to let itself get caught again.

Francisco, like Lucia, had a strong sense of honesty. As the story of Fatima unfolds, one learns that all three children were ready to die in the Administrator's boiling oil rather than tell a lie and deny the beautiful Lady's apparitions, or reveal secrets which Heaven had not authorized them to tell.

Olimpia once related a story about her son's honesty. On one occasion she had instructed Francisco to take the sheep to another's land to graze. He answered, "Are you going to make me steal?" Even though his mother slapped him on the ear for his response, Francisco took the sheep to the place only after receiving permission from the owner of the land—his godmother.

Jacinta, who was but seven years old when Our Lady first appeared, was an exceptionally beautiful child. Her light brown eyes and hair were quite fair for a Portuguese child, and her features were very delicately formed. Jacinta's personality was very different from that of her brother

Francisco.

Before the Mother of God appeared to the shepherd children, Jacinta had a disposition which in some ways made her the least attractive of the three. Being the youngest, she was the pet of the family—spoiled, to say the least. She was demanding and possessive and usually got her own way. If she did not get her own way at playing games, she would become sulkly and separate herself from the other children until Lucia restored her spirits, usually by giving in to her demands.

The association of the three children before the apparitions was based more on close blood relationship than on natural attraction. Lucia, with her strong personality, was not attracted to Francisco's quiet and submissive temperament. If Jacinta fared any better with Lucia, it may have been because the older girl at least admired Jacinta for demanding what she wanted. Not until after seeing God's Mother did the three develop a close affection for one another. This affection was to become deeply spiritual, and it has remained in the heart of Lucia all the long years she has had to remain on earth after the death of her cousins.

All three of the children loved music. Francisco spent hours sitting on a large rock, playing tunes with his little reed flute to which Lucia and Jacinta sang or danced. Lucia claims that before the apparitions, the young people of Fatima had an immoderate love for dancing.

Senhora Maria Rosa Santos, Lucia's mother, had a great respect for the authority of the parish priest. When a priest assigned to Fatima preached against dancing, it was especially Lucia's mother who forbade her older daughters to attend dances. This had an effect on the three shepherd children who had formerly developed their own dance games. Maria Rosa's strict compliance also influenced others in the village to obey the priest.

Francisco and Jacinta recognized the leadership ability of their older cousin Lucia, and they frequently sought her out to join them in their games. A favorite place to amuse themselves was at the well located in the "backyard," the lower part of the grounds near Lucia's home. There they would play dib-stone or buttons. After the apparition of the Angel, the well became a religious meeting place for the three children. There they would discuss spiritual things and pray. The well remains a place of pilgrimage to this day.

Because of her excellent memory, Lucia only needed to hear a story once and she could repeat it in great detail. This made her popular with all the neighborhood children, and they spent hours hearing her retell Bible stories she had heard from her mother. The account of the Passion of Jesus Christ especially interested the children, and it touched Jacinta deeply. Maria

Rosa herself told many stories on winter evenings as parents and children gathered around the fireplace. All this made for close family bonds, and provided an opportunity to instruct and form the children in the true Faith.

Maria Rosa's teaching gifts rubbed off on her youngest daughter who shared the truths of the Faith with all the children in the village. Village children sometimes came to Maria Rosa to hear her teach catechism. It is little wonder that Lucia was permitted to make her First Holy Communion and Confession at the early age of six. This permission is particularly noteworthy because the local parish priest was still requiring that children reach the age of ten or eleven years old before receiving these Sacraments. Until she reached the age of eleven, Lucia was required to renew her Solemn Communion each year with the First Communicants.

In her love for small children, Lucia would often gather up to fifteen children around her and teach them religious games. They imitated parish processions, ending these with "Benediction." The processions even moved through the village to the accompaniment of a children's band and the singing of hymns. In many respects, Lucia was a real leader of a prayer cell.

Lucia's games with the children were hindered when she reached her seventh year, as she had to take her sister Caroline's place in tending the sheep so that the older sister could become a wage earner. Francisco and Jacinta were very unhappy at this, and they begged their mother to permit them to take their flock and accompany Lucia during the day. However, Olimpia would not permit children so young to be gone all day in the countryside.

Each evening Francisco and Jacinta sat by the roadside to await their cousin's return, and Jacinta would greet Lucia by scattering petals of wild flowers over her. Then off the three would go to the threshing floor to await the appearance of the moon (Our Lady's "lamp") and of the stars (the "candles" of the angels). From their earliest years, their parents had instilled in the children a great devotion to these holy spirits, the angels.

A first unusual apparition was experienced by Lucia already in 1915, two years before the appearance of Our Lady. Lucia was about eight at the time, and was herding sheep with three other girls named Teresa Matias, Rosa Matias, and Maria Justino. It occurred after the noon lunch, when the children had begun to pray the Rosary. Suddenly the girls saw something in the shape of a person, like a white cloud with a sheet wrapped around it; it appeared over the tops of the trees which were at their feet in the valley below them.

This strange figure appeared twice during the days that followed. Lucia kept silent, but the other girls told about the events—only to be laughed at and reprimanded for lying. Lucia said that she would have forgotten about that first unusual experience had it not been for the later apparitions with their very definite shapes and messages, which took place when she was with Francisco and Jacinta.

Francisco was about eight and Jacinta just over six years of age when finally their mother gave in to their begging to accompany Lucia. About twenty sheep were placed in their charge, and off they ran to share the good news with their cousin. The three planned their daily meetings; the first out in the morning would wait at the Barreira Pond near the village. There the children would decide on the pasture land for the day.

During the day the hills echoed with their songs and games. The children found that "Maria," the name of God's Mother, was the word that echoed and re-echoed best through the hills. They sang secular songs of the village, but there were also favorites among hymns, such as "Virgin Pure," and "Angels, Sing with Me."

Their mothers instructed the children to be sure to say the Rosary each day while they herded their sheep. But they loved their games so much, and each day passed so quickly, that even the Rosary suffered, as they found a short cut to this prayer. A decade of the words "Our Father" and "Hail Mary," without the complete prayers, and they were through in no time! All this was to change when Our Lady instructed them as Mother and Catechist.

But first, the children received three visits from a beautiful angel. Being so very young, and lacking formal education, Lucia was not able to give a specific date when the first apparition of the Angel took place on a hill called the Loca do Cabeco. She said that it must have been spring. The Angel appeared to the children three times, the second time being about midsummer, and then finally in October or toward the end of September. At that time, as Lucia remembered, "We were no longer returning home for the midday rest."

As the purpose of this book is to present the *message*, rather than simply the *story* of Fatima, only a brief summary of these events is given in this chapter. Many other details on the apparitions of the Angel and Our Lady along with an explanation of their significance, are set forth later in the book.

The appearances of the Angel had a profound effect on the the children. Following the angelic apparitions, they spent long hours in their parish church on their knees, their heads bowed to the ground, saying the prayers taught them by the Angel. They offered up acts of mortification for the conversion of poor sinners. When the congregation left after Holy Mass, Lucia, Francisco, and Jacinta would remain. They would go around the interior of the church on their knees in penance. The Angel's message was taking effect, and the children were being prepared for the appearances and message of the Mother of God the following spring. What was to happen in the souls of these three children was not just for themselves, but rather for the whole world. Jacinta, the "bright star of Fatima," was to have a particularly significant role in the spread of the Fatima messages both during her short life and in the years after her death.

Each of the six visits of Our Lady was not long. The words she spoke were not many. Yet the message of Fatima, like the Scriptures, is so rich and so far reaching that many decades have not been sufficient time to digest it. Following is a brief summary of the wonderful events of 1917.

THE FIRST APPARITION
(May 13, 1917)

In 1917, the Portuguese people were living in an explosive political and social atmosphere. In addition, they were suffering from World War I, with many of their husbands, sons, and lovers dying in battle. Nevertheless, May 13th of that year was a lovely Sunday, and Lucia, Francisco, and Jacinta went straight home after the Sacrifice of the Mass to take their sheep to the Cova da Iria. Animals must be fed on Sundays as well as on the other six days of the week. In reality, it was little work for the three shepherds, for their days at pasture were spent in song and games, enjoying one another's company.

The day was clear, with no clouds to be seen in the sky. But suddenly, there came a flash of lightning. In that mountainous part of Portugal it is possible for an approaching storm not to be seen on the other side of the mountain. As usual, Lucia was the leader in giving the signal for the children to gather the sheep and return to their homes in Aljustrel. The children guided the sheep down the hill. About halfway down, they saw another flash of lightning.

After taking but a few steps further, they saw a Lady over a little holm oak tree. She was dressed in white, more brilliant than the sun, radiating light brighter and more intense than that from a crystal glass filled with clear water and penetrated by the most dazzling rays of sunlight. Amazed, they stopped before the apparition; it was about a meter and a half away—so close that the three of them were actually within the light which the beautiful Lady radiated. Then she spoke: "Do not fear; I will not harm you."

"Where do you come from?" Lucia asked.

"I come from Heaven."

"And what do you want of me?"

"I have come to ask you to come here six months in succession, on the 13th, at the same time. Then, I will tell you who I am and what I want. Then I will come back a seventh time."

"Am I going to Heaven too?"

"Yes, you are."

"And Jacinta?"

"She, too."

"And Francisco?"

"He, too, but he must pray many Rosaries."

Then Lucia remembered to ask about two girls who had died recently; they were friends of Lucia, and had frequently been in her house, learning to weave with her older sister. "Is Maria das Neves already in Heaven?"

"Yes, she is." (Lucia thinks she was about 16 years old when she died.)

"And Amelia?" (About 18 or 20 years of age.)

"She will be in Purgatory until the end of the world."

Our Lady continued, "Do you want to offer yourselves to God to bear all the sufferings which He wants to send you, as an act of reparation for the sins which offend Him and as pleas for the conversion of sinners?"

"Yes, we do."

"You will have a lot to suffer then, but God's grace will be your comfort."

It was as she said these last words, "the grace of God," that she opened her hands, permitting the children to see themselves in God. Then by an interior impulse, they fell to their knees and repeated: "*Most Holy Trinity, I adore Thee. My God, my God, I love Thee in the Most Blessed Sacrament.*"

After a moment, Our Lady added: "Pray the Rosary every day, to obtain peace for the world and the end of the war."

Then she started to ascend, going toward the east until she disappeared in space.

The children experienced great liveliness and joy after the apparition of Our lady, in contrast to the weakness and compelling silence they felt after the apparitions of the Angel in 1916.

Being the oldest, and feeling responsible, Lucia cautioned the others about the need for silence regarding the Lady from heaven, lest the three children be called imposters. Jacinta, however, could not remain quiet, and told the story. Lucia's mother reacted in a most severe manner when the news reached her house; she accused her daughter of lying. The happiness of Lucia's home life ended at this point; the reaction of her own family was the beginning of the suffering foretold by Our Lady.

THE SECOND APPARITION
(June 13, 1917)

The appointment which Our Lady made to meet the children for the second time fell on the Feast of St. Anthony, the patron of the district of Fatima. This would be a day of great celebration. Thousands of boys and girls, not only from the immediate district but from outside as well, would meet around the Fatima church. In Portugal, St. Anthony is considered the saint of marriage par excellence, and his Feast day was the occasion for the meeting of young people from far and wide for the purpose of courtship and then marriage.

Although it was especially the young people who came to celebrate St. Anthony's Day, the parents came too, in order to watch over them, though perhaps from a distance. Lucia's mother thought the attractions of the day would cause Lucia to forget all about the promised appearance in the Cova da Iria. Senhor Marto and his wife, Olimpia, had left early in the morning to go to a distant fair.

The feast was marked by loud fireworks calling all to the celebrations. But at the right time, Lucia, Jacinta, and Francisco left the worldly celebrations of the feast—the fireworks, the music, the flirting of their sisters and friends. Off they went to the little holm oak tree. The news of the apparition had spread, and in spite of the feast, about fifty other people had gathered in the Cova da Iria.

Our Lady appeared as she had promised. Lucia again asked: "What do you want of me?" (These were to be Lucia's words of greeting to Our Lady at each of the apparitions.)

"I want you to come here on the 13th of next month, to pray the Rosary every day, and to learn to read. Later, I will tell you what I want."

Lucia asked for the cure of a sick person. Our Lady answered: "If he is converted he will be cured during the year."

"I would like to ask you to take us to Heaven," said Lucia.

"Yes, I will take Jacinta and Francisco soon, but you must stay longer. Jesus wants to use you to make me known and loved. He wants to establish in the world the devotion to my Immaculate Heart."

"Shall I stay here alone?" Lucia asked sadly.

"No, daughter. Are you suffering a great deal? Do not be downhearted. I shall never leave you. My Immaculate Heart will be your refuge and the way that will lead you to God."

As she opened her hands, the children again saw themselves immersed in God. Jacinta and Francisco were seen in that part of the light ascending toward Heaven, while Lucia was seen in the part which radiated towards the earth. In front of the right hand of Our Lady appeared a heart encircled by thorns which seemed to pierce it. The children understood that the Heart was the Immaculate Heart of Mary, outraged by the sins of humanity and seeking reparation.

THE THIRD APPARITION
(July 13, 1917)

To inquiries about the apparitions, the three young shepherds would only answer: It is a very beautiful Lady, unequalled. She says that it is necessary to say the Rosary every day and to do penance. The fifty witnesses at the June apparition had helped spread the news, and interest began to spread throughout the country. Meanwhile, the parish priest seemed almost hostile to the children. This was certainly in the plan of God. When Lucia's mother took her daughter to the priest to discuss the apparitions, Lucia listened to the priest say that they could be a trick of the devil. Lucia spent an anxious night after hearing that; she awoke from her dreams terrified. She decided not to go to the Cova on the 13th of July. But at the last minute, an inner prompting changed her mind, and the three children arrived at the little holm oak tree before the appointed hour. Along the way, they were bothered with countless questions and petitions to give Our Lady. The crowd had now grown from the fifty in June to about two or three thousand. People were praying the Rosary.

The sun darkened somewhat and a gentle, pleasant breeze blew. Some of the people present saw a little grey cloud hover over the holm oak tree on which the children said the Lady had appeared. Some people heard a sound, a hum. This helped give proof to some that the children were indeed experiencing something supernatural. There was a flash of light, and then Our lady appeared. As was the case with all the apparitions, Francisco saw but did not hear Our Lady. Only Lucia and Jacinta saw and heard, and only Lucia spoke. Lucia asked again: "What do you want of me?"

"I want you to come here on the 13th of next month, to continue to pray the Rosary every day, in honor of Our Lady of the Rosary, to obtain peace in the world and the end of the war, because only she can help."

"I want to ask you to tell me who you are, and to perform a miracle so that everyone will believe that you appear to us."

"Continue to come here every month. In October I will tell you who I am and what I want, and I will perform a miracle for all to see and believe."

Here Lucia made some requests for other people. Our Lady said that it was necessary for these people to pray the Rosary to gain these graces during the year. And Our Lady continued: "Sacrifice yourselves for sinners and say often, especially whenever you make a sacrifice: *'O my Jesus, it is for love of Thee, in reparation for the offenses committed against the Immaculate Heart of Mary, and for the conversion of poor sinners.'* "

On saying these words, she opened her arms as in the two previous months. The reflection seemed to enter the earth, and the children saw a sea of fire; in that fire were devils and lost souls. Lucia later gave a detailed picture of Hell as the children had perceived it; this will be reported in the chapters ahead. At this time Our Lady also spoke of her Immaculate Heart, and gave a warning and promise for the world. This too will be described later in the book. The vision of Hell and the Immaculate Heart devotion were the first two parts of a three-part secret which Our Lady gave the children. The first two parts were held in confidence for many years; the third part has still not been revealed to the world at large, but is kept in the Vatican archives. The author of this book has personally discussed the Fatima secret with Bishop John Fenancio, the second Bishop of Leiria-Fatima, who said he held the secret, sealed in an envelope, in his own hands. Bishop Venancio did not read it, but he saw that it was properly delivered, being eventually given to the Pope.

After the vision of Hell, the three Fatima children acted more like adults than children. Their games diminished, and they became ever more aware of the mission which Heaven was giving them. Remembrance of the horrifying vision in fact became the occasion for grace to transform their souls; this was especially true of Jacinta.

After giving the children the secret, Our Lady continued: "When you pray the Rosary, say after each mystery: *'O my Jesus, forgive us; save us from the fire of Hell; take all souls to Heaven, especially those most in need.'* "

There was a moment of silence, and then Lucia asked: "Do you want anything more of me?"

"No, not today."

And as usual, Our Lady began to go up towards the east, until she disappeared in the immense distance.

THE FOURTH APPARITION
(August 13/15, 1917)

The political atmosphere in Portugal at this time was affected by the intense influence of Freemasonry and other similar organizations which were directing the government and its administration. They waged a quiet but implacable war against the clergy, and against Catholics in general. When the apparitions reported at Fatima were becoming known, those in control in the government saw that they might compromise the work of de-Christianization and laicization which the secret organizations were working so hard to accomplish.

Artur de Oliveira Santos was the Mayor of the district of Vila Nova de Ourém at this time. He also was both Mayor and Deputy Judge of the district, and had long been an active Freemason. Holding both administrative and juridical posts, he plotted to take secret action against the Fatima events. He eventually persecuted the three children, and afterwards carried out persecutions of the pilgrims.

The Mayor ordered the parents of the three Fatima seers to appear with the children at the town hall on August 11th. Manuel Marto went alone, saying that the long difficult trip would have been too much for Jacinta and Francisco. Lucia went with her father, riding on a donkey. The road was so rough that at times she fell to the ground. Artur de Oliveira Santos thought that he could drag out of Lucia what the Lady had said, but whether he used kind words or threats, he could not succeed.

Francisco and Jacinta received Lucia back home with great joy because they had been told that the Mayor would have her killed. Nothing like that happened, but the Mayor was not one to give up easily. On August 13th, when there was to be another apparition, he went to Fatima in his carriage. First he went to the priest's house. Then he continued on to Aljustrel where he met the parents of the children.

Arriving in Aljustrel, the Mayor pretended that he had been converted and that he too wanted to go to the apparition site. "Well, we're all going there. I'll take the children with me in the car. . . . Seeing is believing, like St. Thomas." When the children, who had a marvelous sense of time, knew that it was nearly time for the apparition, they brought the animals home and made ready to go to the Cova. They told the Mayor that it was not necessary for them to ride in his car. But he insisted, saying, "It's better, because that way we'll get there in no time and nobody will bother you on the way." To the children's parents, he said: "We'll go on to Fatima, to the priests's house. I want to ask them some questions there."

At the priests's house, Lucia was questioned by the parish priest, but she refused to state that she had been lying. She said: "If liars go to Hell, I will not go to Hell, because I do not lie and I only say what I have seen and what the Lady has told me. And as for people who go there [to the Cova], they only go because they want to; we do not ask anyone."
The questioning continued:

"Is it true that the Lady told you a secret?"

"Yes, but I can't tell it. If Your Reverence wants to know it, I will ask the Lady, and if she allows me, I will tell you."

The Mayor added: "Those are supernatural things. Let's get on." The Mayor got up, went out of the room, and forced the children to get into the car before their parents' eyes. Years later, Senhor Marto commented on the incident: "It was well organized. It was well arranged. And it couldn't be helped."

The Mayor, instead of going toward the Cova da Iria, took the road to Vila Nova de Ourém, where he arrived about an hour later. Pilgrims along the way recognized the children and threw stones at the carriage. The Mayor then covered the children with a rug to hide them from the pilgrims. Meanwhile, the five to six thousand people who were gathered in the Cova became angry upon learning that the children had been kidnapped by the Mayor. Thinking, incorrectly, that the parish priest was in a plot with him they becanme angry at the priest as well.

The crowd at the Cova was calmed when suddenly there came a clap of thunder, followed by a flash of lightning. Many saw above the tree a small white cloud which soon disappeared. Obviously, although she knew that the three children were not there, Our Lady kept her own appointment and did not leave the faithful without the signs which they had seen at the previous apparitions.

At Ourém, the children were shut in a room and told they could not come out until they told the secret. They were questioned and offered pieces of gold to reveal it. They were also taken to prison and threatened with being left there if they did not tell the secret. Then they were taken back to the court and told that they would be fried in oil if they did not reveal it. The Administrator told a man to make ready a pan with boiling oil. He summoned the children one by one, beginning with Jacinta. The children believed they were going to their deaths. But after a couple of days, having gotten nowhere, the Mayor left the children off at the priest's house, on the terrace. The people rejoiced to see them.

There has been disagreement over exactly when the August apparition took place, since the children were in jail on the 13th. It is now more commonly held to have taken place on the 15th. This time, the apparition was at Valinhos, near Aljustrel. As always, Lucia asked Our Lady: "What do you want of me?"

"I want you to continue going to the Cova da Iria on the 13th, and to continue praying the Rosary every day. In the last month, I will perform a miracle so that all may believe."

"What do yo want me to do with the money which the people leave in the Cova da Iria?"

"Make two platforms; you carry one with Jacinta and two other girls dressed in white; let Francisco carry the other with three other boys. The money for the platforms is for the Feast of Our Lady of the Rosary, and what is left over is to help build a chapel which you must have built."

"I want to ask you for the cure of some sick people."

"Yes, some I will cure during the year."

Looking sadder, Our Lady said: "Pray, pray a great deal and make many sacrifices for sinners, for many souls go to Hell because there is nobody to offer sacrifices and prayers for them."

THE FIFTH APPARITION
(September 13, 1917)

As the saying goes, God writes straight with crooked lines. The imprisonment of the children had an effect which the persecutors of the Church and of the Faith had not anticipated. The press reported what had happened on August 13, and the thousands of pilgrims who had gone to the Cova da Iria became justifiably provoked. Thus, interest arose throughout Portugal, and tens of thousands of people came to Fatima on September 13. They came on every form of transport—cars, carriages, donkey-carts, and their own two legs, for in 1917 there were few automobiles in Portugal, and roads were very primitive.

Among other seminarians who went to Fatima in September was one who was later to play an important part in Fatima. He is now known as Canon Dr. Galamba de Oliveira of the Diocese of Leiria. He was then a seminarian of fourteen years, and on vacation. This is his account:

The land was covered with bushes, with a few larger trees here and there, and was divided by stone walls, according to the custom of the country, either to mark boundaries or just to clean the soil. We climbed onto a wider one, half in ruins, so as to see better. It was on the slope between the place of the apparitions and the place where today there is a church.

Lower down, the people gathered around the grotto and the little shepherds, who could hardly be seen.

I did not notice anything near the place, but after the apparition, I can't say the exact moment, I looked up to the sky, perhaps because someone told me to, and I saw, about a meter above the earth, a sort of luminous globe which soon began to descend towards the west and from the horizon went up again towards the sun.

We were very moved. We prayed earnestly for we knew not what. Everyone present could see the same globe except for a colleague of mine, also a priest now, from Torres Novas. I took him by the arm to show it to him, but at that moment I lost the said globe from sight before he could see it, which made him say in tears, "Why is it that I can't see it?"

Before or after, but certainly on the same day, we—but I don't know if this is true of all those present—began to see a fall of rose petals or snow drops which came from above and disappeared a little way above our heads, so that we couldn't touch them.

I didn't see anything else, but it was enough to comfort us and we left with the certainty, like an intuition, that there was the finger of God.

Maria dos Anjos, Lucia's sister, and still living in 1981 as the final pages of this book were written, also was present in the Cova da Iria that September 13th, and has shared with the author as late as 1980 a similar account of the September events. She described seeing a small star approach from the east and come to rest above the holm oak tree, as well as small flowers—like olive tree flowers in the spring—which were falling and which the people attempted unsuccessfully to catch.

The great message of the September apparition was:

Continue to pray the Rosary in order to obtain the end of the war. In October Our Lord will come too, as well as Our Lady of Sorrows and of Carmel, and St. Joseph with the Child Jesus to bless the world. God is pleased with your sacrifices, but He does not want you to sleep with the cord on, only to wear it during the day.

The children had been wearing a knotted rope around their waists for mortification.

THE SIXTH AND LAST APPARITION
(October 13, 1917)

By October, the news of Fatima had spread even more; in particular, the people had learned that a miracle was to happen. Our Lady had not forbidden the children to relate this prediction. The spread of the news upset Maria Rosa Santos so greatly that she told Lucia on the 12th that they should both go to Confession since they were both going to die: "If the Lady does not work the miracle, the people will kill us." To this, Lucia answered: "If you want to go to Confession, I will go too, but not for that reason. I am not afraid that they will kill us. I am quite certain that tomorrow the Lady will do all that she promised."

Between seventy and a hundred thousand pilgrims from the north to the south of Portugal came to the place of the apparitions on October 13, 1917. Neither the silence of the clergy, the threats of the civil authorities, nor the sacrifices involved in making the long journey could stop them. At the last moment, Maria Rosa decided to go as well, "If my daughter is going to die, I want to die beside her."

When the time came to depart, it was raining hard, and everything was muddy. After working their way through the rain and thick mud and the crowds of people, the children finally reached the Cova da Iria. Along the way, many people had attempted to interrupt them with requests for Our Lady.

Upon reaching the holm oak, and moved by an interior impulse, Lucia asked the people to shut their umbrellas and to pray the Rosary. Soon after that there was a flash of light, and Our Lady appeared above the holm oak tree. Lucia asked: "What do you want of me?"

"I want to tell you that I wish a chapel to be erected here in my honor; I am the Lady of the Rosary. Continue always to pray the Rosary every day. The war will soon end, and the soldiers will return to their homes."

"I have many things to ask you: the cure of some sick persons, the conversion of sinners, and other things. . . ."

"Some yes, not others. It is necessary for them to amend their lives, to ask for forgiveness of their sins." Then with a sad expression on her face, Our Lady said: "Do not offend the Lord Our God any more for He is already deeply offended." And opening her hands, she made them reflect onto the sun; while she arose, the reflection of her own light continued to be projected onto the sun.

In recalling the event later, for her Bishop, Lucia wrote:

Here, Your Excellency, is the reason why I cried out to the people to look at the sun. My aim was not to call their attention to the sun, because I was not even aware of their presence. I was moved to do so under the guidance of an interior impulse.

Lucia has described what followed:

> When Our Lady disappeared in the immense distance of the firmament, beside the sun we saw St. Joseph with the Child Jesus and Our Lady robed in white with a blue mantle. St. Joseph and the Child Jesus seemed to bless the world, for they made the Sign of the Cross with their hands. A little later this vision vanished, and I saw Our Lord, and Our Lady who appeared to me to be Our Lady of Sorrows. Our Lord seemed to bless the world in the same manner as St. Joseph. This apparition disappeared, and I saw Our Lady again, this time resembling Our Lady of Mt. Carmel.

At the predetermined hour, the rain stopped, and the thick mass of clouds broke asunder. The sun looked like a disc of dull silver, and began dancing wildly. The people shouted out: "Miracle!" It seems that the majority of the people saw the sun trembling and dancing, whirling around like a catherine wheel; it descended almost low enough to burn the earth with its rays. Many thought the end of the world had come, as the sun seemed to fall upon them. People reported color changes in objects on earth, caused by the rays of the sun. Some expressed sorrow for their sins aloud. Some who had come to ridicule now believed.

After the great miracle of the sun which Our Lady had performed "so that all may believe," the events of Fatima became the subject of national attention in Portugal. It would take at least thirteen years before Church authorities would make an official declaration, and many clarifications were still necessary. The Church always has to act with prudence and caution in exercising the responsibility entrusted to her by Christ. The political issues of the times added to controversy surrounding the apparitions.

The first publication on the subject of Fatima came from the pen of Father Formigão, in 1921. His full name and title were: Dr. Manuel Nunes Formigao Cónego de Si Partriarcal de Lisboa (Canon or theologican of the Cardinal Patriarch of Lisbon). He also wrote under the pen name of "Visconde de Montelo." His work was entitled *Os episódios maravilhosos de Fátima* ("The Marvelous Event of Fatima"). Dr. Formigão had repeatedly questioned the children; these interrogations, together with this personal impressions, have contributed much to spreading an understanding of Fatima.

Father Formigão originally wanted to spread devotion to Our Lady of Lourdes in Portugal. He was at first a non-believer in the Fatima events, but was suddenly converted on September 13, 1917, when he went to the Cova to make a study and even expose the "fraudulence" of the reported apparitions. Father Formigão became such an apostle of Fatima, and had such an influence in the formation of the Sanctuary and its events in its early years, that in Portugal he has been called the "Soul of Fatima."

Our Lady had predicted that Jacinta and Francisco would go to heaven soon. They both became ill about the same time, in August of 1918, when almost everyone in the Marto family became ill with influenza. The influenza epidemic had been going all over Europe, and it finally broke out in Portugal; many people died from the disease.

Jacinta and Francisco never really got over the effects of the influenza, and they fell very ill again on December 23, 1918. Francisco developed bronchial pneumonia, and Jacinta developed pleurisy. Even after the children became very sick, they continued to do penance in reparation to Jesus and Mary and for the conversion of sinners. People felt a special presence of God whenever they came near Jacinta or Francisco, who were suffering terribly and offering it up to God and the Immaculate Heart of Mary in reparation.

On April 2nd of 1919, Francisco became more seriously ill and knew that he would not remain on earth much longer. He cried out: "Mother, Mother mine, must I die without receiving the Hidden Jesus?" Thus Francisco expressed his wish to receive Holy Communion. His father went to get the parish priest, only to find the priest ill. Another priest came and promised to bring Holy Communion the next morning.

Desiring to go to Confession before Holy Communion, Francisco sent his sister Teresa to get Lucia. He questioned Lucia: "Did you ever see me commit any sin? Ask Jacinta the same thing." Having examined his conscience thoroughly with the help of Lucia and Jacinta, Francisco was prepared to received the Sacraments.

After Francisco received Holy Communion, he said to Jacinta: "Today I am happier than you are, for I have the Hidden Jesus in my heart!" To Lucia, he said: "I am going to Our Lord. When in Heaven, I shall beg Our Lord and Our Lady to take you there soon too. I am sure I shall feel lonely without you. What would I not give for Our Lord to take you quickly!"

Jacinta said to Francisco: "Give my love to Our Lord and Our Lady. Tell them I will suffer as much as they wish to convert sinners and in reparation to the Immaculate Heart of Mary."

That evening Francisco saw a beautiful shining light at his door. When Lucia left that evening she said: "Good-bye then, Francisco, until we meet in Heaven." Francisco died the following morning, April 4th of 1919, at 10:00 a.m., without having seen either Jacinta or Lucia again.

When Jacinta became so ill that she could no longer go to the church to visit Jesus in the Tabernacle herself, she would send Lucia in her place. She worried much about the war Our Lady said would break out if people did not stop offending God. Our Lady told Jacinta when Francisco would die, and her heart was heavy when God took him. She told Our Lady that she herself was willing to remain some time longer upon earth in order to convert more sinners by continued suffering. Our Lady then told her that she would go to a hospital, not to get well, but to suffer a great deal.

Thus Jacinta knew that when they took her to the hospital at Vila Nova de Ourém she would not be cured but would only suffer more. Our Lady revealed to her that she would go to yet another hospital to suffer more for the love of God and for the conversion of sinners; she told Jacinta that she would die alone at this second hospital, and that she would never see Lucia or her parents again. Shortly before going to the hospital in Lisbon, Jacinta said to Lucia:

> It will not be long now before I go to Heaven. You will remain here to announce that God wishes devotion to the Immaculate Heart to be established in the world. When you are to say that, do not hide yourself; tell everybody that God concedes us His graces through the Immaculate Heart of Mary; that people should invoke her, that the Heart of Jesus wishes the Heart of Mary to be venerated at his side. Let them ask for peace through the Immaculate Heart of Mary, for God has given it to her. Ah! If only I could put into people's hearts the flame that is burning within my own heart and that is making me love the Hearts of Jesus and Mary so much!

Jacinta's parting with Lucia was heartbreaking when in mid-January of 1920 she left Aljustrel for Lisbon. Our Blessed Lady appeared to Jacinta again repeatedly in Lisbon with messages that amaze those who have read them.

Her last day on earth was Friday, February 10th of 1920. About 6:00 p.m. that evening Jacinta felt worse and asked for a priest. The priest from the near-by church came about 8:00 p.m. and heard her confession. Jacinta pleaded for Holy Communion, saying that she was going to die. The priest, thinking she was not that close to death, promised to bring her Communion the next morning. Jacinta died peacefully at 10:30 p.m. She was alone, just as Our lady had foretold. Only after her death did the staff at the hospital discover that they had been caring for one of the seers of Fatima.

Back in Fatima, when the church bells began to toll, Lucia clasped her hands over her heart and cried out in an anguished voice that the bells must be signalling Jacinta's death. Without another word she turned and fled from the house and ran to the Loca do Cabeco, where she flung herself upon the ground and wept as if her heart would break. She did not return home until nightfall, her eyes red from crying.

A little more than five months after Jacinta died, a Bishop was appointed to take over the newly formed Diocese of Leiria-Fatima (August 5, 1920). The ever-increasing crowds, as well as the reports of conversions to God and marvelous cures, caused the Bishop to look kindly upon the events.

With the permission of Lucia's mother, the Bishop decided to send Lucia to an orphanage school at Oporto, run by Sisters of St. Dorothy. Before the morning of May 16, 1921, Lucia made a round of farewells to the places she loved so well, the place that had become so dear because of the apparitions of the Angel and of Our Lady. She visited the graves of her father and of Francisco. On returning from these places she went to the Marto home weeping. She bade a silent good-bye to Jacinta's room.

Lucia went to bed after supper but was up again in a few hours. Accompanied by her mother and a poor laborer who was going to Leiria, and without taking leave of anybody, she set out at two in the morning. They passed the Cova da Iria, where Lucia said a last Rosary. Then, as long as she could see the place, she kept turning back to bid it a last farewell.

At Vilar (Oporto) she pursued her studies and was regarded by her teachers and classmates as an ordinary child. In 1925 she left Vilar to become a postulant in the order of St. Dorothy at Tuy, Spain. It was there that the Most Holy Virgin Mary appeared to Lucia with the Child Jesus. The great intimacy between Our Lady and Lucia was manifested on this occasion by Our lady resting one hand on her shoulder, while in the other hand she held a Heart surrounded with sharp thorns. At the same time the Child Jesus complained of the thorns with which ungrateful men pierce the Heart of His Mother at every moment. It was then that Our Lady gave details about the five First Saturdays, which will be discussed in a later chapter.

On December 15, 1926, the Child Jesus again appeared to Lucia, asking her if she had spread the devotion to the Immaculate Heart of His Mother. And in what has commonly been called the "Last Vision," Our Lady appeared to Lucia in June of 1929 to ask for the consecration of Russia to her Immaculate Heart, promising by this means to prevent the spreading of Russia's errors and to bring about that country's conversion.

In 1948 the Pope permitted Lucia to change orders, and she was admitted into the Carmelite Order that same year, receiving the Carmelite habit and beginning the novitiate on May 13th. Since then, with the exception of the brief time when Pope Paul VI called her from her convent in Coimbra to come to the Cova on May 13, 1967, when he himself was in Fatima,

Sister Lucia has remained in the cloistered convent. She is not permitted to meet the public except with permission which only the Pope can grant, and which has rarely been given. Her immediate family members, however, may always visit her.

The most authentic record of the Fatima events is to be found in the *Memoirs* of Sister Lucia (*Memorias E Cartas Da Irma Lucia*: an English translation of Lucia's *Memoirs*, under the title, *Fatima in Lucia's Own Words*, is available from Ravengate Press, Box 103, Cambridge, MA 02138). In preparing this book I have frequently drawn from these *Memoirs*, attempting to point out their great implications for today. An edition of this work printed in Portugal carries a foreword which states:

> The history of Fatima involves some difficulties, as is natural. The New Testament, to say nothing of the Old, carries with it problems which have provoked endless researches throughout nearly two thousand years. Nevertheless, no sensible Christian decides to disdain the Holy Scripture in spite of so many difficulties which have not yet been clarified and probably never will be.
>
> It is ridiculous to scorn Fatima because of two or three difficulties. The way we must follow through is to study the events carefully and afterwards to accept the Heavenly Message and try to live accordingly. Another more subtle temptation is that Fatima is a private revelation; therefore there is no reason to spend time on it since we have the REVELATION.
>
> Fatima, like all other true apparitions of Our Lady, is a work of God and God leaves nothing to chance. As in Israel, from time to time, God sent prophets to remind His People of their eternal destiny, so after Christ's coming, God in His utmost sapient Providence used apparitions of Christ and of Our Lady—strong enough in themselves to have world-wide influence—to recall the attention of His children to the eternal truths of the REVELATION, which was very often forgotten or distorted due to human passions. Let us remember that in Christ's time most of the priests and doctors of law, in spite of their frequent readings of Holy Scripture, had wandered so far from the true meaning of the REVELATION that they were expecting a political Messiah to set Isreal free from Roman bondage.
>
> *Mutatis mutandis*, is not something like this going on in our day?
>
> As a matter of fact, are there not some priests and Bishops who pretend to turn the Church into an institution of social assistance and means of development of underdeveloped people or countries?
>
> There are many who attack the authentic Magisterium under the pretense of liberating the Church from medieval structures.
>
> But the most dangerous error that has led many priests to leave

the priesthood is the pagan naturalism that pretends to achieve super-natural goals solely by human means. Therefore they do not care about prayer and penance, but trust only in action, action, action.

Is not such a mentality in conflict with the eternal words of Christ, "For apart from Me you can do nothing. . . .If you dwell in Me, and My words dwell in you, ask what you will, and you SHALL HAVE it"?

There are some, too, who pretend to banish all responsibility for sin, fictionalizing strange theories. Christ has already fulminated against such baseless intents (Mt. 7:15-23).

The apparitions of Our Lady at Fatima—are they not a strong ad-monition against the above-mentioned distortions of the REVELATION?

As stated earlier, this book will not have as its chief purpose the retell-ing of the *story* of Fatima. One can hear the story and miss the *message*. Our purpose is to go beyond the story and beyond the *Memoirs* of Sister Lucia, though frequently we must refer to them, just as we always go back to the Scriptures. In the Scriptures God gives His Revelation to man within the context of "salvation history," and at Fatima, where He reaffirms His Will for men, He does it within the context of the lives of three shepherd children.

On the twenty-fifth anniversary of Fatima, His Eminence the Cardinal Patriarch of Lisbon wrote:

> In Fatima everything has been the work of God. . . . The miracle of Fatima is not the work of man. It has grown in spite of every kind of human opposition directed from the beginning to suppress the message of the three innocent children; in spite of the hostile incredulity of their own family, the prudent reserve of the Church, and the fiery persecution of the authorities. But now, when only twenty-five short years have gone by, the good news of "Our Lady of Fatima" has gone all over the world. . . .
>
> We were among those who, at the beginning, paid no attention to what was happening in Cova da Iria. . . .
>
> The children disappeared from the scene, but the pilgrimages to the Cova da Iria did not cease. By the invocation of the Mediatrix of All Graces, who appeared there, miracles of healing are performed, such as no human science or power could have worked. . . .
>
> Saint Paul says that the Christians are a letter of Christ, ministered by us, and written "not with ink, but with the Spirit of God" (II Cor. 3:1-3). Imitating him, we can say that "JACINTA" is a letter of the Ho-ly Virgin, to be read by souls. Better than words does it say what Our Lady came to do in Fatima and what she wants of us.

What happened in Portugal proclaims the miracle and is a token of what the Immaculate Heart is preparing for the world.

And today, the fact of Fatima is even more evident than when the Cardinal Patriarch wrote on the twenty-fifth anniversary: "The Immaculate Heart of Mary worked the miracle of Fatima. Who can doubt that God's finger is there after having seen for a quarter of a century the extraordinary and continual *FACT* of Fatima?"

Note that the Cardinal said "fact" and not "facts," for to appreciate Fatima one must grasp the *whole* of Fatima—just as in appreciating the Catholic Church one must grasp the fullness of the Catholic Faith. This is done in simple fashion at first, and then to ever greater depths. The "fact" of Fatima is seen not only in the three apparitions of the Angel and the six apparitions of the Blessed Virgin Mary. The "fact" of Fatima is not simply the building of a sanctuary as a place of pilgrimage and cures, a place where prayers and penance continually rise upward. The fact of Fatima includes all these things and much more.

The fact of Fatima re-echoes the totality of the Catholic Faith; it proclaims again the life, death, and resurrection of Our Lord and Savior Jesus Christ. It directs souls back to the Gospels, back to the supernatural in a modern scientific world engrossed in the natural, worshipping itself and its scientific discoveries.

The fact of Fatima is its message. I propose to explore that message, and I hope to lead my readers to live it.

2.
The Miracles of Fatima

In answer to Lucia's request for Mary to "work a miracle so that everybody will believe that you are appearing to us," Our Lady said: "In October . . . I will perform a miracle for all to see and believe." She made that promise on July 13, 1917. In her first apparition on May 13th she had told the children: "I have come to ask you to come here for six months in succession, on the thirteenth day, at this same hour." What we have then is a promise from Heaven, made at least three months in advance, for a miracle to be performed at a precise day, hour, and place.

Word of the "beautiful Lady" appearing in the Cova da Iria in the parish of Fatima had spread throughout Portugal, thanks to Jacinta who did not keep her agreement to remain silent. By October the crowds would number up to 100,000 in a mountainous land where traveling conditions were primitive—especially for the poor peasant people of the farms and villages.

What happened on that 13th of October was not simply one miracle, but several, as will be seen from the following accounts. The well known miracle of the sun took place at the promised hour of noon, peace time, as Our Lady did not keep her appointment according to European clocks set to war time. In keeping with her mission as Our Lady of Peace, she always followed true sun time.

In this chapter dedicated to the miracles of Fatima, especially the promised miracle "for all to see and believe," I shall offer a few out of many eye witness accounts. As noted in the official findings of the Canonical Commission established by the Bishop of Leiria-Fatima, the reports of the good and common people of deep faith were not disregarded. My first account shall be of an eighty-year old native Portuguese lady, Erminia Caixeiro, whose testimony was given to me in writing on October 30, 1974 after I traveled with her to Portugal. Erminia was still living in New York state, at the time of the writing of this book, and still continues to communicate with me. Fifty-seven years after the miracle she wrote:

In July 1917, my husband had to go to Reguengo do Fetal to fill out papers for the military service as he was still a subject and citizen of Portugal. It was then that he heard rumors of the apparitions of the Blessed Mother to the three shepherd children every 13th day of the month since May. He did not believe any of this. To him it was too far-fetched. His father and mother were very devout people, not educated, yet not illiterate. They could not convince him this was true and it disturbed them.

My husband had strayed away from the Church and the religion but he never failed to say his rosary. He had never lost his love for the Blessed Mother. He was very close to her. He had gone through some questionable experiences. So when he went into the town square again, conversation turned to the apparitions.

He had cousins, one was a priest and they assured him this was no figment of the children's imagination. It was very real. The children had been seized and imprisoned and suffered many injustices and were threatened with punishment if they did not stop going to the Cova. In spite of it, the children held strongly to their stories. Also he was told that on October 13th, 1917 the Blessed Mother would perform a miracle, that all should come to see for themselves. When he came home he told me of these appearances of the Blessed Mother.

So on the morning of October 12, 1917 we left with our two children, Maria and José, my husband carrying one child and I the other on horseback. We were on the road all day, arriving in Reguengo, five miles from Fatima, late in the afternoon. We took our children to my husband's mother so that she could care for them. She had gone to all the other apparitions on the 13th day of each month from June to September. However, she herself had never seen anything but did hear the children speak to our Blessed Mother.

As we were traveling from Reguengo to Fatima, we saw people on foot, on donkey, on mules, on horseback. Some and most were barefoot,

plodding in the mud, making camp wherever it was convenience. Some
people were soaked to the skin and hungry. They came from far, the mountains, villages. The road was filled with people. It was a pilgrimage.

We made camp in the evening in the Cova where our Mother appeared
to the children. It rained all night, very heavy, and everyone was soaked
and covered with mud. The next day, October 13th, it was still raining
and the sky was very grey. Everywhere one looked, the people were many.

Some were praying, singing, and some on their knees. Some were
standing and holding their umbrellas for coverage, patiently awaiting the
arrival of the children as the Blessed Mother always appeared at 12 o'clock
precisely.

At five minutes to twelve, the children arrived and announced to the
people that they should close their umbrellas. Almost instantaneously the
rain stopped as though they had turned a faucet off. They also asked all
the men to remove their hats. A man next to me refused to do so. A few
seconds went by and the sun came out. Then the man took his hat off
and said, "Now I believe. No one could do that."

There was a great silence that came over the crowd. The sun was radiant with colors surrounding it. People's clothes were of gold hue and
immediately their soaked clothes were dry. The sun started to spin and
descend toward the earth like a spiral. Just as fast it ascended back into
the sky.

Everyone in the crowd was frightened and screaming and begging God
to forgive them. The blind and crippled were asking for favors of cures.
I saw a lot of crutches being dropped and I saw a few people who were
blind since birth regaining their sight. Everyone was in a state of exhilara-
tion and happiness.

At no time did I see the Blessed Mother. I was only a few feet away
from where the children were kneeling.

After the miracle the children told the people they must say the Rosary
every day. If not, the world would be engrossed in a terrible war and
we would suffer much. Only through prayer could we enjoy peace among
nations; that God her Son was very unhappy with us.

I say the Rosary at 12 o'clock every day for special indulgences. In
prayer Our Lady has asked me to do things for world peace, for the conversion of sinners and of souls; my daily sacrifices are for non-believers.

I am now 80 years old, a widow. I was 23 when I saw the miracle.
I am the mother of twelve children. . . I am very busy to help propagate
the Rosary to help souls. . . .

Now let us turn to a scientist who will present his testimony of the miracle
of the sun of October 13, 1917. The following account was written by Dr.
Joseph Xavier Proenca de Almeida Garrett, a professor of the University
of Coimbra.

I am going to tell briefly and concisely, without toning down the truth in any way, what I saw at Fatima on October 13, 1917. The hours that I shall speak of are those of official government time in use at that period which synchronized our time with that of other warring nations. I do this for greater accuracy, for it was not easy for me to state with precision the exact moment at which the sun reached its zenith.

I got there at noon. A fine and persistent rain had been falling all morning and now, driven by a strong wind, it bade fair to drench everything. The sky was very dark and overcast, foreboding heavy rains of long duration.

I stayed on the road under the shelter of the automobile a little above the place where the apparitions were said to have taken place, not daring to venture on the muddy ground of the freshly tilled field. I was a little more than a hundred meters from the wooden beams surmounted by a rustic cross. I saw very clearly around this structure the large circle of the crowd with open umbrellas, resembling a vast bed of shields.

After a little more than an hour (at 1:00 p.m.) the children for whom the Virgin had marked the place, the day, and the hour of the apparition arrived. We could hear the hymns intoned by the people who surrounded them.

At a given moment this confused and compact mass of people closed their umbrellas, thus uncovering in a gesture of humility and respect which surprised me and made me admire them since the rain continued to fall in torrents on their heads and drenched them. They told me later that when those people went down on their knees in the mud, they were obeying the voice of a child.

It must have been one-thirty when there arose at the very spot where the children were a column of smoke, thin, tenuous and bluish. It rose about two meters in the air above their heads and then vanished. This phenomenon lasted for several seconds and it was perfectly visible to the naked eye. Since I did not check the time of duration, I cannot say whether it lasted more or less than a minute. The smoke vanished abruptly and after a certain time the phenonemon was repeated a second and a third time. At each of the three times and especially at the last, the thick planks that had been erected stood out clearly in the gray atmosphere.

I trained my field glasses on the spot. I could see nothing but the column of smoke; but I was convinced that it was produced by someone swinging a censor of burning incense. Since then, trustworthy persons have assured me that this had occured on the thirteenth of the five preceding months and that neither then nor this time had anyone burned anything or made a fire.

While I was looking at the place of the Apparitions, in a serene and cold expectation of something happening and with diminishing curiosity because a long time has passed without anything to excite my attention,

I heard a shout from thousands of voices and saw the multitude which stretched out at my feet, here and there concentrated in small groups around the trees, suddenly turn its back from the point towards which up to then it had directed its attention and anxieties, and turn to look at the sky in the opposite direction.

It must have been nearly two o'clock by the legal time and about midday by the sun. The sun, a few moments before, had broken through the thick layer of clouds which hid it and shone clearly and intensely. I turned to the magnet which seemed to be drawing all eyes and saw it as a disc with a clean-cut rim, luminous and shining, but which did not hurt the eyes. I do not agree with the comparison which I have heard made in Fatima—that of a dull silver disc. It was a clearer, richer brighter color, having something of the luster of a pearl. It did not in the least resemble the moon on a clear night because one saw it and felt it to be a living body. It was not spheric like the moon nor did it have the same color, tone, or shading. It looked like a glazed wheel made of mother-of-pearl. It could not be confused, either, with the sun seen through fog (for there was no fog at the time), because it was not opaque, diffused or veiled. In Fatima it gave light and heat and appeared clear-cut with a well-defined rim.

The sky was mottled with light cirrus clouds with the blue coming through here and there but sometimes the sun stood out in patches of clear sky. The clouds passed from west to east and did not obscure the light of the sun, giving the impression of passing behind it, though sometimes these flecks of white took on tones of pink or diaphanous blue as they passed before the sun.

It was a remarkable fact that one could fix one's eyes on the brazier of heat and light without any pain in the eyes or blinding of the retina. The phenomenon, except for two interruptions when the sun seemed to send out rays of refulgent heat which obliged us to look away, must have lasted about ten minutes.

The sun's disc did not remain immobile. This was not the sparkling of a heavenly body for it spun round on itself in a mad whirl. Then, suddenly, one heard a clamor, a cry of anguish breaking from all the people. The sun whirling wildly, seemed to loosen itself form the firmament and advance threateningly upon the earth as if to crush us with its huge and fiery weight. The sensation during those moments was terrible.

During the solar phenomenon, which I have just described in detail, there were changes of color in the atmosphere. Looking at the sun, I noticed that everything around was beoming darkened. I looked first at the nearest objects and then extended my glance further afield as far as the horizon. I saw everything an amethyst color. Objects around me, the sky and the atmosphere, were of the same color. An oak tree nearby threw a shadow of this color on the ground.

Fearing that I was suffering from an affection of the retina, an improbable explanation because in that case one could not see things purple colored, I turned away and shut my eyes, keeping my hands before them to intercept the light. With my back still turned, I opened my eyes and saw that the landscape was the same purple color as before.

The impression was not that of an eclipse, and while looking at the sun I noticed that the atmosphere had cleared. Soon after I heard a peasant who was near me shout out in tones of astonishment: "Look, that lady is all yellow!"

And in fact everything, both near and far, had changed, taking on the color of old yellow damask. People looked as if they were suffering from jaundice and I recall a sensation of amusement at seeing them look so ugly and unattractive. My own hand was the same color. All the phenomena which I have described were observed by me in a calm and serene state of mind and without any emotional disturbance. It is for others to interpret and explain them. [Taken from a letter of Dr. Garrett to Dr. Formigão who had asked for an account of what he had seen on October 13, 1917; see *Os episódios maravilhosos de Fátima*.]

Dr. Almeida Garrett said that after careful consideration he had placed the number at the Cova at over one hundred thousand. The testimony of this learned scientist demonstrates how difficult it was to describe the marvelous signs witnessed that day.

Secular newspapers had not been friendly to reported apparitions taking place at Fatima. Nevertheless, the Lisbon newspaper *O Seculo* of October 15, 1917, carried the following report as given by Avelino de Almeida:

From the height of the road where the people parked their carriages and where many hundreds stood, afraid to brave the muddy soil, we saw the immense multitude turn towards the sun at its highest, free of all clouds. The sun called to mind a plate of dull silver. It could be stared at without the least effort. It did not burn or blind. It seemed that an eclipse was taking place. All of a sudden a tremendous shout burst forth, "Miracle, miracle! Marvel, marvel!"

Before the astonished eyes of the people, whose attitude carried us back to biblical times, and who, white with terror, heads uncovered, gazed at the blue sky, the sun trembled and made some brusque unheard-of movements beyond all cosmic laws; the sun danced, in the typical expression of the peasants.

On the running board of the bus from Torres Novas, an old man whose stature and gentle, manly features recall those of Paul Deroulede, turned toward the sun and recited the *Credo* in a loud voice. . .I saw him later addressing those about him who still kept their hats on, begging them vehemently to take their hats off before this overwhelming demonstration of the existence of God. Similar scenes were repeated at other places. A lady, bathed in tears and almost choking with grief, sobbed, "How pitiful! There are men who still do not bare their heads before such a stupendous miracle!"

Immediately afterwards the people asked each other if they saw anything and what they had seen. The greatest number avowed that they saw the sun trembling and dancing; others declared that they saw the smiling face of the Blessed Virgin herself; they swore that the sun turned around on itself as if it were a wheel of fireworks and had fallen almost to the point of burning the earth with its rays. Some said they saw it change colors successively.

The reporter for the newspaper, *Ordem*, wrote:

> The sun was sometimes surrounded by blood-red flames; at other times it was aureoled with yellow and soft purple; again it seemed to be possessed of the swiftest rotation and then seemed to detach itself from the heavens, come near the earth and give forth a tremendous heat.

Inácio Lourenco was nine years old at the time and lived in the village of Alburitel, ten miles from Fatima. Years later when he was a priest he remembered the experience vividly. We quote this account as given in Father John De Marchi's book entitled *Fatima: The Facts:*

> About noon we were startled by the cries and exclamations of the people going by the school. The teacher was the first to run outside to the street with all the children following her. The people cried and wept on the street; they were all pointing towards the sun. It was "The Miracle" promised by Our Lady. I feel unable to describe it as I saw it and felt it at the time. I was gazing at the sun. It looked so pale to me. It did not blind. It was like a ball of snow rotating upon itself. All of a sudden, it seemed to be falling, zigzag, threatening the earth. Seized with fear, I hid myself amidst the people. Everyone was crying, waiting for the end of the world.
>
> Nearby, there was a godless man who had spent the morning making fun of the simpletons who had gone to Fatima just to see a girl. I looked at him and he was numbed, his eyes riveted on the sun. I saw him tremble from head to foot. Then he raised his hands towards Heaven, as he was kneeling there in the mud, and cried out, "Our Lady, Our Lady." Everyone was crying and weeping, asking God to forgive them their sins. After this was over, we ran to the chapels, some to one, others to the other one in our village. They were soon filled.
>
> During the minutes that the miracle lasted, everything around us

reflected all the colors of the rainbow. We looked at each other and one seemed blue, another yellow, red and so on. It increased the terror of the people. After ten minutes, the sun resumed its place, as pale, and without splendor. When everyone realized the danger was over, there was an outburst of joy. Everyone broke out in a hymn of praise to Our Lady.

If the miracle that happened on October 13 was a natural occurence, a true physical disturbance in the sun, then it should have registered on astronomical equipment. Atheists who came to scoff but instead were awestruck at the miracle testify that it was not due to mass hallucination. Those who were within a radius of thirty-five miles around Fatima and saw the miracle testify to the same. People who were expecting no miracle joined as one with the multitude of witnesses to the existence and power of God.

It is to be noted that the extraordinary events of Fatima did not end on October 13, 1917, nor, for that matter, have they ceased since that time. This is true with regard to miracles of grace and conversion that continue to take place there and throughout the world through Mary's intercession.

Later, the Bishop purchased the land of the Cova da Iria; it comprised 120,000 square meters, which included a little of the surrounding property. This was done in accord with the people's desire to have a large church built at the site of the apparitions in honor of Our Lady of the Rosary of Fatima. A hospice for sick pilgrims was also to be built near the chapel of the apparitions.

The first official act of worship performed in the Cova took place on October 13, 1921, when the Sacrifice of the Mass was offered in the open air under the porch of the little chapel. To the present day, the chapel—with its sides open to the air, but with a roof overhead—marks the exact spot of the little holm oak tree on which Our Lady appeared. (In 1981-82 extensive renovations took place in the Cova da Iria which were completed in time for the May 13, 1982 pilgrimage of Pope John Paul II.) These early activities on the part of the Bishop manifest the favorable actions on the part of the church authorities even before the final approval of the apparitions.

Most Catholics are aware of the famous water of Lourdes. Many, however, have not yet heard about the water of Fatima. Water is a scarcity in Portugal, and this was especially true of the Cova da Iria, which is situated atop a mountain. The Bishop recognized early that there would be a difficulty in establishing a water supply in the Cova. He could not allow buildings to be started without it; the ever-growing number of pilgrims coming to the site made water a necessity. Great efforts had been made, but none could be located.

The Bishop of Leiria wondered if he would be obliged to have expensive pipes laid down the mountain, all the way to Vila Nova de Ourém, in order to bring the needed water. Or, if the mountain could not produce water naturally from dug wells, perhaps cisterns would be the answer.

However, another attempt was made to find underground water. The workmen had dug hardly half a day when they hit rock. The decision was made to blast the rock, but before the work was finished, water came up abundantly. It was considered a miracle. The people of the serra and pilgrims from everywhere also regarded the water itself as miraculous, and they filled their vessels from the constantly flowing fountain.

Dr. José Alves gave the following report:

> They came here with their bottles and their pitchers which they filled and took home for their sick to drink and wash their wounds in. Everyone had the greatest faith in Our Lady's water and she used it to cure their pain and wounds. Never did Our Lady do so many miracles as at that time. I saw people with terrible legs, running with pus, but they washed them there and left their bandages behind because Our Lady cured them. Others knelt and drank that earthy water and were cured of internal diseases.

On July 15 of 1927, Antonio Pavilon, Mayor of Ourém, sent an official note to the *regedor* of the parish of Fatima to have the ditch covered; he called it "an immediate danger to public hygiene." Dr. Alves and Pavilon then paid a visit to the Cova knowing that otherwise nothing would be done. The Mayor said to the parish priest: "The place is disgusting. It must be covered over at once. It's a disgrace to the parish." Father Ferreira answered: "Faith never hurt anyone yet. It's a miracle already that such dirty, impure water does no harm to those who drink it, apart from the fact that people declare miracles to have occurred in the place."

Fearing the reaction of the people, the two officials threw onto the parish priest the burden of having the well covered. The following year another note was sent calling for action as soon as possible, for the well was "a menace to public health and sanitation, in view of the fact that the said water is full of dirt and microbes." This preoccupation with the well at the Cova seemed strange in light of the fact that many other water supplies of the same kind existed in the area.

The Bishop ordered that the well should be deepened and covered. The work was carried out under the supervision of the Mayor, the parish priest, and the sub-delegate of Public Health. Dr. Alves finally declared the water to be drinkable, and, after the little open-air Chapel of the Apparitions, the fountain was the first of the buildings to be erected in the Sanctuary.

At the present time, in the midst of the Cova, near the little chapel, water can be obtained from the same spot through faucets now provided there. And in the midst of this plentiful supply of water from an area which was thought to be completely dry, there now stands a tall pillar atop which is a bronze statue of the Sacred Heart of Jesus with hands raised in blessing.

During the months of the apparitions, Lucia, Francisco, and Jacinta had been asked by pilgrims to petition Our Lady for the cure of sick persons. Lucia would try hard to remember the requests; Our Lady answered: "Some yes, but not others. They must amend their lives and ask forgiveness for their sins." Our Lady announced that some would be cured within the year.

In the early years after the apparitions, *La Voz da Fatima* had already registered more than eight hundred attested cures; among these were cures of tuberculosis, blindness, meningitis, pleurisy, paralysis, various kinds of ulcers considered incurable, bone fractues, cancers, etc. Frs. Barthas and Da Fonseca, S.J., began in 1922 to record case histories of various cures. These men also speak of "moral miracles." In their words,

> Mary sometimes cures the body, but she more often cures the soul. There are invisible miracles, produced in the secrecy of the heart, the conscience, or the reason. Marvels of grace in the spiritual order are infinitely varied, but they blossom in the soul and are preceptible only to those in whose favor they are wrought, They are published, if at all, to only a few.

The author of this book leads pilgrimages of teenagers and young adults from throughout the United States and Canada to Fatima each year, and can testify to the miracles of grace which take place in souls there. I have spent night after night at Fatima until 12:00 or 1:00 in the morning hearing the confession of these young people and witnessing their tears of repentant love.

Father John De Marchi, presently a missionary in Ethiopia and personal friend, tells about his first pilgrimage to Fatima during the years of World War II. He arrived within the precincts of the Fatima Sanctuary about 8:30 p.m., and went to the retreat house. Anxious to make an extensive tour of the Sanctuary grounds in the Cova da Iria, he decided to do so before the evening ceremonies began. He had hardly left the house, however, when he was asked to hear a man's confession.

Father De Marchi sat on a stone to hear the man's confession, and immediately noticed a long line of people "looking like ants and . . .forming as if by magic from nowhere." He recalls:

Struggling against my impatience, I strove to remember that Fatima is the place of sacrifice and penance, and comforted myself with the thought that it must end some time. Once more I was mistaken. The line stretched interminably on, not only in front of me, but also in front of other priests who were sitting on the stones which at that time, when building operations were not complete, strewed that part of the Sanctuary.

The last penitent was heard about 2:00 a.m. He was a young father of twenty-five or thirty who had walked for eight days with his wife as they carried their child. Their little daughter had been born blind, and the doctors said she could not be cured. The young father continued,

> We made a novena and every night we put a few drops of Fatima water into her eyes. On the last day, just when we weren't thinking about it at all, I passed in front of her and she turned her head and followed me with her eyes. I nearly lost my head and shouted to my wife: "Maria! Come! Our prayers have been answered!"

The young father explained that the family had come on foot, "to fulfill a promise."

> You see, my wife and I both promised to come here on foot if Our Lady would cure our little daughter. . . .The doctors said she could not be cured, but now she sees. . . . And so, Father, here we are. We waited a few days so as to be here on the twelfth. [The big days of pilgrimage in Fatima are the 12th and 13th, especially May through October. At these times, hundreds of thousands come, many walking from one to two weeks to get there in fulfillment of some promise made to Our Lady. Food supplies are little more than barley bread and some wine. Many spend the cold nights sleeping in the open air. In recent years every weekend, especially during the warmer months of the year, sees celebrations on a smaller scale representative of the 12th-13th of May-October.]

Similarly, in 1970, an American couple and their daughter, Elise, visited Fatima on the twelfth and thirteenth of the month. Nine years of age, Elise had never been able to speak. A priest asked to offer Mass for Elise at the tomb of Jacinta Marto. Jacinta's tomb is situated in a side chapel to the left of the high altar in the Basilica. After Mass, which a handful of friends attended, the priest asked the little girl to step inside the altar rails and kneel with him on the tomb of Jacinta. "Elise," he said, "say after me, 'Jesus.' " Without any hesitation she did so. "Now Elise, say 'Mary and Jacinta.' " She pronounced them perfectly and with great clarity. These were the first words she had ever uttered: Jesus, Mary and Jacinta. Early the next morning as the bells of the Basilica rang out the famous Fatima Ave Maria, Elise stood on her bed and sang the familiar chorus, along with the chimes, at the top of her voice.

Today Elise, who is personally known to me and whose parents are friends, is a vivacious and beautiful young woman. Together with her parents she works to promote Our Lady's messages and the cause for Jacinta's beatification and canonization. She now speaks English, Portuguese, and is learning French. What experts were unable to bring about was suddenly accomplished at the tomb of Jacinta.

This is but another beautiful example of Our Lady's answers to faithful prayer at Fatima. She cares for both our bodies and our souls. Though her spiritual cures are her greater gifts, we know that she is interested in all aspects of our lives. In all things, Mary's great desire is to draw us to her Son, for His glory and the eternal salvation of all men.

3.
Fatima and the Holy Angels

Fatima reaffirms for us the constant teaching of the Church regarding the existence of angels. Although Catholic teaching and practice should go hand in hand, today there seems to be a wide gap between the two. How often has the reader heard a sermon on the angels? How often has a confessor or spiritual advisor exhorted his penitents and those under his care to pray for the intercession of the angels and of one's guardian angel in particular? How many continue their prayers to their guardian angels, much less to the nine choirs of angels, beyond the time of preparation for First Holy Communion?

The word "angel" means "messenger," "sent." The angels are individual persons, though they do not have bodies. Each angel is a pure spirit, and his very being moves with the speed of thought. The angels' place in the staircase of creation is between God and men, and their primary task is the glorification and service of God. In addition, God has appointed angels over different aspects of His creation, and to each of His human creatures He has given a particular guardian angel. To each of these guardian angels God has given a mission to guide and care for the soul entrusted to him. This mission can be compared to the vocation, or calling which each man receives in the plan of God.

The intervention of heaven on earth in the second decade of the twentieth century shows an angel carrying out a particular mission from God. The angel came to prepare the shepherd children for Our Lady's visit. Much of the world has not well heard the message of Fatima, much less lived it, but our openness to Our Lady's message will greatly deepen when, in imitation of the children of Fatima, we open ourselves to angelic preparation.

In the spring of 1916 the Angel appeared to Jacinta, Francisco, and Lucia for the first time. They saw a light whiter than snow, revealing the form of a young man. The form was transparent and much brighter than crystal which is pierced by the rays of the sun. The brightness of the Angel was a reflection of the light of God. His youth displays to us the eternal life of the angels and saints in heaven—a life spent in adoration of God, to which the angels labor to bring us also.

The Angel said, "Do not be afraid. I am the Angel of Peace. Pray with me." Thus we are told that the angels, especially our guardian angels, pray with us. This is a call to join them in a community of prayer. By uniting our prayers with those of the angels, we will more easily accomplish the complete surrender of ourselves to God. Remember that every good angel has made a profound submission to Almighty God, and that the Archangel Michael drove from heaven all angels who refused to serve the Lord.

Kneeling down, the Angel bowed his countenance to the ground. By a supernatural impulse, the children did the same as they repeated after him this prayer: "My God, I believe, I adore, I trust and I love Thee! I beg pardon for those who do not believe, do not adore, do not trust, and do not love Thee." (Our prayers should likewise involve our total person, body and soul; the reverent attitude of the body joins with the prayer of the heart and soul.) Having repeated these words three times, the Angel rose and said: "Pray thus. The hearts of Jesus and Mary are attentive to the voice of your supplication." Then the Angel disappeared.

The supernatural atmosphere which enveloped the three was so intense that for a long time they were scarcely aware of their own existence; they remained in the same bodily position and repeated the same prayers. So intimate and intense was their feeling of the presence of God that they remained silent about their experience.

The prayer of the Angel echoes the prayer which is prayed by the angels, saints, and the faithful on earth at Mass: Holy, Holy, Holy. This beautiful spirit shows us something of the great adoration of God which must take place in Heaven. The Angel also prays for sinful men, for those who do not render to God the worship and love which they owe.

Later that year, the same Angel suddenly appeared to the children a second time. He spoke: "What are you doing? Pray! Pray a great deal! The Hearts of Jesus and Mary have designs of mercy for you. Offer up prayers and sacrifices constantly to the Most High."

To Lucia's inquiry, "How are we to make sacrifices?" the Angel replied:

Make everything you do a sacrifice, and offer it to God as an act of reparation for the sins by which He is offended, and in supplication for the conversion of sinners. Bring peace to your country in this way. I am its Angel Guardian, the Angel of Portugal. Above all, accept and bear with submission the sufferings sent you by Our Lord.

Sister Lucia explains,

These words made a deep impression on our minds, like a light making us understand who God is, how he loves us and desires to be loved, as well as the value of sacrifice, how pleasing it is to Him, and how, on account of it, He grants the grace of conversion to sinners. For this reason, from that moment we began to offer up all that mortified us, never seeking other ways of mortification and penance, except to remain for hours, with our foreheads touching the ground, repeating the prayer the Angel had taught us.

The work of the angels is seen in the effect this second angelic visitation had on the children. Their efforts to lead us to an understanding of the value of sacrifice for the glory of God and the salvation of souls are evident in the impression the three so vividly received. The spirit of prayer is intensified by the second apparition. The children are carried far beyond their initial attitude toward life—from the time before the first apparition when they had been so wrapped up in their carefree games in the countryside. But they are to be transformed more deeply still in the months ahead.

The first apparition led the shepherd children to a deeper prayer life, and in the second the Angel told them to make many sacrifices. In the third apparition, they—and we—are shown that only through an intimate union with Jesus Christ in the Most Blessed Sacrament of the Holy Eucharist can we reach great holiness.

The Angel held in his hands a chalice surmounted by a Host, from which some drops of the Precious Blood were falling into the chalice. Leaving the chalice and the Host suspended in the air, the Angel prostrated himself on the ground and repeated this prayer three times:

O Most Holy Trinity, Father, Son and Holy Spirit, I adore Thee profoundly, I offer Thee the Most Precious Body, Blood, Soul and Divinity of Jesus Christ, present in all the tabernacles of the world, in reparation for the outrages, sacrileges and indifference by which He is offended. By the infinite merits of the Sacred Heart of Jesus, and the Immaculate Heart of Mary, I beg the conversion of poor sinners. [Note that the Mother of God is not infinite, nor is she the essential source of grace. Her activity as Mediatrix is completely subordinate to Christ's activity as Mediator.]

The Angel then arose and gave Holy Communion to the children. He gave the Host to Lucia, and he gave Francisco and Jacinta the chalice to drink from. Doing so, he said: "Take and drink the Body and Blood of Jesus Christ, horribly outraged by ungrateful men. Repair their crimes and console your God." After this, the Angel again prostrated himself, as did the children, and again prayed thrice beginning, "Most Holy Trinity. . ." They repeated the prayer.

In a century that was to witness among many Catholic people a weakening of faith in the Real Presence of the God-Man in the Holy Eucharist, we note that the three children felt so intensely the presence of God that they were completely overwhelmed and absorbed by it. For a considerable time they were unconscious of their bodily senses; even for some days afterwards, their physical actions were impelled, as it were, by that supernatural Being. They felt immersed in that world with which the angels are familiar.

The angels, like Our Lady, wish to lead us to the Eucharistic Jesus. The Angel had prepared the children for their Eucharistic union with Our Lord: "The Hearts of Jesus and Mary have designs of mercy for you. Offer up prayers and sacrifices constantly to the Most High." The children were to be given a mission in and for the world, but only in union with Our Eucharistic Lord could they carry it out. By His power they would become apt instruments of God's mercy. The third apparition prepares them for their mission of holiness. Their holiness will come into fuller bloom under the guidance of Mary, the Mother of the Church.

In the third angelic apparition, the central mystery of our holy Faith unfolds for the children. They see most clearly that the angels join men in adoring God in the Holy Eucharist, and that they adore God wherever Jesus Christ is sacramentally present in Catholic tabernacles the world over. The guardian angel of each one of us surely joins us when we kneel in adoration before the tabernacle, or at the Consecration of the Mass. In fact, the guardian angel leads and inspires such adoration. Thus the Angel of Fatima joined the chilren in adoration, communicating with them in their acts, or rather, first leading them to such acts of faith, trust, love and adoration.

We can compare what happened in the Cova da Iria to what happened in other humble surroundings 1900 years earlier in Bethlehem. Angels announced to the shepherds good news, and led them to our Divine Lord and to His Mother. In poverty, unattached to the world, in the silence of the countryside, the shepherds find God.

The angels have often played a role in the history of salvation. They were active in Isreal, and their mission continues on into the life of Christ and the Church. The Angel Gabriel came to Mary with the message that she was the chosen Mother of the Holy One, and it was an angel who told Joseph not to put Mary away, since the Child she was carrying within her was of God. Christ Jesus in the Garden of Olives, sorrowful unto death, was comforted by an angel.

When Christ freely surrendered Himself in the Garden of Olives to His captors, He reminded Peter, "Thinkest thou that I cannot ask My Father, and he will give me presently more than twelve legions of angels?" (Mt. 26:53) An angel kept guard at the empty tomb upon the resurrection of Our Lord, and two angels had to remind Peter and the other disciples not to look for the risen Jesus in the empty tomb, but rather to look in Galilee. As Our Divine Lord ascended into Heaven, it was the angels who said to the apostles: "This Jesus who it taken up from you into heaven, shall so come, as you have seen Him going into Heaven" (Acts 1:11). Further, an angel appeared to Peter in a dream, directing him regarding the baptism of the pagan centurion, Cornelius.

As the holy angels were the precursors of the first coming of the Lord, so they will be for His second coming. We see that in Apocalypse 12:12, after the great battle, Satan, who had deceived the world, is hurled down in defeat. Just as Fatima announced the ultimate triumph of the Immaculate Heart, which is the triumph of her Son, so the final book of Sacred Scripture presents to us the triumph of Heaven.

The strong voice of the first angel announcing the judgment is heard in Apocalypse 14:7. "Fear the Lord, and give Him honor, because the hour of His judgment is come; and adore ye Him, that made heaven and earth, the sea, and the foundations of waters." At Fatima, the angel announces that the sins of men outrage their God. He calls souls who love God to make Eucharistic reparation, so that we may be more familiar with Divine mercy than with Divine justice. It is an angelic call to the members of the Church to complete in themselves what is lacking to the sufferings of Jesus Christ.

Angels are seen in Sacred Scripture preparing all the actions desired by God for the final glory of His Son Jesus Christ and of His Holy Mother Mary. To remove the angels from our consciousness and not to work together with them is to miss the harmony of God's approach to man and of man's response to God, according to the plan of the Almighty. But those who actively and consciously accept their angel come to live in the presence of a truly celestial companion. In the Old Testament, God says, "Behold I will send My angel, who shall go before thee, and keep thee in thy journey, and bring thee into the place that I have prepared" (Ex. 23:20).

Jacinta, whose short life was especially touched by the vision of Hell, was also deeply devoted to the holy angels. She apparently had an experience of hearing angels sing, for she said that angels do not sing as men do. Her favorite songs were "Salve Nobre Padroira" (Hail Noble Patroness), "Virgin Pura" (Virgin Pure), and "Anjos, Cantai Comigo" (Angels, Sing with Me). Certainly her openness to the Angel's message contributed to her unusual spiritual transformation, which stands out even among the Fatima children.

From all eternity God chose each man's guardian angel just for him. God did this in His infinite love. The guardian angel has perfect awareness of his mission and responsibility toward you. His vocation is to stay by our side, protect and inspire you, and to lead you in the true way of life, to the Way which is Jesus.

Each one of us has a vocation from God. How important it is to teach young people that their guardian angels too have a "vocation," a mission, in their regard, and will assist them in finding their own vocations in the eternal plan of God. A young person who will entrust himself in faith and love to his guardian angel's care will hardly go astray in his chosen place in life for time and for eternity. It is very wise for a young person to consciously open himself to his angel's guidance in his choice of vocation. Then he will choose rightly according to God's will and plan.

Adults who have already found their vocation in life should consciously remain open to their angels, knowing that once God has given an office in life, He will supply all the graces we need to live that vocation perfectly. Our angels have an important role in helping us to use these graces wisely. As we know from the prayer we learned as children, our guardian angels are given to us "to light, to guard, to rule and guide." Moreover, God surely sends His angels to faithful priests to assist them in their Eucharistic duties. God also uses angels to awaken in souls the vocation to the priesthood so as to perpetuate the presence and action of Our Eucharistic Lord.

The faith of Christians in the world in recent decades has weakened in many cases. This is because the life of prayer has weakened. As the Angel of Fatima first led the children to pray, so a constant mission of the holy angels is to lead us to prayer. Fatima reminds us to grow accustomed to the holy angels as companions. By ignoring our angel we hinder the purpose for which God has given each of us this celestial companion. The holy angels are honored to be near a soul in the state of sanctifying grace, as they too share in the very Divine life. When we are aware of the action of the holy angels, and in particular of our guardian angel, we open ourselves to the action he desires on our behalf as he communicates to us his heavenly inspirations. We develop an habitual attitude of desiring to communicate with out angel, accepting his happiness and his values of eternity as compared with those of earth. Our Lord has said: ". . . for I say to you, that their angels in Heaven always see the face of My Father who is in Heaven" (Mt. 18:10).

I have led hundreds of young people to Fatima for intensive education and spiritual formation. Before I even meet them, I pray to their guardian angels. My first efforts on Fatima Youth Pilgrimages have been to inspire youth to become open to their guardian angels and to love purity—reclaiming this virtue, if necessary, through the Sacrament of Penance. The transformation which takes place in a great many of these young people becomes apparent to others, and especially to their parents.

People are not able to probe the meaning of Fatima because they are not pure enough. To understand Fatima one must be pure. Heaven has repeatedly brought its special messages to the world through children, through youth who have retained their purity. Children are completely open to Heaven's message because of their purity, and it is important that Fatima be taught to them. Heaven is addressing itself to those who, like the three little children, are child-like enough to be open to the message of the Angel and of Our Lady. With the downgrading, or at least the ignoring of the place of the holy angels in the life of the church, there is in evidence less and less the love and practice of purity. Though this is not the greatest virtue, it has often been called the "angelic" virtue, and the angels can certainly help us toward its better understanding and practice.

There is a movement in the Church known as *Opus Sanctorum Angelorum* (The work of the Holy Angels). In this movement, which has been authorized by the Church, a "promise to the Guardian Angel" is made. It is a real commitment to one's guardian angel. While Sacred Scripture and the constant teachings of the Church form the essential motivation for this devotion, it is likewise true that the message of Fatima serves to inspire us to study in prayer the work of the holy angels and their place in our spiritual lives. We can only comprehend and respond to them in the light of Divine faith.

When God calls a soul to make a promise to his guardian angel, that person becomes more open in grace to grow in a supernatural vision of life.

Of course, the guardian angel must respect man's liberty, the great gift which God has given to each human person. If God respects the freedom of the will, surely the angel must do the same. Therefore, one who makes the promise to his guardian angel finds that things do not change in themselves. There are still difficulties, temptations, joys, and sorrows. What changes is oneself. By the grace of God, through the intercession and inspiration of his guardian angel, one can see things in a new way, accept them in a new way, and all things can have a supernatural effect.

One dedicated to his angel may on occasion fall into sin, but realizing the presence of his angel, he will more quickly seek Divine forgiveness, seeing the futility of remaining in darkness when light is available. When we truly realize that our guardian angel is our constant companion, all is done in his presence, and we will experience good thoughts, actions, interior graces and supernatural joy. Even our relationships with other humans will become enlightened with the light of the angels, so that we see others as God sees them. The angels lead us in faith to grow in love and grace unto the glory of God. But if we are not open to the good angels, the bad angels, the devils, have more power over us. Pope Paul VI, who understood well the message of Fatima and authorized the Movement of the Holy Angels, once remarked that the smoke of Satan was sifting into the very crevices of the Church. To Peter, Jesus said, "Simon, Simon, behold Satan hath desired to have you, that he may sift you as wheat"(Lk. 22:31).

The message of Fatima begins with light and it will end with light. First there is the Angel of Light, then the Lady of Light from whose hands come a brilliant lift—a light that immersed the three children in God and empowered them to endure all sufferings in order to carry out the designs of mercy which God had for them for the salvation of the world. And in the final apparition, with the spinning of the sun, Our Lady brought enlightenment even to atheists and those of little faith. Like the Angel of Portugal, the other angels try to guide us toward the supernatural light which they can see and which we all hope to see in Eternity.

ACT OF DEDICATION

Eternal High Priest of the Holy Church and of all men,
Eternally begotten by the Father
Breathing the Spirit from eternity to eternity.

You are the Lord of heaven and earth,
Yours are all creatures, angels and men, and all nature.

You created angels before men,
You will come with Your angels to judge all men.

Give these, Your powerful Spirits, to us as friends and helpers
That they may be our light in these days of darkness,
That they may be our deliverers from the snares of the evil one.
Let us hold fast their hand and let their strength become our strength.
Through your angels, let these words in Your sight be a dedication to You,
O Lord, of all that we are and have.

Our union with the angels leads us to a stronger union with You,
because the strength of Your angel strengthens our hands which enclose You.

Let these words be written in Your heart, heavenly Father,
as a dedication of the world (the diocese, the parish, the family),
to You through Your angels.

Let these words be written on Your pierced hands, Lord Jesus Christ,
as witness of this dedication.

Breathe, Holy Spirit, Your spirit of re-creation over these words,
as words of the Church which you lead and guide.

And You most Holy Trinity,
through the prayers of Mary, Queen of all Angels,
shower the grace of Your blessing over this dedication. AMEN.

4.
Fatima and Eucharistic Reparation

When Bishop Venancio, the former administrator of the diocese in which Our Lady appeared, was asked to summarize the Fatima message, he answered: "Fatima is reparation, reparation, reparation, and especially Eucharistic reparation." He added that Eucharistic reparation includes such things as visits to the Most Blessed Sacrament, holy hours and vigils, but that the highest form of Eucharistic reparation is the offering of the Sacrifice of the Mass. Our Catholic Faith tells us that Holy Mass is the perpetuation of the Sacrifice of the Cross.

Reparation is atonement to God for sins committed against Him by ourselves and others. Every sin is an offense against God; justice and love demand that we make reparation to God. Jesus made reparation to God the Father for our sins when He died on the Cross, and it is God's Will that we also make reparation to Him, in union with His Beloved Son. We do this every time we make an Act of Contrition or any time we pray or perform good actions for the love of God. While anything that is not sin can be offered to God to atone for sin, the best form of reparation is Eucharistic reparation. As mentioned above, this includes first of all the Mass, then adoring Jesus in the Most Blessed Sacrament. Jesus' perfect act of reparation, His sacrifice of Calvary, is perpetuated at every Sacrifice of the Mass, and we join our hearts with Jesus as He offers Himself to God through the words of the priest. Then, by receiving Jesus with love in Holy Communion, we can make up for the hatred and indifference which men show Him.

As members of the Mystical Body of Christ, we can and should offer prayers and sacrifices to God in reparation to Him for the sins of other members of His Mystical Body. We also offer reparation for the sins of the whole world. In this way we can win from Jesus graces to save souls. On the Day of Judgment we may be surprised to meet souls in Heaven who would not have been saved without our prayers and sacrifices. Let us look, then, at the actual messages and happenings of 1916 and 1917 to determine why Fatima can be summarized as "reparation and especially Eucharistic reparation."

As indicated in the previous chapter, the Angel of Fatima came three times to Jacinta, Francisco, and Lucia before God's Mother made her first appearance in the Cova da Iria. The reality of God, His existence, His holiness, our lowliness as creatures, all comes through strongly in the apparitions of the Angel. But it was in his second visit that the Angel said those words which, by Sr. Lucia's own account, made such a deep impression on the children. "Make everything you do a sacrifice, and offer it to God as an act of reparation for the sins by which He is offended. . . ." And, as we have seen, in the third visit the Angel demonstrated the highest form of reparation is in the Holy Eucharist. The children had just said their Rosary and the prayer, "My God, I believe, I adore. . ." when suddenly the Angel appeared with the chalice surmounted by a Host.

The drops of Blood make us realize that Our Lord is really present in the Eucharist, as well as that the Eucharistic sacrifice is truly the Sacrifice of Calvary. The fact that the Angel appeared after the children had said the Rosary reminds us of the words of Pope Paul VI in *Marialis Cultus*: "Meditation on the mysteries of the Rosary. . .can be an excellent preparation for the celebration of those same mysteries in the liturgical actions and can also become a continuing echo thereof." While it is best to pray the Mass prayers during the Mass itself, Pope Paul stated that the Rosary is a worthy preparation for the Eucharistic Sacrifice.

Here we recall again the Angel's awesome message when he too prostrated himself on the ground and said that he offered the Christ in the Eucharist "in reparation for the outrages, sacrileges and indifference by which He is offended." We note that the children did not receive under both species, indicating the Catholic doctrine that Jesus is present whole and entire under either the form of bread or the form of wine. Moreover, in the presence of the Blessed Sacrament the Angel adored the entire Trinity, not simply Jesus Christ, the Second Person, for the three Persons in God are inseparable. Then, as he gave Holy Communion, the Angel presented the ideal of reparation: "Take and drink the Body and Blood of Jesus Christ, horribly outraged by ungrateful men. Repair their crimes and console your God."

We must see a relationship between what the Angel first told the children and what God's Mother later related to them. During the winter months between the apparitions of the Angel in 1916 and the spring of 1917, the children made frequent visits and acts of Eucharistic reparation in their parish church. They grew in spirituality during those months, and then in May of 1917, they were ready for further growth. It was then that Our Lady, the Catechist, came.

The Angel had told them they should make everything they did a sacrifice. The Angel taught them Eucharistic reparation in adoring and receiving Our Lord in Holy Communion. When Our Lady first came in May of 1917, she asked whether the children wished to offer to God all the sufferings God desired to send them in reparation for the sins by which He is offended and in supplication for the conversion of sinners.

At her very first apparition Our Lady communicated a light that penetrated to the inmost recesses of the children's hearts, making them see themselves in God, who was that light, more clearly than they could see themselves in a mirror. Their spirituality was directed to reparation and to the Holy Eucharist in that very first visit. By an interior impulse, they cried out these words: "*Oh, Most Holy Trinity, I adore You. My God, my God, I love You in the Most Blessed Sacrament.*" Only then did Our Lady instruct them, "Pray the Rosary every day. . ." First, she intensified their realization of the reality and presence of God and to move them to adore God in the Most Blessed Sacrament. They were to offer their sufferings in reparation to God and for the conversion of sinners, in union with the Holy Eucharist. Again, in her second visit, Our lady made the children understand that her Immaculate Heart was outraged by the sins of humanity and that she wanted reparation.

The question may here arise as to whether Mary wants reparation to herself rather than to God. But we must remember that Mary said that Her Immaculate Heart was the way that leads to God. The reparation we make to the Immaculate Heart of Mary is ultimately reparation to God. Mary's Heart is inseparable from the Sacred Heart of Jesus. At this visit she herself said:"My Immaculate Heart will be your refuge and the way that will lead you to God."

On the third visit, July 13, 1917, Our Lady returned to her theme of reparation when she said, "Sacrifice yourselves for sinners, and say often, especially when you make some sacrifice: Oh Jesus, it is for love of You, for the conversion of sinners, and in reparation for the sins committed against the Immaculate Heart of Mary." During this visit Our Lady again made reference to Eucharistic reparation. After the terrible vision of Hell and the prediction of war and persecution of the Church and the Holy Father, Our Lady said she would come again to request the "Communion of Reparation" on the first Saturdays.

The message of Mary continues what the Angel introduced. Mary asked for the following reparation prayer to be said after each decade of the Rosary: "Oh my Jesus, forgive us; save us from the fire of Hell; take all souls to Heaven, especially those most in need." In August, there was again the request for reparation: "Pray, pray very much and make sacrifices for sinners, for many souls go to hell because they have nobody to pray and make sacrifices for them." In September Our Lady again mentioned sacrifices. It is the ongoing theme of her appearances, together with the request for the daily Rosary. According to Father Messias Coelho, a Portuguese Fatima scholar, although Our Lady smiled continuously at Lourdes, the only time she smiled at Fatima was in September when she said to the children: "God is pleased with your sacrifices."

In October Mary asked for a chapel to be built in the Cova in her honor—and what is a chapel essentially for but to offer the Sacrifice of the Mass? Moreover, St. Joseph and the Child Jesus both made "the Sign of the Cross" with their hands in this last apparition, and what is the Mass but the perpetuation of the Cross? In the little chapel where formerly the little holm oak tree stood, one Mass after another is now offered, and a priest must make reservations to get his turn. Many Masses are also offered in the Basilica of Our Lady of the Rosary of Fatima overlooking the Cova.

Even after the 1917 Fatima messages, events continue to emphasize the Holy Eucharist. Recall that back in July of 1917 Our Lady had said she would come again to ask for the Communion of Reparation to bring about the triumph of her Immaculate Heart. In October Our Lady told the children, "Do not offend the Lord Our God any more, because He is already so much offended." Avoidance of sin indeed goes hand in hand with reparation; our reparation would not be true if it did not include a sincere effort to renounce sin.

On December 10, 1925, when Lucia was a Dorothian nun, Our Lady came to her with the Child Jesus. She again asked for reparation to her Immaculate Heart—and thus of course to Jesus—through the devotion of the five First Saturdays, which includes Holy Communion received in the spirit of reparation.

But there is still more. In June of 1929, at Tuy, Spain, that remarkable apparition took place which showed how the basics of our Catholic Faith tie together with the Holy Eucharist as central. In the words of Sister Lucia:

> Suddenly the whole chapel was illumined by a supernatural light, and a cross of light appeared above the altar, reaching to the ceiling. In a brighter light at the upper part of the cross could be seen the face of a man and his body to the waist [God the Father], on his breast there was a dove also of light [God the Holy Spirit] and, nailed to the cross, was the body of another man [God the Son]. A little below the waist, I could see a chalice and a large Host suspended in the air, on to which drops of blood were falling from the face of Jesus Crucified and from the wound in His side. These drops ran down on the Host and fell into the chalice. Our Lady was beneath the right arm of the cross, and in her hand was her Immaculate Heart. (It was Our Lady of Fatima with her Immaculate Heart in her left hand without sword or roses, but with a crown of thorns and flames.) Under the left arm of the cross, large letters, as if of crystal clear water which ran down over the altar, formed these words: "Grace and Mercy."

The Mother of the Church is seen in this apparition. The entire Blessed Trinity is involved in the Holy Eucharist, which is shown as the same Sacrifice as that of the Cross. Jesus Christ is perpetuating the action of the Cross so that grace and mercy flow over the altar out to the world for the salvation of poor sinners. Our Blessed Mother, the Mother of the Church, manifested herself as Our Lady of the Holy Eucharist. She stands there interceding beneath the right arm of the Cross, with her Son on the Cross just above her and with the Most Precious Blood falling from both the Crucified Jesus and His other presence in the Holy Eucharist, into the chalice onto the altar to bring grace and mercy to mankind. Mary holds the Rosary, representing the mysteries of Christ upon which we are to meditate, those same mysteries of the Rosary which the Pope said were celebrated in the Mass. Here we have a summary of the Fatima message.

A balanced spirituality is concerned with both God and neighbor. Sometimes these two aspects are described as the "vertical" and the "horizontal" relationships. An exclusively vertical devotion would aim directly and only at God, unmindful of our union with one another in the Mystical Body of Christ. Then again, if one became completely devoted to others, he would be in danger of neglecting his duties to God and thus of making his religion entirely horizontal. Both directions are necessary. The Cross upon which Jesus died is a combination of a vertical and a horizontal symbol, and therefore represents the balance we seek.

The Angel focused on both the vertical and the horizontal in his first apparition. The vertical: "My God, I believe, I adore, I trust and I love Thee!" The horizontal: "I beg pardon for those who do not believe, do not adore, do not trust and do not love Thee."

Both these aspects are present in our attitudes as we adore God perfectly in, with, and through Jesus Christ in the Sacrifice of the Mass, which is the perfect and highest form of reparation. It is perfect, because it is Jesus Himself who is the chief Priest, the main offerer of every Holy Mass as His Sacrifice of the Cross is perpetuated on earth. Though Jesus does not die over again, His one sacrifice of the Cross is perpetuated and re-presented at each Holy Mass; at each Mass we have an opportunity to receive more deeply the fruits of Jesus' sacrifice.

In the words of the *General Catechetical Directory* issued by the Vatican:

> This sacrifice is not merely a rite commemorating a past sacrifice. For in it Christ, by the ministry of the priests, perpetuates the sacrifice of the Cross in an unbloody manner through the course of the centuries. In it too He nourishes the faithful with Himself, the Bread of Life, in order that, filled with love of God and neighbor, they may become more and more a people acceptable to God.

This document reminds us of the accuracy of the word "transubstantiation" to describe the substantial change of bread and wine into the Body, Blood, Soul and Divinity of Jesus Christ. This in turn reminds us of the expression which the three Fatima seers used for the Real Presence of Our Savior in the Most Blessed Sacrament. They spoke of Jesus present in the Tabernacle of their parish church as "the hidden Jesus." The *General Catechetical Directory* speaks too of the *hidden* Real Presence of Jesus in the Holy Eucharist:

> . . .Accordingly, under the appearances (that is, the phenomenal reality) of the bread and wine, the humanity of Christ, not only by its power but by itself (that is, substantially), united with His Divine Person, lies hidden in an altogether mysterious way.

This is the Mystery of Faith. Jesus is in all the tabernacles of the world wherever a validly ordained priest has consecrated bread and wine. The

General Catachetical Directory referred to Catholics as "having been nourished with the Victim of the sacrifice of the Cross. . . ." We should therefore have "a genuine and active love" for others.

We can be sanctified only through the Holy Eucharist. Jesus Christ has said,

> Abide in Me, and I in you. As the branch cannot bear fruit of itself, unless it abide in the vine, so neither can you, unless you abide in Me. I am the vine; you the branches: he that abideth in Me, and I in him, the same beareth much fruit: for without Me you can do nothing. (John 15:4-5)

Through an intimate union in love with Jesus Christ in the Holy Eucharist, our souls are saved and sanctified and we are called to serve as instruments in drawing other souls to the same fountain of divine life. Moreover, Our Lord foretold triumph through the Holy Eucharist when He said:

> Amen, amen I say to You: Except you eat the Flesh of the Son of Man, and drink His Blood, you shall not have life in you. He that eateth My Flesh, and drinketh My Blood, hath everlasting life; and I will raise him up in the last day. For My Flesh is meat indeed: and My Blood is drink indeed. He that eateth My Flesh, and drinketh My Blood, abideth in Me, and I in him. As the living Father hath sent Me, and I live by the Father; so he that eateth Me, the same also shall live by Me. This is the Bread that came down from Heaven. (John 6:54-59)

It is revealed at Fatima that in the end the Immaculate Heart of Mary will triumph; that triumph will be a Eucharistic one. Mary triumphs when souls are sanctified—led not simply to the Immaculate Heart of Mary, but through her to the supreme Sacrifice perpetuated in the Holy Eucharist where her Son always abides.

It is ineteresting that some say, "Devotion to the Immaculate Heart of Mary summarizes the Fatima message." But, if we spell out the meaning of devotion to the Immaculate Heart of Mary, we see that this includes that love for God and neighbor which the Holy Eucharist brings about. How could one be truly devoted to the Immaculate Heart of Mary without also cherishing a devotion to the Eucharistic Jesus?

Whether, like Father Alonso, we see the Immaculate Heart of Mary as the center of the Fatima message, or whether we look to the summary of Bishop Venancio who sees "Eucharistic reparation" as the essence of the message, we are essentially aiming in the same direction: *Fatima is devotion to the Immaculate Heart of Mary leading us to her Son, Jesus Christ, in reparation for Sins and for the conversion of all poor sinners, especially through Eucharistic Reparation.*

The message of Fatima calls for all to accept Mary as spiritual Mother and her Immaculate Heart as model in loving God and neighbor. And when men accept Mary as the Mother of the Church and model in love, which means model of unity with God and neighbor, this leads of necessity to Eucharistic reparation. This is no new doctrine. Our American Bishops said in their 1973 Marian pastoral, "The authenticated appearances of Our Lady . . . serve as reminders to us of basic Christian themes: prayer, penance, and the necessity of the sacraments. . . ."

Is Fatima being preached in the parishes? If the Gospels are preached, if the reality of the Holy Eucharist as Sacrifice and Sacrament is preached, if we are reminded of the substantial and real living presence of Jesus Christ Our Savior and Redeemer in the Eucharist, if there is preached that at Holy Mass there is offered to God the Father the same Sacrifice of the Body and Blood of Jesus once offered on the Cross, and that He is offered in atonement for our sins and the sins of the world, then, indeed, Fatima is being preached though the word "Fatima" never be used. Since "Fatima is a reaffirmation of the Gospel" (Pope Pius XII) every sermon and lesson that reaffirms our Faith in the doctrine of the Holy Eucharist is an answer to Our Lady's call.

Hardly two hundred feet from the Chapel of the Apparitions in the Cova da Iria, the very spot where God's Mother appeared to ask for prayer and sacrifice, there is today another chapel where sisters observe perpetual adoration of Our Lord in the Most Blessed Sacrament. In a small chapel, with the Eucharistic Lord always contained in the monstrance over the tabernacle, one will always find a nun kneeling in adoration and reparation. This has taken place ever since 1960, the year Pope John XXIII opened the third part of the Fatima secret.

The sisters, covered with a white veil before their Eucharistic Lord, are nonetheless popularly called the "Blue Sisters" because of the bright blue color of the habit they wear around the Cova. The Blue Sisters are properly named the "Reparation Religious of Our Lady of Dolors of Fatima." I requested a brief history of the founding and purpose of the order and received the following explanation:

About 1900, a young Portuguese priest, having received a laureate in theology and canon law from the Gregorian University in Rome, stopped at Lourdes on the way home in order to entrust to the Blessed Mother the apostolic field opening to his zeal. Kneeling at the grotto, he made a vow: to spread in Portugal devotion to Our Lady of Lourdes.

In 1917, like a lightning bolt from the north to the south of the country, the news of the apparitions of Fatima spread. This "Apostle of Our Lady of Lourdes," Dr. Manuel Nunes Formigao, fearing it to be some plot of the devil, went to the Cova da Iria with the purpose of unmasking the trick and defending the Mother of God. He was in Fatima on September 13, 1917, the day of the fifth apparition, and the Blessed Mother made her devoted apostle feel that the apparitions at Fatima were not a human work, but a manifestation of Divine mercy.

In February of 1920, Jacinta was slowly dying in a hospital ward. Our Lady appeared to her and gave her grave revelations concernig punishments that God would send to the world if there were not souls to make reparation to God, offended by the sins of humanity. The Blessed Mother appointed Dr. Formigao, the same priest who had made the vow at the grotto at Lourdes, as the man to whom the seer would communicate the said secret. Upon receiving that Divine message a light burst upon the heart of this priest: It was necessary for souls to make the vow of making reparation for the sins that saddened the Heart of Jesus and the Immaculate Heart of Mary, and to realize as perfectly as possible the ideal of the message of Fatima.

Thus, on January 6, 1926, the cradle of a newborn congregation was settled in Lisbon. In May of 1934 the motherhouse was definitely fixed near the Sanctuary of the Cova da Iria. On May 4, 1940, the Feast of the Finding of the Holy Cross, the Bishop of Leiria sent to Fatima the good news that he had received from the Holy See the authorization for the canonical erection of the Repairing Religious of Our lady of Dolors of Fatima.

The principal aim of the new congregation is to repair, particularly by adoration of the Holy Eucharist, the offenses made to the Sacred Heart of Jesus and to the Immaculate Heart of Mary, and also to recognize that an intense interior life can be harmonized with the lively wish of providing for the necessities and exigences of the present hour. The Repairing Religious of Fatima devote themselves also to works of the social apostolate, such as orphanages and workhouses for girls, the apostolate of the press, and help for Catholic action organizations. Also within the basic scope of this institute is prayer for the Christianization of families.

Our Lady opened to souls a new yet old road of perfection, the message of Fatima *lived* and the souls which tread generously by that road shall have in the Heart of Mary the sure shelter to take them to the Heart of God.

5.
The Church and Fatima

At the time of the Fatima apparitions, the Church in Portugal was laboring under an atheistic government. Soon after the Fatima events, the diocese of Leiria-Fatima was restored by the Holy See. And on May 3rd, 1922, after suffering imprisonment and torture from the government, Bishop José Alves Correi da Silva published a pastoral letter in which he stated the following:

> In this diocese of Leiria, there can be no fact connected with our holy Religion to which our pastoral action is or could be indifferent.
>
> Practically every day, but more especially on the thirteenth of each month, great numbers of people go to Fatima. These people are drawn from every social category and they go there to thank Our Lady of the Rosary for the benefits they have received through her mediation.
>
> It is well known that in 1917 a series of phenomena occurred there, witnessed by thousands of people of all kinds and foretold by some unlettered children to whom, it was affirmed, Our Lady had appeared and made certain recommendations. From that time there has never ceased to be a flow of pilgrims to the place.
>
> Of the three children who said they were favored by the apparitions, two died *before our appointment to this diocese*. We have questioned the

remaining seer several times.

Her story and her replies are always *simple and sincere;* in them we can find nothing contrary to faith or morals. We ask, could this child, now fourteen years old, exercise an influence which could explain such a continuous concourse of people? Could her personal *prestige* alone draw such multitudes of human beings? Could any precocious qualities in her attract vast crowds to herself alone? It is most improbable that such could be the case since we are dealing with a child of most rudimentary education, and without instruction of any kind.

Moreover, this child has now left her native place and has not been seen there again; yet the people go in ever increasing numbers to the Cova da Iria.

Could one explain it perhaps by the natural beauty or picturesqueness of the place? On the contrary, it is a lonely and deserted spot, without trees or water, far from the railway, almost lost in the serra and destitute of scenic beauties.

Do the people go there because of the chapel perhaps? The faithful have constructed a *tiny cell*, so small that it is impossible to celebrate Holy Mass inside, and in the month of February of this year some unfortunate people, may Our Lady forgive them, destroyed the chapel with explosives during the night and set fire to it.

We have advised against its reconstruction for the moment, not only with the idea of further attacks in mind but also to test the motives which draw so many people to the place.

And yet, far from diminishing in numbers, the crowds are ever greater.

In answer to the demand implied in this pastoral letter, the Bishop of Leiria-Fatima nominated a commission to study the case. He set up a canonical inquiry; two it its members were Rev. Dr. Formigão and Rev. Dr. Marques dos Santos.

The diocese of Leiria celebrated the seventh centenary of the death of St. Francis of Assisi in October of 1926. The Apostolic Nuncio was present at the ceremonies and visited Batalha, a centuries-old national shrine in Portugal, and later visited the place of the Fatima apparitions in company with the Bishop of Fatima. There exist no records of the impressions which the Nuncio communicated to the Holy See. What is certain is that three months later, on January 21, 1927, the privilege of a special Votive Mass of Our Lady was conceded to Fatima by the Holy See.

The final meeting of members of the commission for the canonical process took place on April 14, 1929. On October 1, 1930, the Bishop of Leiria issued a pastoral letter entitled *The Divine Providence.* In it he solemnly declared that the visions of the three seers were worthy of belief.

The pastoral letter approving of the Fatima apparitions contained the following memorable paragraphs:

> As little by little the crowds continued to increase extraordinarily, and as the diocese of Leiria, canonically erected in that year, was then administered by His Eminence the Cardinal Patriarch of Lisbon, Dom Antonio Mendes Belo, of happy memory, His Grace the Archbishop of Miliene, now Bishop of Villa-Real and then Vicar-General of the Patriarchate, ordered an inquiry to be made into the happenings.
>
> On our taking charge of the diocese as its bishop in 1920, we could not ignore what had passed and therefore, by our order of May 6th, 1922, we appointed a commission of priests freely to take evidence in favor of or against the events and to submit the report to us. Two members of this commission were called by God to His presence, but the others continued the work. Recently they submitted a long report which we have examined with great care.
>
> * * *
>
> Our Holy Mother the Church having entrusted to our care the Bishopric of Leiria, and it being our duty as bishop to care for the faithful entrusted to us, and following the example of the venerable prelates in such cases, we now pronounce our decision, while humbly declaring that we submit our judgment to the Holy See.
>
> Referring to the small number of the wise, the powerful, and the noble among the Christians of the primitive Church, St. Paul adds, "But the foolish things of the world hath God chosen, that He may confound the wise; and the weak things of the world hath God chosen, that He may confound the strong. And the base things of the world, and the things that are comtemptible, hath God chosen, and things that are not, that He might bring to naught things that are: That no flesh should glory in His sight. . . . That, as it is written: 'He that glorieth, may glory in the Lord.' "(1 Cor. 1:27-29, 31).
>
> History upholds these observations with facts. The Apostles chosen by Our Lord to preach the Christian doctrine to the whole world were fishermen; St. Gregory VII, the champion of the liberty of the Church, belonged to a poor peasant family. St. Joan of Arc, who liberated France, and the Blessed Bernadette de Soubirous, the happy seer of Lourdes, were poor shepherdesses.
>
> At Fatima it is the same. The place chosen for the apparitions is stony, without any attraction whatsoever. Portugal is rich in beautiful spots, verdant lands, superb panoramas. Cova da Iria, besides being a real hollow, had nothing attractive about it. The child seers were humble creatures from our mountain lands, modestly dressed, without instruction, not being able to read, and with a rudimentary religious knowledge.
>
> They were not nervous, but affable and loving in the midst of their naturalness, fond of the family, obedient to their parents, happy!. . .

One could not discern in them any self-interest or the spirit of vanity. They would not accept alms or presents which people wished to give them. And when we decided to take upon ourselves the direction of the works and the religious movement, they honorably handed over to us, in their original form, the money and the objects of value which the people used to leave on the site of the apparitions.

Their parents possessed a little property, and today continue to support themselves as before. They worked for their living, and continue to do so today. In nothing is their life altered after the lapse of thirteen years.

The children, when questioned jointly or separately, answered with the same precision, without noticeable contradictions, to the questions whether official or private, to which they were subjected.

They were imprisoned by the representative of the administrative authority, and threatened that they would be roasted, but not even then would they deny what they had declared.

They said nothing against faith or morals, according to the words of the Apostle, "No man, speaking by the Spirit of God, saith Anathema to Jesus" (1 Cor. 12:3).

Finally, the two younger children, brother and sister, fell ill with the pneumonic influenza, which carried away so many in the whole world, and both died edifying deaths, while Lucia, the only surviving seer, freely and voluntarily, without any coercion or persuasion, after obtaining her mother's consent, embraced the religious life.

It is likewise necessary to consider the circumstances which accompanied the visions. [Already reviewed earlier in this book.]

* * *

The argument of persecutions, which are a sign that the works are of God, was not wanting either in the case of the apparitions of Fatima.

* * *

The seers of Fatima were imprisoned by the authorities, and threatened with being cast into a cauldron of boiling oil.

It is common knowledge that the authorities did all they could to prohibit the pilgrimages, creating diffulties in the passage of the people, while certain publicists ridiculed and scoffed at the ardent faith of the good Portuguese people.

Belief in the apparitions resisted all violence, which after all, but served to increase fervor and to propagate the graces and favors which Our Lady showers on those who ask her.

And let it not be said that Fatima was an invention of the clergy; if the government with all its might and prestige could not succeed in vanquishing faith in Our Lady of Fatima, how could our humble clergy, despoiled by the revolution of all their possessions which Christian piety had handed to the Holy Church for her maintenance, clergy so often persecuted and calumniated, the lowest and poorest in this diocese of Leiria, how could they have the power to create a religious movement at Fatima which today has extended to the whole of Portugal and so consolingly develops in so many foreign countries?

Besides this, His Eminence the Cardinal Patriarch, Dom Antonio Mendes Belo, whom may God grant eternal happiness, prohibited the clergy from encouraging or taking part in any religious manifestation relating to Fatima, wise precautions which we too upheld for some time after our entry into this diocese.

But let us return to the Divine Master's sentence quoted above [in the first half of the letter not included here]: ". . .though you will not believe me, believe the works" (Jn. 10:38).

* * *

The sick come here at the cost of so many sacrifices, so much trouble! How many marvelous cures have not been wrought there through the intervention of the Virgin most Holy? And what a spirit of resignation do the sick not manifest even when they have not obtained the cure of their physical ills!

And while the infirm of body come to Fatima in thousands, greater still is the number of the morally afflicted. Our Lady is the Health of the Sick and the Refuge of the Sinners. How many wayward hearts have not found pardon there! How many of those who had abandoned the Faith of their Fathers, or were indifferent to it, found it again there!

Oh! If the confessionals of Fatima were not rigorously sealed with the sacramental seal, ever inviolable, what marvels of grace would they not be able to reveal to us!

* * *

In virtue of the consideration made known, and others which for reason of brevity we omit; humbly invoking the Divine Spirit and placing ourselves under the protection of the most Holy Virgin, and after hearing the opinions of the Rev. Advisers of this diocese, we thereby:

First, declare worthy of belief, the visions of the shepherd children in the Cova da Iria, parish of Fatima, in this diocese, from the 13th of May to October 1917.

Secondly, permit officially the cult of Our Lady of Fatima.

In this chapter we have shown how carefully the Bishops of Portugal labored to guide their people at a time in history when the Church was under a certain persecution and its freedom could have been totally destroyed, had they acted less prudently. All secular newspapers in Portugal at the time of the apparitions were anticlerical in tone. A study of the documents issued at various times indicates too how the Church worked in close harmony with Heaven to make the message of Our Lady most credible.

From the early years of Fatima, the Bishops became ever more conscious that what had happened in their small country was not for themselves alone, but rather was for the entire world. Beginning at a point between East and West, from Fatima the message goes out to all the world.

On July 25, 1966, the Bishop of Leiria-Fatima issued a pastoral letter to answer those who wanted to know the content of the third part of the Fatima secret. This was occasioned by press reports in Europe and Brazil, reports which were later picked up and which still circulate in America.

The Bishop wrote as follows:

> We feel well, dear diocesans, how difficult it is, and even dangerous, to broach this subject. But we cannot help doing so, although in few words, because now and then there appear certain affirmations, and they assume certain attitudes which can only prejudice the message of Fatima, which is all light. . . .
>
> Fatima's mission is not to fill with fantasies those who live, or wish to live, in dreams or hallucinations. Fatima is a diaphanous light that comes from the East.
>
> Neither does Fatima agree with auguries of universal catastrophies. Fatima cannot be reduced to sensational prophecies of terrible wars. Much less can her message, essentially one of peace, be directed against any country in particular, principally this well beloved nation, a victim, besides, of a known body of doctrine, very contrary to her dearest traditions. Fatima can never be a name given to party factions in which lands and politics are merely at stake.
>
> * * *
>
> We wish to say, dear diocesans, that nobody can place in Fatima, in spite of all her immense power of intercession before God Our Lord, an illusory hope that has not been consolidated in the holy fear of God, origin of her own love (Ecclus. 25:16), in persevering prayer based on the infinite merits of Christ, and in the intercession of Our Lady. It is always within these great Christian truths that Fatima works the prodigies of divine mercy in these times of the Church.
>
> It is in this meaning that her eschatologic future has to be unfolded. It is in this perspective that Fatima must be understood, and in this they acquire full significance in these consoling words: "And in the end my Immaculate Heart will triumph."

The Bishop of Leiria-Fatima understood the world-wide significance of the shrine in his diocese and the message it represents when, on the occasion of the golden jubilee of the apparitions, he addressed a pastoral letter to his people. We quote from it as follows:

> Charismatic manifestations, granted that they are private—and here

we refer to those that are authentic—in the teaching of the Fathers and
Doctors of the Church, have an indispensable mission in the Church of
God. They do not increase the deposit of Faith, sealed with the death of
the last Apostle; rather, they are the perennial actualization of the Gospel
in daily life. This theological perspective most adequately expresses Fatima,
the extension and universality of whose misson is unparralleled in the
history of the Church. Fatima is, in fact, an admirable synthesis of Catholic
dogma in its spiritual richness.

The supernatural in Fatima takes on the features of the Gospel. The
Infant of Bethlehem, the shepherds with their snow white gifts, the Angels
singing, the sick on the roads of Galilee crying out: "Jesus, Son of David,
have pity on me. . .," the humble house at Nazareth, the noisy crowds
following Christ. . .the strong scenes of the Passion of Our Lord. . .and
lastly the glorious apparitions of the Risen Christ. All is enveloped in that
sweet light from the virginal breast of her who "kept all these words,
pondering them in her heart" (Luke 2:19).

Fatima presents to our eyes the great and ineffable Christian dogmas,
their power of suggestion and conviction taking hold of us: the Most Holy Trinity, the Indwelling of God in the souls of the just by grace, the
Mystery of the Redemption of Christ, the mystery of iniquity and sin,
the sense of the solidarity of Christians in the Mystical Body of Christ
making reparation, the intercession of the angels and saints, the ineffable
Mystery of the Eucharist, the unique place of the Blessed Virgin, interceding for us, showing us the maternal solicitude of her Sorrowful and
Immaculate Heart, the great dogmas of Heaven and Hell. . .we might
go on forever. . . . Fatima is a summary of the Gospel.

Pope Pius XII stated: "Fatima is a reaffirmation of the Gospels." On May
13 of 1946, he sent a Papal Legate to Fatima to crown Our Lady's image
and proclaim her "Queen of the World."

Jacinta could not understand why the Holy Father did not come to Fatima,
especially since the children saw so many other people coming. This youngest
seer, who developed a most profound love and life of prayer and sacrifice
for the Holy Father, and who had mystical experiences of seeing the Pope,
was not to have her desire materialize until forty-seven years after her death.
On May 13th of 1967, the Vicar of Christ, Pope Paul VI, went to Fatima
for the fiftieth anniversary of the Fatima apparitions. This same Pope had
spoken of Fatima with great tenderness when the Bishops of the world were
gathered together for the Second Vatican Council:

While we turn in ardent prayer to the Virgin, that She may bless the
Ecumenical Council and the entire Church, hastening the hour of union
of all Christians. our glance opens on the endless horizons of the whole

world, the object of the most lively care of the Ecumenical Council, and which our venerated predecessor, Pius XII of venerated memory, not without inspiration from on high, solemnly consecrated to the Immaculate Heart of Mary. Today, we consider it particularly oppurtune of recall this act of consecration. Bearing this in mind, we have decided to send a special mission to Fatima in the near future in order to carry the golden Rose to the Sanctuary of Fatima, more dear than ever, not only to the people of the noble Portuguese nation—always, but particularly today, dear to us—but also known and venerated by the faithful throughout the entire Catholic world. In this manner we intend to entrust to the care of this heavenly Mother the entire human family, with its problems and anxieties, with its legitimate aspirations and ardent hopes.

O Virgin Mary, Mother of the Church, to you we commend the entire Church and our Ecumenical Council.

The above words of Pope Paul VI were spoken on the occasion of the promulgation of the Dogmatic Constitution on the Church.

The Pope's Legate, His Eminence Cardinal Costa Nunes, arrived in Lisbon on May 11th of 1967. The following day, the 12th, he came to Fatima by way of Batalha, and along the route he was the object of the greatest attention on the part of official authorities and pilgrims on account of his position as Legate of the Pope. The Pope himself was due to arrive on the 13th. In the evening there was a solemn reception ceremony in the Sanctuary. Then the letter of the Legate's appointment by the Supreme Pontiff was read in public for the first time; this was a letter of orientation as to how he would fulfill this function. A throb of intense joy swept over the hearts of all on hearing of the ardent enthusiasm and devotion with which the Pope spoke of Our Lady and wove a loving crown for her of titles of praise. This letter remains as one of the most powerful responses of the Pope and the Church to the heretical tendency to ignore or despise the Most Holy Virgin Mary. A portion of the Pope's letter read to that vast throng of pilgrims in the Cova follows:

In the discharge of this mission and with the well-known fluency of your words, full of warmth and enthusiasm, it will indeed by your duty to jubilantly praise and exalt to the highest Mary, the Mother of Christ, the most resplendant aurora of whom was born the Sun of Justice, [Mary, the] solid foundation of the confidence of the human race and the cause of its perpetual joy, miracle of the most ineffable beauty in the plane of nature and of grace, crown of the saints, Queen of the world, column of the orthodox Faith, Mother of the Church, never-failing helper and deliverer of the People of God.

How well the Pope answered those who after Vatican Council II were either ignoring or downplaying the official position of the Church regarding the ever-Virgin Mother of God.

His Holiness Pope Paul VI more than once indicated that his trip to Fatima as a humble pilgrim was of world-wide significance; he came to pray for peace in the universal Church and for peace in the world at large. Vatican II had ended a few years before. The Pope had spoken of Our Lady of Fatima at the Council and even entrusted the Council to her, and now it was obvious that some would distort the true intention of the world's twenty-first Ecumencial Council and attempt to change the One, Holy, Catholic and Apostolic Faith. Yet we know that Almighty God will never permit His Church to be destroyed.

I am convinced that the significance of Fatima, in its depth, is only beginning to penetrate the masses of the faithful. All the popes since 1917, with their finger on the pulse of the world, have seen that the Finger of God is there. They have known the significance of the Fatima message. Weigh well then these words spoken by Pope Paul VI when he spoke during the Sacrifice of the Mass at Fatima:

> You all know our special intentions which have characterized this pilgrimage. Now we recall them, so that they give voice to our prayer and enlightenment to those who hear them. The first intention is for the Church: the Church, One, Holy, Catholic and Apostolic. We want to pray, as we have said, for its internal peace. The Ecumenical Council has revitalized the heart of the Church, has opened up new vistas in the field of doctrine, has called all her children to a greater awareness, to a more intimate collaboration, to a more fervent apostolate. We desire that these be preserved and extended.
>
> What terrible damage could be provoked by arbitrary interpretations, not authorized by the teaching of the Church, disrupting its traditional and constitutional structure, replacing the theology of the true and great Fathers of the Church with new and peculiar ideologies; interpretations intent upon stripping the norms of Faith of that which modern thought, often lacking rational judgment, doesn't understand and doesn't like. Such interpretations change the apostolic fervor of redeeming charity to the negative structures of a profane mentality and of mundane customs. What a delusion our efforts to arrive at universal unity would suffer if we fail to offer to our Christian brethren, at this moment divided from us, and to the rest of humanity which lacks our Faith in its clearcut authenticity and in its original beauty, the patrimony of truth and of charity, of which the Church is the guardian and the dispenser?
>
> We want to ask of Mary a living Church, a true Church, a united Church, a holy Church. We want to pray together with you, in order that

the aspirations and efforts of the Council may find fulfillment through the fruits of the Holy Spirit, the Font of the true Christian life, Whom the Church celebrates tomorrow at the feast of Pentecost. . . .

His Holiness, surely aware of Our Lady's words regarding the spread of atheistic Communism, the "errors of Russia" which would spread throughout the world if men did not turn in prayer and penance back to Jesus Christ, continued as follows:

Faith in God is the supreme light of humanity; and this light not only must never be extinguished in the hearts of men, but must renew itself through the stimulus which comes from science and progress. This thought, which strengthens and stimulates our prayer, brings us to reflect, at this moment, on those nations in which religious liberty is almost totally suppressed, and where the negation of God is promulgated as representative of the truth of these times and the liberation of the people, whereas this is not so. We pray for such nations; we pray for the faithful of these nations, that the intimate strength of God may sustain them and that true civil liberty be conceded to them once more.

The Pope continued: "In this way, the second intention of our pilgrimage fills our hearts: the world, peace in the world! . . .But you can easily see that the world is not happy, is not tranquil, and that the first cause of its uneasiness is its difficulty in entering into harmonious relationships, its difficulty in following the paths of peace."

The Pope continued to speak of the world being full of tremendously deadly armament. While the world, he indicated, has progressed scientificaly and technically, it has not kept pace morally: "Therefore, we say: the world is in danger. For this reason we have come to the feet of the Queen of Peace of ask for the gift, which only God can give, of peace." The Pope indicated that in seeking peace we should not simply look for miracles from God to do it for us. Peace, he said, "has need of free acceptance and of free collaboration."

Was not the Pope calling upon the world to live the message of Fatima when he continued:

Behold, my brothers and children, who listen to us here, behold the immense and dramatic picture which the world and its destinies present to us. It is the picture which Our Lady opens up before us, the picture which we contemplate with frightened eyes, but ever trusting knowledge, the picture to which we ever draw near and to which we pledge ourselves, following the counsel which Our Lady gave us—that of prayer and of penance—and which God desires that this picture of the world shall never again have to face wars, tragedies, and catastrophies, but the conquest of love and the victory of peace.

Ten years later, for the sixtieth anniversary of Fatima, Pope Paul VI was still mindful of its importance. As his personal representative, the Supreme Pontiff sent His Eminence Humberto Cardinal Madeiros, Archbishop of Boston, to the May 13, 1977 celebrations. Cardinal Medeiros also delivered a message of world-wide significance, as heaven calls for a new world, a re-Christianizing of society.

The death of Pope Paul VI at 9:40 p.m. Rome time, on August 6th, 1978, just three hours and ten minutes after suffering a heart attack, was a shock to the world as it came so suddenly. I was in Fatima at the time. In the days following, the many bells of the Basilica in the Cova rang out periodically in disharmony. They were deliberately set to ring that way to express the sorrow felt so keenly in Fatima at the passing of the Pope who had come there in 1967 as a humble pilgrim to pray for peace in the Church and in the world.

The following Sunday, August 13, usually the time when the pilgrims, due to harvest work, come in the least numbers, a crowd estimated at from 700,000 to 800,000 was present for the Holy Sacrifice of the Mass in the Cova. The altar on the steps of the Basilica was draped in cloths of sorrow, and the chair Pope Paul had used there in 1967 sat empty. But the Chair of Peter was soon filled with the election of Patriarch Albino Luciani of Venice on August 26, 1978. He took the name of John Paul I and immediately gained the affection of the world, becoming known overnight as "the smiling Pope."

It soon became apparent that Pope John Paul I would be a Marian Pope and that God had again permitted a man to be elevated to the papacy who was devoted not only to Our Lady, but to God's Mother in her messge given at Fatima. Within the year before Cardinal Luciani became Pope, he had visited Sister Lucia. Of that visit, he wrote:

> . . .one might ask why a Cardinal would be taking such interest in a private revelation? Does he not know that everything is already contained in the Gospel, and that even approved revelations do not constitute articles of Faith? I know all that very well. But let us not forget this article of Faith, contained in the Gospel: "Signs will accompnay those who believe" (Mk. 16:17).
>
> If today it has become fashionable to observe the "signs of the times" of which the present day seems to abound, then it would also seem

legitimate to refer (with human faith) to a "sign" witnessed on the 13th of October, 1917, and attested to even by non-believers and anti-clericalists. And it would also seem opportune to pay heed to those things which this unique sign pointed to. And what were they?

First: To repent of one's sins and to avoid offending Our Lord any further.

Second: To pray. Prayer is the means of communication with God but today the means of communication which prevail are those strictly between men (TV, radio, cinema, press) and these seem determined to do away with prayer, communication with God. . . .

Third: To recite the Rosary. Naaman the Syrian, the great general in the Old Testament story, disdained the simple bath in the Jordan River suggested by the prophet Eliseus. Some of us act precisely like Naaman: "I am a theologian, a mature Christian, steeped in the reading of the Bible and the spirit of the liturgy: what need have I of the Rosary?" Yet what are the fifteen mysteries of the Rosary if not biblical? And what are the Our Father, Hail Mary, and Glory if not Bible united to prayer, thus being of immense good to the soul? The Bible studied for more love of research serves only to bring about pride and aridity: it is not completely rare that a biblical scholar loses the Faith.

Fourth: Hell exists, and people go there. At Fatima Our Lady taught this prayer: "O my Jesus, forgive us our sins, save us from the fires of Hell; lead all souls to Heaven. . ." There are many important things in this world, but none more important than meriting Heaven by a good life. It is not Fatima, but the very Gospel which tells us: "For what doth it profit a man, if he gain the whole world, and suffer the loss of his own soul?" (Mt. 16:26).

In his short reign, Pope John Paul I had said that God is "as much a mother as He is a Father." It seemed an apt expression. God had become man in Jesus Christ through the woman Mary, who reflects the light of God as does the moon the sun. The warmth, the tenderness, and the womanly compassion of God's Mother are a reflection of God Himself. In the concluding remarks of his homily on the day of his installation, Pope John Paul had spoken of God's Mother as a "shining Star."

At the Pope's funeral, Carlo Cardinal Confalonieri, Dean of the College of Cardinals, said that John Paul I had "passed as a meteor which unexpectedly lights up the heavens and then disappears, leaving us amazed and astonished."

One can only speculate as to why God does things and permits things, for as the heavens are above the earth, so are God's thoughts and ways above our own. Whatever were heaven's reasons, it seems that the short lovable reign of Pope John Paul I prepared the world to accept its first non-Italian

Pope in 455 years.

On October 16, 1978, Cardinal Felici appeared on the central balcony of St. Peter's to announce: "We have a Pope." The world was presented with the fifty-eight-year-old Cardinal Karol Wojtyla of Cracow, Poland, who took the name of Pope John Paul II. It was providential. The world that had been falling more and more under the hammer and sickle was given a gifted Pope from Poland, a Catholic country whose government was atheistic and Communist. There stepped forth a Pope deeply devoted to the Mother of God, and one who had directed priests, religious, and laity to retain and grow in a strong Catholic Faith in spite of the persecutions of a government which was subservient to Russia.

Coming from the Eastern bloc, from a nation where the people nonetheless remained strong practicing Catholics, this Pope had experienced first-hand what Our Lady of Fatima had prophesied: the spread of the errors of Russia to the nations of the world. In Poland, certain responsible job positions have been reserved exclusively for non-believers. At the time of Pope John Paul II's election, several teaching institutes had reached the point of requiring candidates to present statements that they were atheists.

When the new Pope stepped onto the balcony of St. Peter's Basilica to give his first Papal blessing to the city and to the world, I and many others devoted to Our Lady of Fatima had multiple thoughts flash through our minds. Will this be the Pope to consecrate Russia to the Immaculate Heart of Mary together with the world's bishops?

In his first address to the College of Cardinals, Pope John Paul II pointed out that as a bishop he had chosen a Marian motto: "Totus tuus"—"Totally yours." This would indicate his personal total consecration to Mary. The dedication of this Pope to the Mother of God is repeatedly revealed in his speeches.

The mind of Pope John Paul II may be seen in his actions while still a Cardinal. Cardinal Wojtyla was the promoter and the second ranking signer of the Polish pastoral letter requesting collegial consecration of Russia to Mary. It is therefore not surprising that Pope John Paul II's first words to the world on that late afternoon of October 16, 1978, should speak of Mary:

> I was afraid of receiving the election to these burdens, but I have taken it in the spirit of obedience toward Our Lord and of total confidence in His most Holy Mother. . .And so I present myself to you all to confess our common Faith, our hope and our confidence in the Mother of the Church, and also to set forth on this road of the Church with the aid of God and with the aid of men.

The words of our present Holy Father then show that he does not ignore the need for the cooperation of men. The readers of this volume then will not make the mistake of simply awaiting miracles of God to straighten out the world and give it peace. We must personally live our consecration to the Immaculate Heart of Mary and make known to the world that God wills this devotion for all.

The new Pope's first trip outside Italy was to the Marian shrine of the Americas, Our Lady of Guadalupe in Mexico. He would go to take part in the third general assembly of the Latin American Bishops. "But before going to the conference site," he explained: "I will make a stop at the celebrated sanctuary of Our Lady of Guadalupe. It is from here, in fact, that I desire to take the higher comfort and the necessary stimulus—the good omens, as it were—for my mission of pastor of the Church. . . ."

Pope John Pual II has called the Rosary his favorite prayer, after the Eucharistic Sacrifice, and has said that he prays the Rosary for guidance in all important decisions. He has continually invoked the Mother of God, praying at her shrines, as he did shortly before the conclave that elected him. Our Holy Father gives constant evidence of his total confidence in God's Mother; he fully realizes that the "errors of Russia" spoken of by Our Lady of Fatima continue as the major threat to the world.

The lack of freedom of speech and of the press in Poland was illustrated by the censorship of a letter from Pope John Paul to the people of his former Archdiocese of Cracow for the first Christmas of his pontificate. The government deleted the portion of the letter which called St. Stanislaus "the defender of the most important rights of man and of the nation." In strongly Catholic Poland, St. Stanislaus is often considered a symbol of the Church's autonomy with respect to civil authority.

It may be that Pope John Paul II is Heaven's sign that the Woman of the Bible who first crushed the head of the serpent through the Fruit of her womb is now ready to defeat Satan and convert Russia and grant a certain period of peace to the world. She has promised: "In the end my Immaculate Heart will triumph."

The hierarchy of the United States have also recognized our Lady's call. In their 1973 pastoral letter entitled *Behold Your Mother*, the American Bishops stated:

> Best known of the twentieth century appearances of the Mother of the Lord is that at Fatima, in 1917. . .the authenticated appearances of Our Lady. . .serve as reminders to us of basic Christian themes: prayer, penance, and the necessity of the sacrament. . . .

In 1982 the Bishops of the U.S.A. at their national meeting overwhelmingly voted to petition the Pope, if he saw fit, to call for the collegial consecration of Russia to the Immaculate Heart of Mary. According to Sister Lucia the collegial consecration will herald the conversion of Russia.

The burden does not lie entirely on the Pope and bishops. It lies on us, on all God's people, to live totally our personal consecration to the Heart of God's Mother and to make her message known. As pointed out in this book, little Jacinta of Fatima, as a very young child, has shown the way to live the Fatima message in personal consecration. How she has done this will be shown in the next chapter.

6.
Jacinta, Mystic and Prophetess

Jacinta is truly the youngest prophet, and if and when she is canonized, which seems inevitable to those who have studied Fatima in depth, she will be the youngest child ever formally canonized by the Church. Her role as a prophet—that is, a messenger from Heaven, and as a mystic—that is, someone who understands the mysteries of Faith through deep union with God or by direct revelation, will then be clearly recognized. Then too, the great significance of Fatima will be demonstrated to the whole world in the most effective way possible—by example.

Note the ages of some of the more recently canonized saints. St. Therese of Lisieux was hardly twenty-five years old when she died; she was declared a saint in 1925. St. Bernadette was canonized in 1913, having died at the age of thirty-five. St. Dominic Savio, who took as his motto, "Death rather than sin," and who was the student of that great apostle of youth, St. John Bosco, was only fifteen years old when he died; he was canonized in 1954. After these three saints, who lived during the latter part of the nineteenth century, we move into the twentieth for a saint who was canonized in 1950. This time it was St. Maria Goretti, who had died in 1902, having reached a little less than twelve years of age. The Church seems to be pointing out to us more and more that great sanctity is attainable even in youth.

Heaven raises up the kind of saints that are needed for the times, and the Holy Spirit moves the Church to publicly declare them saints. In a time when the catechesis of youth has often been neglected, when some have even proclaimed that Christianity is only an adult Faith and have advocated delaying the teaching of basic doctrines and reception of the Sacrament of Penance, and at a time when youth are nevertheless becoming interested in mysticism (both true and false), Jacinta's example would speak loudly and clearly to both the parents and young people of today.

Let us recall again the words of the Cardinal Patriarch of Lisbon on the twenty-fifth anniversary of Fatima:

> . . .Saint Paul says that the Christians are a letter of Christ, ministered by us, and written not with ink, but with the Spirit of the Living God (II Cor. 3:1-3). Imitating him, we can say that "JACINTA" is a letter of the Holy Virgin, to be read by souls. Better than words does it [the life of Jacinta] say what Our Lady came to do in Fatima and what she wants of us.

Much of our understanding of Jacinta's mission has come from Lucia, who is now a nun. Sister Lucia has commented that when souls are given special revelations from Heaven, they are also given lights to penetrate the message. She has written that this was especially true of Jacinta: "Jacinta seemed to have this discernment to an extremely high degree." Lucia has also said, "I think myself, Jacinta was the one who received from Our Lady a greater abundance of grace, and a better knowledge of God and of virtue."

Sister Lucia has stated that the following question has come to her from various quarters: How is it that Jacinta, small as she was, let herself be possessed by such a spirit of mortification and penance, and understood it so well? Sister Lucia answered as follows:

> I think the reason is this: firstly, God willed to bestow on her a special grace, through the Immaculate Heart of Mary; and secondly, it was because she had looked upon Hell, and had seen the ruin of souls who fall therein.
>
> Some people, even the most devout, refuse to speak to children about Hell, in case it would frighten them. Yet God did not hesitate to show Hell to three children, one of whom was only six years old, knowing well that they would be horrified to the point of, I would almost dare to say, withering away with fear.
>
> Jacinta often sat thoughtfully on the ground or on a rock, and exclaimed: "Oh, Hell! Hell! How sorry I am for the souls who go to Hell! And the people down there, burning alive, like wood in the fire!" Then, shuddering, she knelt down with her hands joined, and recited the prayer that

Our Lady had taught us:
"O my Jesus, forgive us; save us from the fire of Hell; take all souls
to Heaven, especially those most in need."

When Francisco died, Jacinta was deeply grieved. She would sit on her
bed in long hours of sadness. When asked why she was so sad she would
answer: "I am thinking of Francisco and of how I would like to see him."
But then she would add that it was more than the thought of Francisco's
death that saddened her. "I am thinking of the war which will come. So
many people will die. . . .So many houses will be destroyed and priests
killed. Listen, I am going to Heaven soon, but when you see that light that
Our Lady told us of, you must go there too."

Lucia replied, "Don't you see that one can't just go to Heaven when
one wants to?"

Jacinta said, "Yes, that's true, but don't be afraid. I will pray very much
for you in Heaven and for the Holy Father and that the war may not come
to Portugal, and for all the priests."

If we look at Jacinta before the apparitions, it is easy to see the great
transformation that came over her, a transformation growing with each appearance of the Blessed Mother and reaching a climax during the last part
of her life.

Jacinta had a great love for dancing, and would vibrate at the sound of
music. She loved flowers, and always gathered a bouquet of wild flowers
whenever she went to the Loca do Cabeco. These flowers—often including
peonies and irises and lilies—would be given to her cousin Lucia or strewn
over Lucia like the flower petals thrown before the Most Blessed Sacrament in processions. The very name "Jacinta" means "hyacinth."

Sister Lucia recalls the great joy that filled Jacinta's heart when she was
chosen to drop her flower petals before Our Eucharistic Lord in a procession of the Most Blessed Sacrament. Lucia had assured her that she would
see Our Lord. Jacinta kept her eyes open, but could not find Him, and so
she refused to drop a single petal. Her little mind had not yet grasped that
the "hidden Jesus" in the Holy Eucharist would not appear as on the holy
cards, where she saw Our Divine Lord pictured as the Good Shepherd, as
Christ the King, etc. Jacinta would sometimes pick up one of the little lambs
as the shepherds marched along with their sheep. This she did in imitation
of Our Lord, the Good Shepherd who searched for the one lost lamb and
placed it on His shoulders to carry it to safety.

Before the apparitions, Jacinta was a possessive child, as is shown by
her attitude to the game called "buttons." She would seek to win all Lucia's
buttons and would have liked to keep them for use in the next day's game.

Only Lucia's threat not to play the game again could move Jacinta to give up her winnings.

Unfortunately, some who have studied Fatima do not see beyond Jacinta's childhood innocence and simplicity; they see Jacinta only as the child who saw and heard Our Lady but who did not speak to Our Lady herself. Yet Jacinta received a great mission from Our Lady, and herself underwent a great transformation. Referring to her character after the apparitions, Canon Galamba asked: "What did people feel when in Jacinta's company?" Sister Lucia answered:

> I can only say what I felt myself, and describe any exterior manifestations of other people's feelings.
>
> What I myself usually felt was much the same as what would be felt in the presence of a very holy person who seemed to communicate with God in everything. Her behavior was always serious, modest and amiable; she seemed to betray the presence of God in all her actions, more like a person of advanced age and virtue than a child. I never observed in her that excessive frivolity or childish enthusiasm usual in children for games and pretty things—that is, after the apparitions. Before then, she was the personification of enthusiasm and caprice! I cannot say that other children used to run after her as they did after me; perhaps this was due to the fact that she did not know songs or stories to teach and amuse them with; or else because the seriousness of her behavior was superior to her age. If children or adults said anything or did anything in her presence that was not quite right, she would reprove them telling them not to do that as it offended God, who was already so deeply offended. If the person, or child, retorted by calling her a "pious Mary" or a plaster saint or such things, as they often did, she would look at them with a certain air of severity, then walk off without a word. Perhaps this was the reason why she did not enjoy more popularity.

At the same time, Sister Lucia added that children did like to be with Jacinta. They embraced each other affectionately in the manner of innocent children. They enjoyed playing and singing with her, but, at the same time, a certain reverence kept them shy of Jacinta.

Women liked to come and sit by her bedside when doing sewing. They stated that they did not know what it was about her that attracted them, but they liked being near Jacinta. And of course they admired her exemplary behavior and great patience. An insincere man once asked Jacinta to pray to Our Lord for him as he was a very bad person. Instantly she replied: "Look here, pray for yourself, for you can also ask. If you are bad, then become better."

Providence had used Jacinta at the beginning of the Fatima events when Our Lady first appeared. Even after promising Lucia that she would not utter a word, she could not contain herself. Something inside her just made her tell her parents, and the news quickly spread throughout the village of Aljustrel and from there all over Portugal and throughout the world. A beautiful Lady was appearing in the parish of Fatima to three shepherd children! Jacinta suffered greatly in her heart when scolded by Lucia and by her brother Francisco who was impatient with her for not keeping silent.

Lucia remembered the trouble that had been stirred up when a mysterious figure, which must have been an angel, appeared to her and two other girls at least a year before the Angel began appearing in 1916 to her and her two cousins. At that very first apparition, perhaps in 1915, the mysterious figure never did reveal himself clearly to Lucia and her two companions. Lucia had kept silent, but the other two talked.

Jacinta developed a great devotion to the Pope, whom she rightly called "the Holy Father," and she added three Hail Marys to her Rosary for him. Sister Lucia writes of a time when the children were taking their siesta down by her parents' well. Jacinta called out to Lucia: "Didn't you see the Holy Father?"

"No."

"I don't know how it was, but I saw the Holy Father in a very big house, kneeling by a table, with his head buried in his hands, and he was weeping. Outside the house, there were many people. Some of them were throwing stones. Others were cursing him and using bad language. Poor Holy Father, we must pray very much for him."

Sister Lucia recalled the time when two priests urged the children to pray for the Holy Father. "Is he the one I saw weeping, the one Our Lady told us about in the secret?" Jacinta asked.

"Yes, he is," Lucia answered.

"The Lady must surely have shown him also to those priests. You see, I wasn't mistaken. We need to pray a lot for him."

Some time later, the children were praying in a cave called Lapa do Cabeco, when Jacinta asked: "Can't you see all those highways and roads and fields full of people, who are crying with hunger and have nothing to eat? And the Holy Father in a church praying before the Immaculate Heart of Mary? And so many people praying with him?" Some days later, she asked Lucia: "Can I say that I saw the Holy Father and all those people?"

"No. Don't you see that that's part of the secret? If you do, they'll find out right away."

"All right! Then I'll say nothing at all."

Jacinta became ill in October of 1918, shortly before her brother came down with the influenza from which he later died. Jacinta contracted bronchial pneumonia, and a kind of purulent abscess formed in the pleura, causing her great pain. She tried to hide her intense sufferings from her mother, but would admit them to Lucia, relating that she was offering it all for the conversion of sinners. "Don't worry, Mother, I am going to Heaven and I shall pray for you very much. Don't cry, because I'm all right."

To Lucia, Jacinta would say: "Don't tell anyone how much I suffer, especially Mother. I don't want her to worry."

Jacinta was reduced from exuberant health and spirits to little more than a thin skeleton. Still she would struggle out of bed to bow her head to the floor when saying the prayer and making the act of adoration taught the children by the Angel. She thought of others, not herself, in her extreme illness.

Sister Lucia gives further examples of Jacinta's penances:

> One day her mother brought her a milk pudding and told her to take it. "I don't want it, Mother," she said, pushing it away. My aunt tried to persuade her but finally went away, saying: "I don't know how to get her to take anything. . . ."
>
> When we were alone I asked her: "How can you disobey your mother like that, and not offer this sacrifice to Our Lord?" When Jacinta heard this she dissolved into tears, which I had the happiness of wiping away, and she said: "I forgot that time!" Then she called her mother and asked her pardon and said that she would take whatever she gave her. The milk pudding was brought back and Jacinta took it without any sign of repugnance. Afterwards she said to me: "You don't know how hard it was to take!"

Her will—or rather her love for the Heart of Mary and for sinners— triumphed. After that experience Jacinta accepted the milk puddings and soups in reparation. She even accepted these over grapes which she would rather have eaten.

The doctors advised the parents of Jacinta to send her to the hospital at Vila Nova de Ourem. The Mother of God had let Jacinta know that no amount of hospital treatment could cure her. Being removed from her family, from Lucia, and from the Cova da Iria would only add to her sufferings. Our Lady told Jacinta that she would go to two hospitals, not to be cured but to suffer more for the love of God and for the conversion of sinners and to make reparation for the sins against her Immaculate Heart.

Jacinta dreaded the hospital as a place that would be dark and lonely.

Her only consolation was that she could suffer more for the conversion of poor sinners. Yes, Jacinta feared the hospital. That is human. She feared the loneliness of being away from home and her beloved Lucia. Our Lord too complained about being left alone in His agony: "Could you not watch one hour with Me?"

It was July of 1919 when Jacinta's father, Ti Marto, placed the thin body of his sick daughter upon the beast of burden and they set off for St. Augustine's Hospital in Vila Nova de Ourem. How difficult a journey that must have been for Jacinta. Likewise, the two months in that hospital were painful. But Jacinta was relieved on two different occasions when her cousin Lucia came to visit her. Lucia asked: "Do you suffer much, Jacinta?"

"Yes, but I offer it all for the conversion of sinners and in reparation to the Immaculate Heart of Mary. I love to suffer for the love of Jesus and Mary, just to give them pleasure! They love people who suffer for the conversion of sinners."

Jacinta had asked her mother, Olimpia, to leave her and Lucia alone at the hospital so they could talk about their spiritual secrets. The visits passed all too quickly, and Olimpia and Lucia were soon on the road up the serra to Fatima again, leaving Jacinta in pain and loneliness.

Regarding the second visit, Sister Lucia wrote: "I found her as joyful as ever, glad to suffer for the love of God and the Immaculate Heart of Mary, for sinners and the Holy Father. She was living her ideal and it was of this that she spoke." By the end of August it was recognized that hospital treatment was doing no good, and was only adding to the expenses of the Marto family. There remained an open wound in Jacinta's side which drained continuously and had to be dressed daily. The wound became infected, and the child gradually wasted away.

When Father Formigão came to visit her after she had left the hospital, he described her condition as follows:

> Jacinta is like a skeleton and her arms are shockingly thin. Since she left the local hospital where she underwent two months' useless treatment, the fever has never left her. She looks pathetic. Tuberculosis, after an attack of bronchial pneumonia and purulent pleurisy, is undermining her enfeebled constitution. Only careful treatment in a good sanatorium can save her. But her parents cannot undertake the expense which such a treatment involves. Bernadette, the peasant girl of Lourdes, heard from the mouth of the Immaculate Virgin in the cave of Massabielle, a promise of happiness not in this world but in the next. Has Our Lady made an identical promise to the little shepherdess of Fatima, to whom she confided an inviolable secret?

The koch bacillus was eating away Jacinta's little body. Still, her thirst for sacrifice did not lessen. She carried her efforts for mortification to what seemed like an extreme. She was moved by great grace.

Father Olivial learned that Jacinta had been getting out of bed to say the prayer of the Angel, but she kept falling because she could not get her head to the floor any more, and therefore was saying it on her knees. He told Lucia to tell Jacinta to maker her offering in bed. Assured that God had revealed His Will through the words of the priest, Jacinta obeyed.

Even in her weakened and sick condition Jacinta still desired to go to daily Mass and visit the Cova where Our Lady had appeared. In the cold days of winter her parents refused to allow her to go to the Cova, but they did permit her to participate in an occasional weekday Mass in the parish church at Fatima which was near Aljustrel where the Marto family lived. When Lucia said to Jacinta: "Don't come today. . . you're not strong enough and it's not Sunday," the sick girl answered: "Never mind, I can go for sinners who don't even go on Sundays."

During the winter months Lucia spent much time with Jacinta. There were no secrets between them, but when adults would come near, the two would become silent about the thoughts they so freely shared with one another. They talked of their mortifications, sacrifices which consoled the Hearts of Jesus and Mary which are too much offended.

Samples of the exchanges of conversation between Lucia and Jacinta were learned years later when Lucia was commanded by her Bishop to write about Jacinta. Jacinta would say: "I was thirsty and I didn't drink and I offered it to Jesus for sinners. In the night I had pains and I offered Our Lord the sacrifice of not turning over in bed and so I didn't sleep at all. Lucia, what sacrifices have you made?"

What an apostle Jacinta is for these times when youth so frequently are taught little about penance and mortification, even during the holy season of Lent. Her sanctification reveals to us that Fatima is not just an entertaining story. It is the Mother of God teaching so as to transform souls—and this youngest soul was transformed so thoroughly. One can understand well what Our Lady taught by witnessing how the children responded. The story of Fatima is meant to transform, to convert, to save us from the eternal fires of Hell so that in, with, and through Our Lady's Son, Jesus Christ, we may live with God in Heaven for all eternity.

Lucia tried to participate in the Sacrifice of the Mass and receive Our Lord in Holy Communion each day. On her way home from the parish church of Fatima she would stop for a visit with Jacinta and sit at her cousin's bedside. Jacinta would ask: "Lucia, have you been to Holy Communion today? Then come close to me because you have the hidden Jesus in your heart.'' She would also say: ''I don't know how it is, but I feel Our Lord inside me and I understand what He says though I can't see Him and hear Him, but I love to be with Him.''

Jesus in the Most Blessed Sacrament was called ''the hidden Jesus.'' When Lucia showed Jacinta a picture of a chalice and Host, Jacinta kissed it, saying:

> It's the hidden Jesus; how I love Him. If only I could receive Him in the church. Can you go to Holy Communion in Heaven? If so, I shall go every day. If the Angel could go to the hospital and take me Holy Communion how happy I should be. . . .

Admitting one day that a picture of Our Lord given her by Lucia was ''ugly,'' Jacinta nonetheless accepted it because it was Our Lord and His Heart was exposed. ''I kiss His Heart. It's what I like best, I wish I had one of the Immaculate Heart of Mary. Haven't you got one, Lucia? I should like to keep the two together.''

The compassion of Jacinta as she was maturing spiritually is shown in her concern for her mother. Noticing sadness on her mother's face upon seeing her ailing daughter, Jacinta would try to console her mother, telling her not to mind, and that she should soon be going to Heaven. When Jacinta heard her mother question Lucia about her one day, she called her cousin to her side, forbidding her to reveal the extent of her sufferings to anyone, especially to her mother—lest she be worried.

As can best be determined, it was sometime near the end of December, 1919, when Our Lady appeared to Jacinta again to tell her that she would soon be taken to Heaven from a hospital in faraway Lisbon. This is how she related it to Lucia: ''Our Lady told me that I was to go to Lisbon, to another hospital, and that I shall never see you again, nor Father and Mother; that I shall have to suffer much and die alone, but that I must not be afraid, because she will come and take me to Heaven. I shall never see you again!'' In tears, Jacinta threw her arms around Lucia. ''You won't even be able to come and visit me. But pray for me very much because I have to die alone.''

Other bits of conversations reveal the feelings in Jacinta's heart. One day Lucia found her kissing the picture of God's Mother and saying, ''Darling Mother in Heaven, must I die alone?'' Attempting to comfort her, Lucia said: ''What does it matter if you die alone, if Our Lady is coming to fetch you?''

''That's true, it doesn't really matter, but sometimes, I don't know how it is. I can hardly remember that she is coming to fetch me.''

"Be brave, Jacinta! You will be going so soon to Heaven, but I. . . .''

"Poor Lucia, don't cry. I shall pray so much for you. You must stay, but Our lady wants it like that.''

"What will you do in Heaven, Jacinta?''

I shall love Jesus and the Immaculate Heart of Mary very much and I shall pray for you, and for sinners, and the Holy Father, and for Father and Mother and the others, and everyone who has asked me to pray for them.''

Jacinta announced to her family that she would go to Lisbon, but her prediction was not accepted in the Marto home. The treatment in St. Augustine's Hospital at Vila Nova de Ourem had been expensive and had done no good, and they knew that St. Augustine's was inexpensive compared to hospitals in the capital city of Portugal. Our Lady, however, kept Jacinta fully informed, and her words always proved true.

When Lucia went to visit Jacinta during her illness before the transfer to Lisbon, she would frequently find a large group of children waiting outside the Marto home. They would not enter alone, for a certain repect held them back. They would not enter until they could accompany Lucia or Senhora Marto, or until Jacinta herself invited them to come in. Then when Lucia would leave, all the children wanted to remain, but Jacinta preferred if only those smaller than herself would stay.

When she was confined to bed with illness, Jacinta would teach the neighbor children the Our Father, the Hail Mary, how to bless themselves, or hymns. She would also say the Rosary with them and teach them not to offend God so as not to go to Hell. Jacinta was in fact a missionary as well as a mystic; everyone who lives in deep union with God desires to bring others to Him also. She was a missionary even within her own home, persuading her mother to allow time for the family Rosary. Lucia's *Memoirs* record how, when the children were jailed for their story, Jacinta succeeded in getting the men prisoners to hang her medal on the wall and pray with them.

Events in the Marto home quickly changed with the arrival of visitors: Father Formigao, and Dr. Eurico Lisboa and his wife. Dr. Lisboa left a record of his experiences as follows:

In the middle of January, 1920, we went for a run to the Cova da Iria in order to try out the new motor car which we had recently bought. On our way through Santarém we went to pay our respects to Dr. Formigão, who we knew could tell us all about Fatima and the events of which he had been a witness. Dr. Formigão, whom we had not known personally before, but who has been our intimate friend ever since, had the kindness to accompnay us to Fatima on that occasion and it was through him that we came to know the seers, Jacinta and Lucia.

After a visit to the Cova with Lucia, in whose company we prayed the Rosary with unforgettable faith and devotion, we returned to Fatima, where we spoke to Jacinta and the mothers of the two seers. They told us about Francisco, who had been a victim of the wide-spread epidemic of pneumonia influenza which had swept with such tragic results through Europe. He has, we learned, realized his only wish since the apparitions, which was to go to Our Lady. He refused all help and advice from the people, who knew him in his life and only desired death, with the least possible delay.

Little Jacinta was very pale and thin and walked with great difficulty. The family told me she was very ill, which they hardly regretted, because Jacinta's only ambition also was to go to Our Lady, whose will it was that she should die in the same way as Francisco.

When I censured them for their lack of effort to save their daughter, they told me that it was not worthwhile because Our Lady wished to take her, and that she had been interned for two months in the local hospital without any improvement in her condition.

I replied that Our Lady's will was certainly more powerful than any human efforts and that in order to be certain that she really wished to take Jacinta, they must not neglect any of the normal aids of science to save her life.

Impressed by my words, they went to ask the advice of Dr. Formigao, who supported my opinion in every respect. It was therefore arranged on the spot that Jacinta should be sent to Lisbon and treated by the best doctors in one of the hospitals of the capital.

And in fact, some days later, on 2nd February, 1920, Jacinta was interned in Ward No. 1, bed No. 38 of the Dona Estefânia [St. Stephen] Hospital, under the care of Dr. Castro Freire, then, and now, one of the most famous children's specialists in Lisbon. The diagnosis was as follows: purulent pleurisy, osteitis of the 7th and 8th ribs.

Divine Providence was at work. Jacinta's words that she would go to a hospital in Lisbon, a second hospital, where she would die alone, were verified. Furthermore, this move would help deflate some ugly rumors. Since Our Lady had announced that Francisco and Jacinta would go to heaven soon (a prediction made in 1917), enemies could have argued that the Martos neglected Jacinta so that the alleged apparitions could be "substantiated" by the deaths of the children.

The Martos themselves consented to the transfer to the Lisbon hospital with reluctance. According to his own account, Jacinta's father announced the news to her in the following manner: "Jacinta, we are going to arrange for you to go to Lisbon, to a hospital."

"Yes, Father, I'm in a fine way to go to Lisbon!"

"It has to be, dear. Otherwise everyone will say that we have neglected to have treatment. Perhaps after all you'll be all right."

"Father, dear, even if I recover from this illness, I should get another straightway. If I go to Lisbon it means good-bye."

He comments: "Indeed she was a sorry sight. Her heart was enlarged and her digestive organs were ruined. It seemed as if she could not recover."

Before leaving, Jacinta asked to be taken to the Cova da Iria. This is the way her mother Olimpia described Jacinta's last visit to the Cova:

> I arranged to take her on a friend's donkey because Jacinta could not have managed the walk. When we arrived at the Carreira Pool (where Jacinta had drunk dirty water as an act of mortification), Jacinta got off the donkey and began to say the Rosary alone. She picked a few flowers for the chapel. When we arrived she knelt down and prayed a little in her own way.
>
> "Mother," she said when she got up, "when Our lady went away she passed over those trees, and afterwards she went into Heaven so quickly that I thought she would get her feet caught!"

Ti Marto arranged the journey to Lisbon. Jacinta's mother was to take her by train. Some ladies were to meet Olimpia and her son Antonio with Jacinta at Lisbon and were to recognize them by a white handkerchief tied to the arm. To his wife, Ti Marto said:

> When you get into the train you must ask the other people to excuse you because your little girl is very ill, and it is because of this that she has an unpleasant smell. Be very careful that she doesn't lean out the window when another train is passing. When you are going through the Rossio Tunnel don't forget to tie on the white handkerchief, and don't worry.

Lucia wrote that the separation from Jacinta was heartbreaking.

> She stayed a long time in my arms and then said, sobbing, "We shall never see each other again! But pray for me very much until I go to Heaven and then I will pray very much for you. Don't ever tell the secret to anyone even if they kill you. Love Jesus very much and the Immaculate Heart, and make many sacrifices for sinners."

The little apostle of the Sacred Heart and the Immaculate Heart was growing in her spirit of asceticism and mysticism which came to full bloom in Lisbon.

In her *Memoirs*, Sister Lucia does not write of what happened at Lisbon. She did not know, for she never visited Jacinta and did not witness Jacinta's last weeks on earth. The material from Lucia's *Memoirs* regarding Jacinta ends when the train pulls from the station on January 21st to take her to Lisbon.

We have Lucia's testimony as to her feelings after her cousin had left:

> What sadness I felt on finding myself alone. In such a short space of time, Our Lord had taken my father, then Francisco, and now Jacinta, whom I would never again see in this life. As soon as I could do so, I went to Cabeco Hill, and there in the grotto among the rocks, alone with God, I gave way to my grief and shed tears in abundance. On descending the hill afterwards everything reminded me of my dear companions: the stones where we had so often sat, the flowers I no longer picked, not having anybody to take them to, Valinhos, where together we had enjoyed the delights of Paradise!

> One day, as if doubting the reality of affairs, and in a half abstracted mood, I entered my aunt's house and directed my stops toward Jacinta's room, calling her. Her sister Teresa seeing me thus, barred the way, saying that Jacinta was not there now. A short time later the news arrived that she had flown to Heaven.

In Lisbon, Jacinta and her mother were first taken in by a nun named Mother Godinho, who ran an orphanage. How delighted Jacinta was to discover that in the orphanage she was under the same roof that housed the Chapel of Our Lady of the Holy Miracles, where the hidden Jesus was present in the Tabernacle. Also, while Olimpia remained in Lisbon she often carried Jacinta in her arms to the altar of the Basilica there—the first one in the world to be dedicated to the Sacred Heart of Jesus. Sometimes Mother Godinho carried her too.

One day Jacinta said, "Oh Mother, I want to go to Confession." They went to the Basilica, and when Jacinta came out of the confessional she said to her mother, "What a good priest that was. He asked me so many things!"

Senhora Marto was anxious to return to Aljustrel where she was needed to care for her eldest daughter, Florinda, who was also seriously ill. After being in the capital about ten days, Olimpia asked one of the doctors his real opinion on the case. His answer was not definite, but he indicated that it might be God's Will to take Jacinta. Realizing that there was almost no hope, Olimpia attempted to persuade others that it would be proper to take Jacinta back home. Only when Father Formigão and Dr. Eurico Lisboa intervened could Olimpia be induced to give up her idea and leave her daughter in Lisbon.

Jacinta did not cry when her mother took leave for Aljustrel. She knew from Our Lady that it was God's Will that she must die without any of her family or relatives at her side. She embraced her mother bravely and said, "Good-bye, Mother, until we meet in Heaven."

When her mother had departed, Jacinta remained a long time in a pensive mood, looking very sorrowful. Remaining at the orphanage, she continued to suffer intensely. A cough kept her awake at night. At the orphanage, Jacinta spent as much time in the chapel as she was allowed. She could not kneel, but sat in her chair with her eyes fixed on the Tabernacle. There she prayed silently.

If people misbehaved in chapel she would tell Mother Godinho that Our Lady was not pleased when people did not show proper respect before the Blessed Sacrament. Mother Godinho wrote:

> I soon began to realize that a little angel had come into my house. Although I had long wanted to see the privileged children of Fatima, I never imagined that I would have the good fortune to shelter one under my roof.
>
> We had some twenty to twenty-five children in the orphanage. Jacinta was friendly with them all but she preferred the company of a little girl about her own age to whom she would give little sermons. It was delightful to hear them, and hidden behind the half-open door I assisted at many of these conversations.
>
> "You must not lie, or be lazy or disobedient, and you must bear everything with patience for love of Our Lord if you want to go to Heaven." She spoke with such authority; hardly like a child.
>
> During the time she was in my house she must have received a visit from Our Lady more than once. I remember on one occasion she said, "Please move over, dear Mother; I am waiting for Our Lady," and her face took on a radiant expression.
>
> It seems that it was not always Our Lady in person who appeared but a globe of light such as had been seen in Fatima, because we once heard her say, "This time it wasn't like it was in Fatima, but I knew it was she."

Mother Godinho carefully recorded the following words on various subjects spoken by Jacinta:

Regarding sin:
The sins which cause most souls to go to Hell are the sins of the flesh. Fashions will much offend Our Lord. People who serve God should

not follow the fashions. The Church has no fashions. Our Lord is always the same.

The sins of the world are very great.

If men knew what eternity is they would do everything to change their lives.

People are lost because they do not think of the death of Our Lord and do not do penance.

Many marriages are not of God and do not please Our Lord.

Regarding war:

Our Lady said that the world is full of war and discords.

Wars are the punishments for sin.

Our Lady cannot at present avert the justice of her Son from the world.

Penance is necessary. If people amend their lives, Our Lord will even yet save the world, but if not, punishment will come.

Regarding priests, religious, and rulers:

You must pray much for sinners and for priests and religious. Priests should concern themselves only with the things of the Church.

Priests must be very, very pure.

Disobedience of priests and religious to their superiors displeases Our Lord very much.

Pray, mother, for rulers.

Heaven forgive those who persecute the Church of Christ.

If the government would leave the Church in peace and give liberty to religion it would have God's blessing.

Regarding the virtues:

Mother, fly from riches and luxury.

Love poverty and silence.

Have charity even for bad people.

Do not speak evil of people and fly from evil speakers.

Mortification and sacrifice please Our Lord very much.

Confession is a sacrament of mercy and we must confess with joy and trust. There can be no salvation without Confession.

The Mother of God wants more virgin souls bound by a vow of chastity.

I would gladly go to a convent but I would rather go to Heaven.

To be a religious one must be very pure in body and mind.

One day Mother Godinho asked Jacinta: "Do you know what it means to be pure?" Jacinta answered: "Yes, yes, I know. To be pure in body means to be chaste, and to be pure in mind means not to commit sins; not to look at what one should not see, not to steal or lie and always to speak the truth even if it is hard." It is to be noted that Jacinta more than once related Our

Lady's words about impurity. Sehnora Marto recalls that Jacinta once said, "Mother, you must never eat flesh [meat] on Fridays, nor give it to us because Our Lady said that sins of the flesh brought people to Hell." She also stated: "Doctors do not know how to cure people properly because they do not have the love of God."

Mother Godinho asked, "Who taught you these things?" Jacinta answered, "Our Lady, but some of them I thought myself. I love to think." One can readily see the wisdom of this little girl who was so closely united with Our Lord. Following are more of the sayings of the little prophetess (not necessarily in the order she spoke them):

> I ask you as an act of charity to make it known to the women throughout Portugal and the whole world that Our Lady requires mortification with regard to food, dress, the eyes, the will, and their person. . . .Not to speak ill of anybody, not to murmer.
>
> Woe to the women wanting in modesty!. . .Women are worse than men on account of the fashions.
>
> Let men avoid persecutions, greed, lies, envy.
>
> Our Lord and Our Lady are very offended by people because they do not obey the Pope, nor the Bishops, nor the priests . . . . [This statement should be interpreted as referring to priests who teach in harmony with the Magisterium, in loyalty to the Pope.] Those who rule in the Church are not as other men. Priests should be as the salt of the earth; Our Lady is always pleading for them; they should be sincere and pure. Our Lady wants them to be respected as her sons. . . . God help those who persecute the Church!. . .
>
> God does not wish the death of the sinner; He wants them to be converted to give glory to God on earth and in Heaven.
>
> Our Lady likes those who mortify their senses, and those who help one another to have faith, hope and charity.
>
> Have faith and hope in God and Our Lady. . .Love St. Joseph and the Holy Spirit, Who can do all things! I love the Child Jesus and St. Joseph.
>
> The world is perishing because the people do not meditate.
>
> God help those who do not amend their lives.
>
> If people only knew what it was to love Jesus and His most Holy Mother.

Jacinta had two sisters, Florinda and Teresa, and when Mother Godinho asked Olimpia if she would like these two daughters to enter the religious life, the woman expressed her natural reaction: "Heavens, no!" Jacinta had not heard this, but shortly thereafter she said to Mother Godinho, "Our Lady would like my sisters to be nuns although mother wouldn't like it, and so she will take them to Heaven before long." The two daughters died shortly after Jacinta's death, at the ages of seventeen and sixteen.

Jacinta even predicted that one day Mother Godinho would visit the Cova da Iria, but that this would take place after Jacinta's death. The nun had a great desire to visit the Cova because she believed the Mother of God had appeared there. As we shall see later, circumstances kept Jacinta's body from being buried in Lisbon as first intended, and Mother Godinho was chosen to accompnay it to the family vault of Baron Alvaiazere in Vila Nova de Ourem; thus she was able to visit Fatima and the Cova da Iria.

One of the doctors who treated Jacinta asked her to pray for him in Heaven. Jacinta agreed to this, but looking at the doctor very seriously, she said, "You too will be going before long." She also predicted the death of another doctor who treated her as well as that of his daughter.

Jacinta had a great love for the priesthood and could not bear to hear people criticize priests. Rather, she asked that people pray for them. On a certain day a priest of good reputation delivered an excellent sermon. Jacinta spoke of him to Mother Godinho, saying, "That priest will turn out badly though you wouldn't think it now." Shortly afterwards he abandoned his vocation and lived in open scandal.

Jacinta came to love the stay at the orphanage and to love Mother Godinho, but God had in mind to require still another sacrifice of her. In an effort to save her, Dr. Lisboa had her placed in Dona Esterfânia Hospital. Jacinta underwent a preliminary examination at St. Josephs's Hospital for general cases. There her great love for modesty revealed itself as she wept finding herself exposed before doctors and students. Later, she was displeased that some boys were in the same ward.

Mother Godinho accompanied her to the children's ward of Dona Estefânia Hospital where she was placed in bed No. 38. Jacinta was now deprived of the solace of the orphanage's Chapel of Our Lady of Miracles. She could no longer live almost under the same roof as the hidden Eucharistic Jesus.

Mother Godinho received some serious reprimands from both doctors and nurses when it was learned that she had accepted a tuberculous patient in the orphanage, as they considered this a serious risk of infection for all the other children. However, it was the great charity of Mother Godinho that led to her decision, since, owing to Jacinta's sorry state, other people scheduled to take her in when she arrived in Lisbon had refused to do so. We have Mother Godinho's wise notes to thank for the deep insights into the mystical experiences of a child who reached great heights of sanctity even before the age of ten.

Sister Lucia never knew Mother Godinho, yet the writings of Mother Godinho and those of Sister Lucia about Jacinta are in striking agreement concerning the child's profound spirituality. Father Messias Dias Coelho now has the original writings of Mother Godinho. One time Jacinta asked the nun to go to the chapel to make reparation to Our Lord. "Look, go to the Tabernacle with another nun, and kneel at each side of it, and pray as the angels do in Heaven." Mother Godinho asked Jacinta, "Have you ever seen the angels adore Jesus?" Jacinta answered that she had heard them sing, but that it was not the way the people sang. Jacinta would remain silent for hours, and when asked what she had been thinking about she would usually reply that it had been about Our Lady, who was so beautiful, or else about Heaven.

Once Jacinta said to Mother Godinho, "Ask the Father to have a medal coined with Our Lady on one side and an angel on the other." After the apparitions of Our Lady in the Cova were approved by the diocese, the Franciscan priest, Father Estevao Maria, had a tiny medal about the size of a pea coined to fulfill Jacinta's request. It did not show an angel, however, but only Our Lady of Fatima on one side, and on the other side it read, "Souvenir of Our Lady of Fatima." Not until years later was it publicly revealed that the Angel had also appeared to the three Fatima children.

After her transfer to the hospital on February 2 of 1920, Jacinta's surroundings were cold and lonely. She suffered from the overly decorative dress of visitors and nurses, dress which was often immodest as well. (This does not refer to modern professional nurses.) Of doctors who were unbelievers she said, "Poor things! If they knew what awaited them!" Jacinta revealed that Our Lady appeared to her at the hospital again and spoke of the many sins of luxury, of the flesh, sins which were causing so many souls to be lost. Our Lady spoke of the necessity of penance for these sins.

Jacinta had brief moments of joy when special visitors came. Her father, Ti Marto, came briefly once. He could stay but a very short time for he had to return promptly to his other sick children in Aljustrel.

About the forthcoming operation intended to save her life, Jacinta dictated a letter to be sent to Lucia. (Sister Lucia could not verify receipt of such a letter.) The operation would do no good, she wrote, for Our Lady had appeared to her and revealed the day and hour of her death.

On February 10, Jacinta's operation took place under the hands of Dr. Castro Freire. Because of her serious condition, only a local anaesthetic could be used. This caused her to suffer greatly. Two ribs were removed from her left side, leaving a wound in which the hand could be inserted. Jacinta called out Our Lady's name at the daily dressings which were very painful.

No one ever heard her complain. Rather, she said, "We must suffer if we want to go to Heaven."

Our Lady did not neglect her specially favored soul during the time at the hospital. Mother Godinho received the confidences of Jacinta, who told the nun that the Blessed Virgin Mary would occasionally appear to her. During the last days before her death, Jacinta said, "Now I'm much better. Our Lady said that she would soon come to fetch me and that she would take away the pain."

Dr. Lisboa stated:

> And in fact with the apparition, there in the middle of the ward, her pain completely disappeared and she began to be able to play and enjoy certain distractions. She liked to look at holy pictures, one among them in particular—given me later as a souvenir—of Our Lady of Sameiro which she said most closely resembled the Lady of the apparitions. I was told several times that Jacinta wished to see me, but as my professional duties were heavy and Jacinta was apparently better, I, unfortunately, put off my visit until too late.

Mother Godinho would visit Jacinta at the Hospital. When she sat at the patient's bedside in the place where God's Mother appeared, Jacinta would object: "Not there Mother, that's were Our Lady stood." On one occasion, one of the nurses purposely stood in that place, as Jacinta constantly looked toward that spot. The nurse related: "She did not say anything but her face took on such an expression of pain that I felt I could not remain there."

Our Lady had once given Jacinta a choice either of dying earlier or of remaining upon earth longer in order to suffer more in reparation and for poor sinners. Jacinta chose to stay longer in order to help save more souls in the spirit of reparation. A few days after the operation, Mother Godinho had asked the doctor's permission to move Jacinta back to the orphanage, since Jacinta too desired this. The doctor responded that it would risk her life, so the request was dropped.

Some women patients considered Jacinta a little odd because of her silence. They did not know her identity. Only to Mother Godinho and two ladies who visited her and who knew who she was did Jacinta speak. It was on February 17 that Jacinta saw Our Lady, who told her that she would soon come to fetch her and take away her pains. It was also at this time that Our Lady gave some important communications which Jacinta related to Mother Godinho. Among them was that impurity, the sin of the flesh, was the sin that sent most people to perdition; that people should not remain obstinate in their sins as they had done up until then; that it was necessary to do much penance, and that people should do without luxuries. In reference to this last apparition of Our Lady to Jacinta, Lucia wrote,

> I have frequently been asked if Our Lady has pointed out in some appari-
> tion the kind of sin that displeased Our Lord the most, owing to Jacinta's
> having mentioned the sin of the flesh in Lisbon. I think now that she must
> have put the same question to Our Lady as she had done to me, and ob-
> tained the answer from her.

There followed a terrible threat to Lisbon if people did not amend their lives. Jacinta desired to confide this to Father Formigão, but since she was unable to do so, she entrusted it to Mother Godinho, together with another secret message to transmit to him. For several years ecclesiastical authorities did not permit the first communication to be released, then later, it was cautiously made public. Mother Godinho was not able to record the exact words spoken by Jacinta, but the following was related as the substance of the message:

> Our Lady is profoundly indignant over the sins committed in Portugal.
> For this reason, a terrible cataclysm of a social order threatens our coun-
> try, principally the city of Lisbon. It appears that a civil war of anarchist
> or Communist nature will break out, accompanied by sacking, assassina-
> tion, fires and devastations of every sort. The capital will be turned into
> a real image of Hell. On the occasion on which the offended Divine Justice
> inflicts such an appalling punishment, all those who could, should flee
> that city. This punishment now predicted should be made known little by
> little with the necessary discretion.

Jacinta stated that Our Lady had repeated her declaration that she would appear a seventh time. The little girl commented that it would not be to her, as she was going to die. She added that Our Lady wore a very sad expression on her face when speaking. The young mystic said, "I am so sorry for Our Lady! I am so sorry for her!"

A study of the sayings of Jacinta brings to light her mystical gifts which were so evident in Lisbon. Even before going there, she had been transformed from a sweet and carefree child into a girl still tender and loving, but also serious, one possessing a spiritual insight similar to that of some of the saints of the Church who reached such heights only when much older.

Jacinta said:

> I love to tell Jesus that I love Him. When I say it often, it seems to
> me that I have a flame in my heart, but one which does not burn me.

I can never get tired of telling Our Lord and Our Lady that I love them so much.

Shortly before going to Lisbon she said to Lucia:

It will not be long now before I go to Heaven. You will remain here to announce that God wishes devotion to the Immaculate Heart to be established in the world. When you go to say that, do not hide yourself; tell everybody that God concedes us His graces through the Immaculate Heart of Mary; that people should invoke her; that the Heart of Jesus wishes the Heart of Mary to be venerated at His side. Let them ask for peace through the Immaculate Heart of Mary, for God has given it to her. Ah, if I could only put into people's hearts the flame that is burning within my own heart, and that is making me love the Hearts of Jesus and Mary so much!

Jacinta said that the world was in a disturbed condition. She said that sinners deeply offended the Divine Heart of Our Lord. If they would amend their lives, He would help them. If not, He would send a punishment such as had never been experienced at any time. She condemned riches, except when used to good purpose. Wars were punishments from God for sins.

With her eyes lowered and her hands clasped Jacinta would often murmer, "Oh, Hell! Oh, Hell! Mother of God have pity on me and on sinners!" The vision of Hell was not revealed to the world until years later when Sister Lucia was informed by Heaven that it was time to reveal the first two parts of the secret: the first part is the vision of Hell and the second refers to the devotion the the Immaculate Heart of Mary. The significance of such words of Jacinta were thus to a great extent lost upon those at the orphanage who heard them.

Jacinta's great love for Jesus in Holy Communion was revealed on more than one occasion. Her First Holy Communion had been received from the Angel of the Holy Eucharist. Afterwards, she longed for the Angel to bring her Holy Communion again, saying that if one could receive Communion in Heaven, she intended to receive Our Lord there every day. There were times when she would cry out: "Am I going to die without receiving the hidden Jesus? If only Our Lady would bring Him to me when he comes to fetch me!" Jacinta commented to Lucia that she was so sorry not to be able to go to Holy Communion in reparation for the sins committed against the Immaculate Heart of Mary. Jacinta's desire for the Holy Eucharist was granted when she reached Lisbon. Her spiritual maturity is evident in her deep devotion to this central Mystery of our Faith, the Mystery in which infinitely perfect adoration and reparation are given to the Blessed Trinity. The mystical union of Jacinta's soul with God was nurtured with the grace she received in this great Sacrament.

Jacinta asked for Holy Communion at Lisbon without revealing the fact that she had not made her First Communion. Actually, she had received her First Communion from the Angel. One morning, to her immense joy, an Indian priest named Father St. Rita Sousa brought her Holy Communion. After receiving, she lay motionless on her pillow, joyful and radiant, her hands joined over her heart. Mother Godinho stated that she looked as if in ecstasy.

It is significant that in all her utterances, never once did Jacinta tell about the appearances of the Angel, or reveal the secret. [Having received permission from Heaven, Sister Lucia revealed the first two parts of the secret to the Bishop of Leiria in 1942.] Once Jacinta asked for prayers for Spain. Then Mother Godinho asked her about Portugal. Jacinta answered: "If they do not do penance nor amend their lives, they too will have to suffer. Our Lady loves this kingdom." Mother Godinho asked: "Did Our Lday not say anything else about our country?" Jacinta replied, "I do not say anything; it is Our Lady who speaks, not I."

The time came for Jacinta's operation. It appeared to have been successful, for her father received word that Jacinta was all right. He related,

I immediately had a letter written to Baron Alvaiazere telling him of this and thanking him and all the good people who had helped to arrange it. The Baron had also received a letter telling him the same news, but about ten days later another letter arrived from him telling me to go and see him at once. I set off for the town and when I arrived the Baron told the servants to get me something to eat and then pulled out a letter and read it to me: Jacinta stood the operation well but they did something and she died.

Dr. Lisboa reported Jacinta's death as follows:

On the evening of the 20th of February, at about 6 o'clock, Jacinta said that she felt worse and wished to receive the Sacraments. The parish priest [Dr. Pereira do Reis] was called and he heard her Confession about 8 o'clock that night. I was told that Jacinta has insisted that the Blessed Sacrament be brought to her as Viaticum but that Dr. Reis had not concurred because she seemed fairly well. He promised to bring her Holy Communion in the morning. Jacinta again asked for viaticum saying that she would shortly die, and indeed, she died that night, peacefully, but without having received Holy Communion.

* * *

Jacinta was laid out in Our Lady's colors according to her wish. .
. . When the coffin left the hospital mortuary, it occurred to me that it
might be wiser to have the body deposited in some special space, in case
the apparitions should later be confirmed. . . .

. . .with the help of the Confraternity of the Blessed Sacrament, some
of whose members happened to be in the sacristy at the time, Dr. Reis
was persuaded to give his permission to let the body remain there [Holy
Angels Church]. Soon afterwards it arrived and was placed humbly on
two stools in a corner of the sacristy. [Portuguese law required that not
more than 24 hours elapse between death and burial.]

The news spread rapidly and soon a sort of pilgrimage of believers
in Fatima began, the faithful bringing their rosaries and statues to touch
Jacinta's dress and to pray by her side. All this profoundly disturbed Dr.
Reis who was averse to his church being used for what might well be
a false devotion. . . .

It had finally been decided that the body should be taken to a vault
in Vila Nova de Ourem and matters were accordingly arranged though
this involved a delay of two days, the funeral being fixed for Tuesday
at 4 o'clock from the Holy Angels Church to the Rossio Station and from
thence by train to Vila Nova de Ourem

* * *

At last Dr. Reis, in order to avoid the responsibility of the open coffin and the pilgrims, deposited the body in the confraternity room above
the sacristy and handed the key to the firm of undertakers, Antonio Almeida
and Co., who had been engaged for the funeral. Senhor Almeida
remembers (years later and) in great detail what passed on that occasion.

In order to satisfy the innumerable requests to visit the body he remained during the whole of 23rd February in the church accompanying
each group of pilgrims—whose numbers were strictly limited—to the room
above, in order to avoid any unseemliness which might occur.

He was deeply impressed by the respect and devotion with which the
people approached and kissed the little corpse on the face and the hands
and he remembers very clearly the live pinkness of the cheeks and the
beautiful aroma which the body exhaled.

At last, on 24th February at 11 in the morning, the body was placed
in a leaden coffin which was then sealed. Present at this act were Senhor
Almeida, the authorities, and several ladies, among them Senhora Maria
Pena, who declared in the presence of various people who can testify to
it today, that the body exhaled a beautiful aroma of flowers as the coffin
was being sealed. Owing to the purulent nature of the disease and the length
of time that the body remained unburied this fact is remarkable.

* * *

I remember that on that day the General Annual Conference of St.
Vincent de Paul took place and that I excused my late arrival on account

of the work of mercy which had claimed my attention, namely, the burial of one of the seers of Fatima. These words provoked an outburst of mirth on the part of the assembly, composed, as may be imagined, of some of the most prominent Catholics of the capital, among them the Cardinal Patriarch himself, who joined in the laugh at my expense. Later he became a great admirer of Fatima and declared that his great desire was to celebrate Mass in the Cova da Iria before he died.

The identity of Jacinta had been kept a secret in the hospital. Her father's name was put down in the entry form as Manoel Marques, instead of Manuel Marto. Her mother's name was simply listed as Olimpia de Jesus. The child was listed as Jacinta de Jesus. Her native place was declared to be Vila Nova de Ourem, and the orphanage at which she had stayed, as 25 Estrela Street, Lisbon. In this manner Jacinta was protected from curious visitors and endless interrogations.

In the detailed account Dr. Lisboa has given us, we can easily detect the hand of Divine Providence. It is obvious the events of Fatima were by no means a trick of the clergy to dupe the faithful, as atheists and other enemies are so prone to claim. Those in responsible positions must always be most cautious regarding reported apparitions lest the credibility of the Church's official teachings be discredited. The author of this book can testify to the frequency of the reports from doubtlessly sincere people that they are witnesses to private revelations. The devil himself can pose as an angel of light in order to discredit the Church.

Senhor Almeida, who assisted at the undertaking procedures, later wrote:

> I seem to see Jacinta still, looking like a little angel. In her coffin she seemed to be alive; her lips and cheeks were a beautiful pink. I have seen many corpses, large and small, but I have never seen anything like that. The beautiful perfume which the body exhaled could not be explained naturally and the hardest sceptic could not doubt it. One remembers the smell which so often makes it repugnant to remain near a corpse and yet this child had been dead three days and a half and the smell of her body was like a bouquet of flowers.

Modern methods of embalming were not then employed in Portugal. It is interesting that years later, at the exhumation of Jacinta's body in 1951, there were again reports of perfume given off by the body.

Nurse Nadeja Silvestre had remained by Jacinta's side until 8 p.m. when she was relieved from duty. She remained with Jacinta for an extra half hour when her place was taken by Nurse Aurora Gomes da Costa who continued the vigil. Jacinta died peacefully at 10:30 p.m. Nurse Aurora could not recollect any details of the death and so it is not certain that she was actually at the side of Jacinta at the time of death. There was great surprise among persons at De Estafânia Hospital when they learned that one of their patients had been one of the Fatima seers. The surgeon who operated on Jacinta became famous as a children's specialist. He later declared that all he could recall of the child was that she had suffered with a resignation beyond her years.

Both Mother Godinho and Senhora D. Amelia Sande e Castro hurried to the hospital when they heard of Jacinta's death. They desired to lay out the body, but were informed that they could not be admitted to the mortuary until a coffin and dress could be provided for the deceased child. A second time they went to the hospital with a priest, Father Baltasor, who greatly wished to see the child. They took the needed clothing with them. Again they had difficulty being admitted to the presence of the body until Dr. Eurico Lisboa intervened. At this time it was covered with a sheet, and they could not touch it, but rather had to await the arrival of the coffin. When Mother Godinho was finally permitted to wash Jacinta's body, in the company and witness of a nurse, the women noticed tears of dried blood on her face.

Among the many wanting to honor the remains of Jacinta were those persons who had refused to take Jacinta into their homes. They now came to pay exaggerated homage to her remains, doubtlessly wishing to make up for their mistake. They had refused to accept a small child into their home, and reports now circulated that the very child they refused was the child who had seen the Mother of God and who had died a holy death.

Nurse Nadeja Silvestre declared her amazement at the difference in appearance of Jacinta in life and in death. In her extreme suffering before she died, Jacinta's face had looked worn and emaciated. But in death, her cheeks had filled out and had taken on a healthy color. "She did not look the same child; she had become radiant and beautiful." When Mother Godinho held vigil beside the coffin, she glanced at the little lamp nearby. She was astonished to see that the lamp contained no oil but still burned brightly.

It was 11:00 a.m. on February 24, 1920, when the body of the little mystic was enclosed in a lead lined coffin and accompanied by Mother Godinho and others to Chao das Macas by train. There Senhor Marto and a large crowd awaited its arrival. Senhor Marto broke down and wept bitterly when the little coffin was taken from the train. Another of his daughters, Florinda, was home gravely ill, and so his wife was not able to be present. Jacinta's parents must have felt an even deeper sorrow from the fact that at this time even many high ecclesiastical authorities had not yet accepted the apparitions which had taken place in the Cova.

The funeral procession continued on to the Vila Nova de Ourem, where Jacinta's remains were placed in the family vault of the Baron de Alvaiazere, where they were to remain for the next fifteen years. It was the custom to ring the church bells on the occasion of a death. Maria dos Anjos, Lucia's sister, was in the kitchen with Lucia when suddenly the church bells of the Fatima church began to toll. Lucia placed her hands over her heart and cried out in anguish that they must be tolling for Jacinta. Immediately she fled from the house and ran to the Loca do Cabeco. There she flung herself upon the ground and wept. Only towards nightfall, we are told, did she return home, her eyes red from crying.

Sister Lucia recalls that her Aunt Olimpia "later, in order to comfort me a little, took me to visit the tomb where the mortal remains of her little daughter lay. But for a long time my sadness only seemed to increase."

A canonical inquiry into the extraordinary facts of Jacinta's life was made on Septmeber 12, 1934, in Leiria. Then it was decided to translate Jacinta's remains from the family vault of the Baron de Alvaiazere in Vila Nova de Ourem to the Fatima cemetery, to be placed with those of Francisco in a little tomb over Francisco's grave. This special construction was ordered by the Bishop of Leiria.

Jacinta's prediction that she would return to Fatima after her death was fulfilled one year later, on September 12, 1935, at the orders of the Bishop of Leiria. Before the departure, the coffin was hurriedly opened. To the astonishment of those present, when its covering was folded back, Jacinta's face was seen to be incorrupt. A photograph was taken and the remains were touched with religious objects. The coffin was then closed and taken to the Cova da Iria, where the Bishop of Leiria was awaiting its arrival. Only four motorcars made up the funeral procession to the place where God's Mother had appeared. In the first was the Baron de Alvaiazere and his son; in the other cars were Jacinta's parents, a couple of priests, and some ladies. At 3:30 p.m. a motorcar bore the coffin, covered with a rich silken pall, to the Chapel of Penance in the Sanctuary at Fatima, where the Archbishop of Evora celebrated the Sacrifice of the Mass. Baron Alvaiazere gave up the priceless relic with regret, saying it had brought many graces to his family.

The photograph taken on this occasion was sent to Sister Lucia by the Bishop of Leiria. It was Sister Lucia's grateful response upon receiving this picture, which brought back so many memories of her cousin, that moved the Bishop to order her to write out all the details she could remember about

Jacinta. The things that Lucia then wrote indicated the great depth of this child, and brought out points which the world needed to know in order the better to understand the Fatima message. At the Bishop's request, Lucia's notes were made into a book by the Rev. José Galamba de Oliveira, Professor at the Leiria Seminary.

The first edition of the book compiled from Sister Lucia's notes was sent to her in May of 1938 for her reaction. She replied with a long letter to the Bishop of Leiria. In part it reads:

> In fact, Your Lordship, Jacinta was deeply impressed by some of the things revealed in the secret, and owing to her great love of the Pope and sinners, she often exclaimed: "Poor Holy Father!. . .I am so sorry for sinners!"
>
> And I now add: if she were living at present, when these things are so near to coming to pass [the war of 1939], how much more impressed she would have been! If only the world knew the moment of grace that is still conceded to it and did penance!. . .
>
> Would that her recommendation to pray for the Holy Father and for sinners were heard and put into practice in every corner of the world!
>
> Your Lordship will surely be surprised at my writing these few words, which seem to indicate something, but it is not I, it is Our Lady who is making use of me. Your Lordship may make use of them as Our Lord inspires you.

Sister Lucia's words are an allusion to the war that was to break out the following year. In a letter to her confessor dated February 6, 1938, Lucia said that God made her understand that the war with all its horrors was about to break out. She said that God had assured her of a special protection of the Immaculate Heart of Mary for Portugal. This was because of the Act of Consecration made to Mary's Heart by the Bishops of Portugal in union with the faithful. The protection was also in response to the prayers and penance offered up each month at Fatima.

The tomb of Jacinta in the Fatima cemetery was ruined by people knocking off fragments to take as relics, and then rain was able to penetrate the interior of the tomb. Alarmed at this damage, the Bishop of Leiria decided to hasten the date for the translation of the body to the Basilica at the Cova da Iria, even though construction on the Basilica had not yet been completed.

On the morning of April 30, 1951, the tomb was opened. The Bishop of Leiria, members of the seers' families, and a few other persons were present. Doctors who were present to examine the remains, along with the workmen who would also serve as witnesses, took solemn oaths that they would state the truth and only the truth.

They found Jacinta's coffin and a large casket, thought to contain Francisco's remains. These were withdrawn and taken to a nearby building which belonged to the Servitas, a new religious order. Witnesses refused to authenticate the remains supposed to be Francisco's. These were declared to be bones of babies, mixed with a few adult bones—surely not those of a boy of Francisco's age. (In Portuguese country districts, babies are buried in the graves of the most recently buried persons.)

There followed months of sorrow in the district because Francisco's remains had not been found. Senhor Marto prayed for a solution; meanwhile he insisted: "Dig deeper. Dig deeper!" Finally the Bishop of Leiria gave orders that the grave under the tomb be reopened, and this was done on February 13, 1952. It was not an easy task, for the foundation was about six feet deep and the lower part was covered with a layer of cement which had to be pierced.

On top of the cement were found some adult bones and skulls. It was Senhor Marto who kept insisting that the layer of cement should be pierced, though others were led to believe that nothing more was to be found. Senhor Marto and his son John assisted in the digging, which was done with caution. To the jubilation of all present, beneath the cement a little coffin became exposed two or three inches below the foundation.

Francisco's father had repeatedly told the Bishop of Leiria that the coffin had been too short for the remains of his son, and that its knees were raised so that the body could fit into it. This was verified when the coffin was opened. The doctors authenticated the remains as those of Francisco, though his body had not remained incorrupt. Rain had penetrated the coffin, and the skeleton broke into little bits when the coffin was removed. Senhor Marto had insisted that Francisco was buried with a fifteen decade rosary, and this proved true also. The beads had become separated and one hundred forty-eight loose ones were found. The rest of them, mixed with a little clay, were still adhering to the little fingers. Having been told by Our Lady to say "many rosaries," Francisco held onto the rosary even in death.

The body of Jacinta had been easily authenticated. The exposed face was found to be incorrupt, as were the hands. The entire body was not examined. The face looked more worn than it had in the photograph taken at the first exhumation on September 12, 1935. Jacinta bore a resemblance to both her parents. Stuck to her head were some little white flowers and part of the Communion veil in which she had been buried some thirty years previously. The cambric dress had turned a light brown, but it had resisted the action of the lime used in burial. Her arms and hands were covered with the veil. Senhor Marto stated that viewing Jacinta's body "was somewhat like looking at a person grown old, whom one had known young."

An eyewitness account of the second exhumation of Jacinta's body, which took place in 1951, was carried in the papers of the time as follows:

> These attracted the attention of all, for they were beautifully white and very even—a great contrast to the color of the skin, and gave a strange charm to the little mouth, missing from all her photographs. Her eyes were sunk deep in their sockets, and the lids gave the impression of having adhered together.
>
> * * *
>
> The expression on Jacinta's face was that of great peace, and all who saw her could not help feeling that they were greatly privileged to have been granted such a favor.

The fact that Jacinta's face appeared much older than she was at the time of her death will cause different reactions. Perhaps one explanation is that her body reflected her spirtual maturity at the time of her death, which came when Jacinta was not quite ten years old.

Jacinta's remains were left in the old coffin, but this was placed inside a new one. The remains were exposed to view for a short time. The translation to the Basilica in the Cova took place on May 5, 1951. Jacinta's coffin was covered with a decorative pall and carried on a hand-hearse, surrounded by bouquets of lilies and roses. Small children headed the procession. The children were dressed in blue and were followed by long lines of seminarians in cassock and white surplus, as well as by inhabitants of Fatima, the Cova da Iria, and surrounding villages. Men on bicycles and in motorcars followed. At the new Basilica the Requiem Mass was offered, followed by the Burial service. The coffin was placed before the high altar. Before it was removed to its present resting place, the congregation were permitted to approach it and touch it with religious objects. Then the cofifn was carried by priests to the vault in the transept which lies to the left as one faces the high altar. A simple, pale pink marble slab with looped metal handles at the corners was drawn over the opening. The ceremonies came to an end. The people crowded round the tomb. They prayed and kissed the slab which they covered with flowers.

Later, another upright slab was placed at the head of the tomb. It read: "Here lies Jacinta Marto to whom Our Lady appeared. *Aqui Repousam os restos mortais de Jacinta Marto a quem nossa sensora apareceu. Hasceu a 11-3-1910 — Morreu a 20-2-1920. Transladada para esta Basilica a 1-5-1951.*"

Francisco's remains were transferred to the Basilca in a similar ceremony in the early morning of March 13, 1952. His remains also rest beneath the Basilica floor opposite those of Jacinta, on the other side of the Basilica. The two seers have separate burial places. This permits those who call upon their intercession to clarify which of the Fatima children they are invoking; thus any graces or miracles granted through their intercession can be clearly attributed to either Jacinta or Francisco, and perhaps used as evidence on behalf of their beatification.

7.
True and False Responses to Fatima

When the Blessed Virgin Mary appeared to the Fatima children on July 13, 1917, she showed them the terrible vision of Hell and added, "You have seen Hell where the souls of poor sinners go. To save them, God wishes to establish in the world devotion to my Immaculate Heart." Not until 1941 did Sister Lucia write of these two parts of the Fatima secret, namely, the vision of Hell and devotion to the Immaculate Heart of Mary. The third part of the secret was also given to the Fatima children at the time of the July apparition. It was written down, but was not to be opened until 1960, and then only by the Pope.

Unfortunately, many Fatima devotees placed so much emphasis on the "third secret of Fatima" that they failed to pay attention to the Fatima message that had already been revealed. Periodically there appear sensational reports, some claiming to contain extracts from the third part of the Fatima secret. These reports bear headlines such as "Fatima's Distressing Message," or "Further Warnings from Our Lady of Fatima." One claims to be taken from an article by Louis Emrich in the October 15, 1963 issue of the German newspaper, *Neues Europa*. It states that the third secret impressed diplomatic circles in Moscow:

> Pope Paul allowed not only Kennedy, but also Khrushchev to read cer-
> tain parts of the *Third Message of Fatima* which the Mother of God had
> revealed on the 13th of October, 1917, to the little Portuguese visionary,
> Lucia. . . . *This extract* from the Third Message of Fatima was also sent
> personally to President Kennedy, Prime Minister MacMillan and Party
> Chairman Khrushchev. . . . The directors of the two blocs of world policy
> were overwhelmed by its content, just as Pope Pius XII, Pope John XXIII
> and Pope Paul VI had previously been.

The various distorted Fatima reports are replete with misinformation and
full of inaccuracies. One report pretending to contain extracts of the third
part of the July secret quotes the Blessed Virgin as saying, "Do not be troubl-
ed, dear child, I am the Mother of God who is speaking to you and asking
that you announce the following message to the entire world in my name."
But the fact is that Our Lady did not reveal who she was until October. In
June, when Lucia asked, "Where are you from," the lady simply answered:
"I am from Heaven." During the first five apparitions, the children never
identified their visitor as the Mother of God. What Lucia said to the lady
on July 13th was the following: "I would like to ask you to tell us who
you are, and to work a miracle so that everybody will believe that you are
appearing to us." Our Lady answered: "Continue to come here every month.
In October, I will tell you who I am and what I want and I will perform
a miracle for all to see and believe."

In June, Our Lady had shown herself holding a heart which the children
understood to be the Immaculate Heart of Mary, and more than once she
referred to "Our Lady of the Rosary," but it was not until October that
she clearly identified herself. At that time she stated, "I am the Lady of
the Rosary." This shows how unrealistic it is to quote Our Lady in her July
apparition as saying "I am the Mother of God"—but one example of the
misinformation often contained in spurious and sensational "reports" on
Fatima.

It causes great wonderment how extensive quotations can be attributed
to God's Mother as related by Sister Lucia when the quotations are so unlike
the authentic Marian message which Sister Lucia has given us. In reading
the *Memoirs* of Sister Lucia one sees her profound respect for the virtue
of obedience, and her desire for all to hear the voice of Jesus in the Holy
Father and the Bishops and priests in union with the Pope. Yet pious people, doubtlessly thinking they are helping the Fatima cause, distribute
literature which puts these words in Sister Lucia's mouth:

One thing, Father, you must make clear to the people though; not to wait or hope for any call to prayer and penance either from the Supreme Pontiff, the Bishops, the pastors, or the superior generals. It is time that each one, on his own initiative, undertake to do works of sanctity. . . .

Neither the style nor the words fit the character of Sister Lucia.

In some spurious writings one can see attempts to melt together many inauthentic apparitions. For instance the following:

If mankind will not oppose these evils, I will be obliged to let the Arm of my Son drop in vengeance. . . . Having exhausted all other means which men have ignored, she is now offering with apprehension, as the last resource of salvation herself in person, her numerous apparitions, her tears and messages given through seers scattered in various parts of the world. . . .

In answer to such confusing reports, it is well to set forth an authoritative voice on the subject of the secret message of Fatima. Cardinal Ottaviani was with Pope John when the secret was first opened in January of 1960. The Cardinal gave a special press conference on February 11, 1967, in which he said: "What matters is the public message . . . as Lucia was charged not only to transmit a secret to the Pope, but also to make known to all the world a public message." This public message bears a solemn and divine assurance of a period of peace to mankind if it is heard and lived. Cardinal Ottaviani analyzed the situation correctly in a few words. The important part of Fatima is not a secret but a *public message*. That public message is not well known, understood, or interpreted. It is necessary to get the message out and make sure it is lived. Such is the purpose of this book. Those who waste time and money on a secret which is not ours to know have not grasped the message which Heaven wants us to know and to live.

Rev. John Ryan of the Reparation Society has rightly made the following observations about the third part of the Fatima secret:

What is its content? . . . We wish, moreover, by posing this question in no way to encourage or augment unwholesome curiosity in this matter. Rather the whole purpose . . . is to offset this in some small way by rehearsing the known facts and to do our little part in answering the lies and libels against Fatima and its message which are being published and circulated by the ton.

Let us begin by stating with certainty what the third secret is not. It does not predict the end of the world, much less its dissolution amid horrifying circumstances. "In the end," said Our Lady, "my Immaculate

Heart will triumph. The Holy Father will consecrate Russia to me, and she will be converted, and a period of peace will be granted to the world. In Portugal, the dogma of the Faith will always be preserved; etc . . .'' Our Lady could not contradict herself in the third part of the secret just after having given us a clear cut and absolute prophecy of the final triumph of her Immaculate Heart, of Russia's conversion and final world peace. Besides, as Bishop John Venancio pointed out when he was Bishop of Leiria, the Fatima message cannot contradict the holy Gospel which tells us that the end of the world is known to God alone. "The message of Fatima," he concluded, "is not, therefore, a message of death, an incitement to panic or terror. It is an affirmation of love and of hope."

What a distortion of this sacred message of the Blessed Mother of God to twist it into a prediction of destruction and gloom! True, Our Lady did speak of the annihilation of certain nations, but whether this meant politically or actually, we do not know. This is to take place during the intermediate period before her final triumph. It is in this period—according to the estimation of Sister Lucia—that we are now living. We should pray, especially through the Rosary and First Saturday devotions and practice daily self-denial in reparation for our sins. Fatima has been fully approved and is quite sufficient. Let us beware of unapproved visions: "For there shall arise false Christs and false prophets, and shall show great signs and wonders, insomuch as to deceive (if possible) even the elect" (Mt. 24:24).

It remains for us to offer what seems to be a safe and sound conjecture on the possible content of the third secret. Throughout . . . we have followed the study of Dr. Joaquin Maria Alonso in the booklet *La Verdad Sobre el Secreto de Fatima*, published in 1976 by Centro Mariano, Cor Mariae Centrum, Victor Pradera, 65 Apdo; Madrid-8, Spain. We continue to follow him in his careful conclusions.

If the dogma of Faith is to be preserved in Portugal (Our Lady's promise introduces the third secret) it seems to imply that the Faith's teachings will be obscured or even totally destroyed elsewhere. This seems to point to a crisis within the Church itself, most probably during this postconciliar period in which we are now living. These internal struggles, much more serious than external persecutions and wars, could well refer to the widespread defection of priests and religious and to negligence on the part of pastors, including even some bishops. It could include the enormous weakening of solid theology due to a hypercritical attitude and erroneous interpretations of Sacred Scripture. This weakness within the Church is shown by its seeming inability to throw off the ever-invading spirit of the world which would reduce the Church to a mere human institution. It is exemplified by those reactionary elements in the Church who criticized Pope Paul's pilgrimage to Fatima in 1967 as a 180-degree regression to those former positions which, they claimed, had been overcome by Vatican

Council II.

These observations of Dr. Alonso do not surprise me. He sees disturbances in the Church today as part of the Fatima message, but he does not see the message as a new gospel. Elsewhere in this book, the author has shown Our Lady of Fatima as a Catechist who reviews the total Catholic Faith at a time when men wish to deny it in a spirit of atheism.

Of course, the heart of the matter is our response to her in faith and love. If enough of us would grant Our Mother's requests, she would be able to turn back the tide of wars and spiritual losses in the world. Undue curiosity about a secret message does not accomplish this.

Other false responses to Our Lady are possible. For example, at the time of the apparitions of the Blessed Virgin Mary to Bernadette Soubirous at the Grotto of Massabielle near Lourdes in Southern France, as many as seventy other apparitions were also reported. None of them survived or proved to be authentic. Likewise, in the twentieth century there are many reports of apparitions. It takes little faith or imagiation to realize that Satan does not want the message of Lourdes or Fatima accepted and put into the lives of people any more than he wants the Gospel practiced. He can distract us from Heaven's call by fostering reports of apparitions all over. This sends some dashing off in many directions, instead of studying and truly living the message of the authentic apparitions. It also distracts from the Gospels and the official teachings of the Church.

The Fatima message has such simplicity and such depth that it is missed by many not willing to open their hearts in obedience, in humility, in prayerfulness. A Portuguese scholar of Fatima, Father Messias Dias Coelho, once told the author of this book: "Only those who pray can believe in Fatima." I interpreted him to mean: "Only those who pray in humility, in love, in obedience . . ." Fatima is so much like the Gospels in their simplicity and depth that many long years of study do not seem to exhaust the depth of the message.

People who have not probed the depths of Fatima, but see it only as a call to pray the daily Rosary, which they say they "already do," sometimes go chasing after every reported, but non-authenticated apparition. They say, or at least imply, that they have already digested the Fatima message, so that now they must "move on to newer revelations."

The author of this book has led many pilgrimages to Fatima, taking up to one hundred and fifty young men at a time, and at other times taking young ladies, and spending more than two weeks at a time in intensive prayer and study. At the end of the two weeks of prayer and study, most young men and women, many of them obviously transformed spiritually, have reported that they never realized the depth of the Fatima message. This was the opening to *continued* study and prayer, and a new and more beautiful relationship of personal love between their souls and Jesus and Mary. It was the beginning too of a newer and deeper appreciation of the Church, of the gospels, of the totality of the Christian message. As Dr. Alonso told me, "What Fatima has to say is the mind of the Church."

Unfortunately, some read the Fatima story and see only a dramatic and interesting story about three children. The intriguing events have a happy ending as it turns out that the children really were telling the truth when they claimed that a "beautiful lady" from heaven was appearing to them. Millions saw the Warner Brothers' movie which in many ways was well done. It has been shown on television repeatedly. But how many have seen beyond the story to the message, and have responded with a real conversion to a life of prayer and sacrifice? How many have accepted the message of Fatima for themselves? How many have tried to spread it to others?

Marto, the humble father of Jacinta and Francisco, realized that the message was intended for more than the transformation of the three children or even all of Portugal. He once made a statement that revealed this insight. The occasion was the translation of Jacinta's remains from Vila Nova de Ourem to the Fatima cemetery, to be placed in a little tomb over Francisco's grave. Before the open tomb, the Bishop of Evora turned to Marto and asked, "Happy father?" The father of Jacinta and Francisco acknowledged that the children were not only his; he replied, "They belong to the whole world."

One who visits Fatima must go as a pilgrim, not as a tourist. Tourists are usually seeking enjoyment or relaxation, but pilgrims come to Fatima in a spirit of prayer and penance, willing to deny themselves. Of the hundreds of thousands who arrive for the twelfth and thirteenth, May through October, many have walked for days, some up to two weeks. They walk over hills and mountains. This is why it is recommended that pilgrims from other countries plan their trip so as to be in Fatima for the twelfth and thirteenth of a month from May through October, so as to experience the reality of the message in the lives of the other pilgrims.

Occasionally one hears of tourists who stop over at Fatima for a day or two. They arrive looking for externals such as a beautiful basilica or art works. They are disappointed, and they sometimes report afterwards: "There's not much to see at Fatima." And they are right. With the natural eyes of the body there is not much to see at Fatima. For those looking for a vacation of worldly recreation, there is not much to do at Fatima. But for those who have studied Fatima in advance, preparing for their pilgrimage by prayer and arriving with a heart open for the graces which the Immaculate Heart desires to give, several weeks at Fatima are not enough.

One who truly makes a pilgrimage to Fatima often experiences an inner conversion and what it really means to be "born again." We speak here not of the popular Protestant concept of being "born again," but of a deep spiritual renewal. This is not merely an emotional experience bringing only natural joy and personal satisfaction. It is the inner, supernatural joy and light that God gives through His Mother. Those who study and meditate on the Fatima message, just like those who travel to Fatima, must search for the light of God which Mary gives, and humbly ask for grace in a spirit of penitence—or they will come away unbelievers in Fatima.

Some, after traveling to locations of other reported apparitions, come to Fatima as one of many other places where Heaven has especially manifested divine grace, so that they may "obtain as many graces as possible." On one occasion I stood at the very spot where Our Lady had appeared at Fatima, within the Capelinha, having just completed the celebration of the Sacrifice of the Mass, and with over a hundred youth gathered at the site of the former "holm oak." There came up a group of people who had just come from another religious site in Europe, of which I had never heard. They were on their way to even another site, and without a word of Fatima, were urging me to take all these young people to other locations where they would "surely experience God." I feared that these travelers were missing the reality of Fatima in its call to the entire world to accept the special graces of the Immaculate Heart.

Admittedly, Europe has more than one site of authentic religious pilgrimage, such as Lourdes and Paray-le-Monial. But some people pay more attention to unauthenticated apparitions. To justify themselves, they usually recall that thirteen years lapsed before Fatima was officially approved by competent Church authority. Since Fatima itself was not approved for thirteen years, these people fell justified in ignoring Church strictures and even condemnations of reported apparitions.

The hand of God is present atop the mountain of Fatima, but God, as in Old Testament times, moves and works in the soul as a gentle breeze. His movement in the soul is hardly detected until one opens his heart to prayer and meditation in silence. One must go to Fatima not simply to receive, but also to give. One must ask as Lucia asked each time the Mother of God appeared: "What do you want of me?" In studying and meditating on the Fatima message, one must have the same spirit, since it is in giving that we receive. Not all can go to Fatima, although it is a special place of grace, but all can open their hearts and ask in prayer for that grace which is Mary's to give.

One of the best ways to come to a deep understanding of the true response to the Fatima message is to look at the lives of the three seers. The spiritual transformation of their lives is evidence both of great graces received and of a faithful answer to Heaven's call. Each of the three children—Jacinta, Francisco, and Lucia—fulfilled a special purpose in the mind of God, as each participated in the message in a somewhat different way. Each child was particularly impressed with different aspects of the message, and even on the more obvious level, the children's participation in the apparitions was not identical. Francisco saw the Angel and Our Lady, but did not hear the words of the heavenly visitors. Both Lucia and Jacinta heard them, but only Lucia spoke.

In the lives of the children we can see a progress through the classic three "stages" or "ways" of the spiritual life—purgative way, the illuminative way, and the unitive way. No one except God can really know at what stage a person is at any particular time, and in real life, of course, a person does not experience the "three ways" as neatly organized or watertight compartments, as described in a book. Also, it is true that the three children received very special graces which gave them, so to speak, a foretaste of the unitive way, that is, of constant deep union with God before they had actually progressed that far in virtue. Nevertheless, in studying their lives we can recognize some of the landmarks in their transformation.

The first stage of the spiritual life is the purgative way. The aim of the soul at this stage is to purify itself in order to attain union with God. This is the beginning of the spiritual life wherein one is still inclined toward sin, has falls, and is attempting to root out sin so as to become free from frequent and deliberate venial sin, or at least to live in the state of grace.

The illuminative way is the second stage of the spiritual life. It is characterized by the following of Christ through the positive exercise of Christian virtues. It takes its name from the deeper insight into the things of God which one has at this time. Jesus said: "I am the light of the world: he that followeth me, walketh not in darkness, but shall have the light of life" (Jn. 8:12). In this stage one is illumined by the light of Christ Jesus, and strives not simply to avoid sin, but to grow in His life.

The unitive way is the third and last stage of the spiritual life, a stage in which the goal is habitual intimate union with God through Jesus Christ. St. Paul expressed it in Sacred Scripture: "And I live, now not I; but Christ liveth in me" (Gal. 2:20). The unitive way is characterized by the theocentric orientation of one's whole life, as the Blessed Trinity dwelling in one's soul becomes the center of all thoughts, affections, words, and actions. This does not necessarily mean that a person speaks of nothing but God, but it does mean that God is constantly present to him in a conscious way. He is constantly faithful to God's grace. He continues to mortify himself, but this becomes much easier. The senses of the body and the imagination have become subject to the will, and the will has become subject to God. In a sense, there is a restoration of our fallen state of original justice before the fall of our first parents. One continues to perform reparation and expiation for one's sins by means of penitential works, but these prayers and penances also are offered more and more for the salvation and sanctification of other men, as one becomes ever more concerned for the members of the Mystical Body of Christ, as well as for those not yet incorporated into Christ's Body.

Whereas in the first stage, the purgative, one works to root out sin, in the illuminative way one endeavors to put on the virtues of Christ; by prayer and good works he develops a fervent love of God. Finally, in the unitive way all one's thoughts, words, and actions center around the Triune God in one's soul. One's life becomes a constant prayer, a lingering thought of God. One lives in constant and close union with Christ, the Head of the Mystical Body.

People grow in age and in intellectual knowledge, but it is often the case that they do not grow in grace and in spiritual perfection. Let us see what was happening in the lives of the Fatima children, as they were emptied of self so as to be filled with the love of God through the Heart of Mary.

The Angel himself pointed to a progression in the spiritual life by the increasing depth of the messages he brought. In his first apparition, the Angel invited the children to pray with him in faith, adoration, hope and love, and to ask pardon for those who do not believe, do not adore, do not trust and do not love God. When the Angel appeared the next time, he repeated his exhortation to pray, but in addition, he told the shepherds to make sacrifices: "What are you doing? Pray! Pray very much! The Hearts of Jesus and Mary have designs of mercy on you. Offer prayers and sacrifices constantly to the Most High." With the third apparition the children were led into a deeper appreciation of the Most Holy Trinity and of the Holy Eucharist, two central Mysteries of our Faith. They were overwhelmed by an experience of the presence of God: "The force of the presence of God was so intense that it absorbed us and almost completely annihilated us."

Before the apparitions of the Angel and of God's Mother, the three shepherds—although well-grounded in the practice of the essentials of the Catholic Faith—acted like normal young children, subject to childhood failings. This is in no way to suggest that they ever lived in serious sin, yet it is true that a profound transformation to a much deeper spiritual life did take place in them.

Francisco was a child who sometimes disobeyed his parents. Jacinta even remembered that he had stolen a tostao (about a penny) from José Marto of Case Velha, and that when the Aljustrel boys threw stones at the ones from Boleiros, he threw some too. These matters Francisco submitted to the tribunal of the confessional.

Jacinta's life is described at length in another chapter, but as a summary, we shall consider her part as one of the three children who participated in a particular way in the Fatima events. In her spiritual transformation, Jacinta reaches out in a special way to other souls, for their conversion. Jacinta was deeply impressed with the words of God's Mother concerning the tragedy of lost souls; many souls had abandoned their Faith for sin. Jacinta was possessive by nature, and before the apparitions, she was not the best sport in playing games. In fact, she pouted at times. She seemed more attached to dancing than to spiritual things before her great transformation. But as she began to be changed, she led her family to pray the Rosary; she corrected her mother for telling fibs. There was a moving away from imperfection and toward prayer as she approached the illuminative way.

One sees a similar transformation in the life of the Little Flower, St. Therese of Lisieux, who advanced from hyper-sensitivity, a certain stage of desiring or even requiring to be spoiled, toward a response to grace whereby the things of the spirit began to dominate her life.

The sorrow which Lucia underwent in her own family was a strong stimulus to spiritual growth. She suffered terribly from her mother's doubts about the beautiful lady from Heaven. Lucia's mother even took the broom after her, and on one occasion dragged her to the priest to confess her "lies." As they walked along to the rectory, her mother preached a sermon to Lucia. Trembling, Lucia responded: "But mother, how can I say that I did not see, when I did see?" She did not want to sin by telling a lie, especially to a priest. As they neared the priest's house, Lucia's mother said: "Just you listen to me! What I want is that you should tell the truth. If you saw, say so! But if you didn't see, admit that you lied."

The children were summoned to the administrator's residence, and even threatened with being boiled alive in oil. The intimacy of Lucia's family was greatly disturbed, and the blame for this was thrown onto her. The Cova da Iria was on a piece of land belonging to her parents. In the hollow it was more fertile, and there the family cultivated maize, greens, peas, and other vegetables. On the slopes grew olive trees, oaks, and holm oaks. But when the reports of the apparitions spread and people began coming by the thousands, the family became unable to cultivate anything at all. Some pilgrims came riding on animals which ate up all they could find. The Cova was wrecked. Lucia's mother would say: "You, now when you want something to eat, go and ask the lady for it." Her sisters chimed in with: "Yes, you can have what grows in the Cova da Iria."

Regarding the children's imprisonment at Ourem, Sister Lucia writes:

> . . . what I felt most deeply and what caused me most suffering on that occasion was my being completely abandoned by my family. . . . After this journey or imprisonment, for I really don't know what to call it, I returned home, as far as I can remember, on the 15th of August. To celebrate my arrival, they sent me right away to let out the sheep and take them off to pasture.

In the later years, Sister Lucia realized God's plan and the place of divine Providence working in all this for her spiritual transformation. She had no recourse but to prayer in love and trust, offering all in reparation.

> Poor mother! Now, indeed, that I understand what her situation really was, how sorry I feel for her! Truly, she was right to judge me unworthy of such a favor, and therefore to think I was lying.
>
> By a special grace from Our Lord, I never experienced the slightest thought or feeling of resentment regarding her manner of acting towards me. As the Angel had announced that God would send me sufferings, I always saw the hand of God in it all. The love, esteem and respect which I owed her, went on increasing, just as though I were most dearly cherished. And now, I am more grateful to her for having treated me like this, than if she had continued to surround me with endearments and caresses.

Lucia's first spiritual director was the Rev. Dr. Formigão, a priest who helped her to advance toward the illuminative way. About the time of the disturbed family situation, the priest visited her. She wrote:

> I liked him very much, for he spoke to me a great deal about the practice of virtue, and taught me various ways of exercising myself in it. He showed me a holy picture of St. Agnes, told me about her martyrdom, and encouraged me to imitate her. His Reverence continued to come every month for an interrogation, and always ended up by giving me some good advice, which was of help to me spiritually. One day he said to me: "My child, you must love Our Lord very much, in return for so many favors and graces that He is granting you."
>
> These words made such an impression on my soul that, from then one, I acquired the habit of constantly saying to Our Lord: "My God, I love You, in thanksgiving for the graces which You have granted me." I so

loved this ejaculation that I passed it on to Jacinta and her brother, who took it so much to heart that, in the middle of the most exciting games, Jacinta would ask: "Have you been forgetting to tell Our Lord how much you love Him for the graces He has given us?"

The children were beginning to develop that constant attention to God which is characteristic of souls in the illuminative way and which comes to full bloom in the unitive way.

Lucia describes a penance which the children adopted:

> . . . As we were walking along the road with our sheep, I found a piece of rope that had fallen off a cart. I picked it up and, just for fun, I tied it round my arm. Before long, I noticed that the rope was hurting me. "Look, this hurts!" I said to my cousins, "We could tie it around our waists and offer this sacrifice to God."
>
> The poor children promptly fell in with my suggestion. We then set about dividing it between the three of us . . . Either because of the thickness or roughness of the rope, or because we sometimes tied it too tightly, this instrument of penance often caused us terrible suffering. Now and then, Jacinta could not keep back her tears, so great was the discomfort this caused her. Whenever I urged her to remove it, she replied, "No! I want to offer this sacrifice to Our Lord in reparation, and for the conversion of sinners."

There were numerous other trials which were of great moment for such small children, as Lucia recounts in her *Memoirs*. All of these contributed to the chidlren's spiritual advancement. When a priest left the parish of Fatima, the news went around that he had left because of Lucia, "becuase he did not want to assume responsibility for these events." Lucia explains, "He was a zealous priest and much beloved among the people, and so I had much to suffer as a result." She adds:

> Several pious women, whenever they met me, gave vent to their displeasure by insulting me; and sometimes sent me on my way with a couple of blows or kicks.
>
> These Heaven-sent "caresses" were rarely meted out to Jacinta and Francisco, for their parents would not allow anyone to lay hands on them. But they suffered when they saw me suffering, many a time tears ran down their cheeks whenever they saw me distressed or humiliated.

Lucia's two cousins were to suffer much in the prolonged illnesses which awaited them. Lucia describes Jacinta's attitude toward sacrifice:

One day, Jacinta said to me: "If only my parents were like yours, so that those people would beat me too, then I'd have more sacrifices to offer Our Lord." However, she knew how to make the most of opportunities for mortifying herself. Occasionally also, we were in the habit of offering to God the sacrifice of spending nine days or a month without taking a drink. Once, we made this sacrifice even in the month of August, when the heat was suffocating. As we were returning one day from the Cova da Iria where we had been praying our Rosary, we came to a pond beside the road, and Jacinta said to me:

"Oh, I'm so thirsty, and my head aches so! I'm going to drink a little drop of this water."

Not that water," I answered. "My mother doesn't want us to drink it, becuase it's not good for us. We'll go and ask Maria dos Anjos for some . . ."

"No! I don't want good water. I'd rather drink this, because instead of offering Our Lord the thirst, I could offer Him the sacrifice of drinking this dirty water."

As a matter of fact, this water was filthy. People washed their clothes in it, and the animals came there to drink and waded right into it. That was why my mother warned her children to drink this water.

At other times, Jacinta would say: "Our Lord must be pleased with our sacrifices, because I am so thirsty, so thirsty! Yet I do not want to take a drink. I want to suffer for love of Him."

Francisco, too, was growing spiritually. It was typical of him to disappear for hours at a time, thinking of God and saying his "many Rosaries." When Francisco had learned that Mary had said he must say "many Rosaries" before going to Heaven he replied: "Oh, my dear Our Lady! I'll say as many Rosaries as you want!"

"And from then on," writes Siter Lucia,

he made a habit of moving away from us, as though going for a walk. When we called him and asked him what he was doing, he raised his hand and showed me his rosary. If we told him to come and play, and say the Rosary with us afterwards, he replied: "I'll pray then as well . Don't you remember that Our Lady said I must pray many Rosaries"

Lucia explains:

Francisco was a boy of few words. Whenever he prayed or offered sacrifices, he preferred to go apart and hide, even from Jacinta and myself.
. . .
If I asked him, "Francisco, why don't you tell me to pray with you,

and Jacinta too?''

"I prefer praying by myself," he answered, "so that I can think and console Our Lord, who is so sad."

I asked him one day: "Francisco, which do you like better—to console Our Lord, or to convert sinners, so that no more souls will go to Hell?"

"I would rather console Our Lord. Didn't you notice how sad Our Lady was that last month, when she said that people must not offend Our Lord any more, for He is already much offended? I would like to console Our Lord, and after that, convert sinners so that they won't offend Him any more."

Sometimes on the way to school Francisco would stop off at the church to pray before the Blessed Sacrament. He would go right into the sanctuary and place his elbows on the altar, getting as close as possible to the Most Blessed Sacrament. He would tell Lucia, "On your way home, come here and call me." That was where she would find him on her return from school.

When he fell ill he often told Lucia:

"Look! Go to the church and give my love to the hidden Jesus. What hurts me most is that I cannot go there myself and stay awhile with the hidden Jesus. . . .

"It won't be long now till I go to Heaven. When I'm there, I'm going to console Our Lord and Our Lady very much. Jacinta is going to pray a lot for sinners, for the Holy Father and for you. You will stay here, because Our Lady wants it that way. Listen, you must do everything that she tells you."

While Jacinta seemed to be solely concerned with the one thought of converting sinners and saving souls from going to Hell, Francisco appeared to think only of consoling Our Lady, who had seemed to him to be so sad.

Sister Lucia writes further:

He said to me on one occasion: "I loved seeing the Angel, but I loved still more seeing Our Lady. What I loved most of all was to see Our Lord in that light from Our Lady which penetrated our hearts. I love God so much! But He is very sad because of so many sins! We must never commit any sins again."

Francisco would even pray instead of eating his lunch. He would climb to the top of a steep rock, and when the others asked him to come down and play he would answer: "Don't come up here; let me stay here alone." And later: "Francisco, don't you want to come for your lunch?"

"No, you eat."

"And to pray the Rosary?"

"That, yes, later on. Call me again."

When I went to call him again, he said to me:

"You come up here and pray with me."

We climbed up to the peak, where the three of us could scarcely find room to kneel down, and I asked him:

"But what have you been doing all this time?"

"I am thinking about God, who is so sad because of so many sins! If only I could give Him joy!"

Lucia also explains:

> In the third Apparition, Francisco seemed to be the one on whom the vision of Hell made the least impression, though it did indeed have quite a considerable effect on him. What made the most powerful impression on him and what wholly absorbed him was God, the Most Holy Trinity, perceived in that light which penetrated our inmost souls. Afterwards, he said:
>
> "We were on fire in that light which is God, and yet we were not burnt! What is God? . . . We could never put it into words. Yes, that is something indeed which we could never express! But what a pity it is that He is so sad! If only I could console Him! . . ."

Through the visitations of God's Mother, Francisco saw God in Mary by a special gift of contemplation. No words were needed. Although a young boy, Francisco surely reveals himself as a contemplative. Already from the time of the apparitions of the Angel, he was given to contemplating. In her *Memoirs*, Sister Lucia writes:

> But it seemed that he had not received an understanding of all that the words meant, for he asked: "Who is the Most High? What is the meaning of 'The Heart of Jesus and Mary are attentive to the voice of your supplications?' " . . . Having received an answer, he remained deep in thought for a while, and then broke in with another question. . . .

Francisco admitted to Jacinta that he too could "no longer talk, or sin, or play or have strength enough for anything." He added: "But what of it? The Angel is more beautiful than all this. Let's think about him." Sister Lucia writes:

> After the third apparition of the Angel, for several days even Francisco did not venture to speak. Later he said: "I love to see the Angel,

but the worst of it is that, afterwards, we are unable to do anything. I couldn't even walk. I don't know what was the matter with me.''

Francisco did not exactly understand what he was receiving when the Angel gave Jacinta and Francisco Holy Communion under the form of wine. He said: "I felt that God was within me, but I did not know how! Then, prostrating themselves on the ground, he and his sister remained for a long time, saying over and over again the prayer of the Angel: ''Most Holy Trinity. . .''.

Lucia's spiritual transformation developed along lines similar in form yet different in detail. Her problems with convincing her own family of the authenticity of the apparitions may have been a providential preparation for her mission as witness to the world. The loneliness which Lucia had to endure at home was highlighted when her mother fell seriously ill and the family was convinced she was going to die. Lucia was pulled away from her mother by her eldest sister and taken to the kitchen, where she was forbidden to go back to the sickroom. "Mother is going to die of grief because of all the trouble you've given her!" Lucia said that this caused her more bitterness than she had ever known before.

A short time later, her two oldest sisters, thinking the case hopeless, said to her: "If it is true that you saw Our Lady, go right now to the Cova da Iria and ask her to cure our mother. Promise her whatever you wish and we'll do it; and then we'll believe." Lucia set out at once, saying her Rosary, and taking back roads so as not to be seen. She recalls:

> Once there, I placed my request before Our Lady and unburdened myself of all my sorrow, shedding copious tears. I then went home, comforted by the hope that my beloved Mother in Heaven would hear my prayer and restore health to my mother on earth. When I reached home, my mother was already feeling somewhat better. Three days later, she was able to resume her work around the house.
>
> I had promised the Most Blessed Virgin, if she granted me what I asked, I would go there for nine days in succesion, together with my sisters, pray the Rosary and go on our knees from the roadway to the holmoak tree; and on the ninth day we would take nine poor children with us, and afterwards give them a meal. We went, then, to fulfill my promise, and my mother came with us.
>
> "How strange!" she said. "Our Lady cured me, and somehow I still don't believe! I don't know how this can be!"

Lucia's mother was one of the last in Fatima to believe the children. Even the miracle of the sun left her with doubts. It took the official proclamation of the Bishop of Leiria-Fatima to remove all her doubts.

The reaction of Lucia's mother, the hesitancy of the priest who did not know what to make of it all, the jailing and threats of the administrator, the unfair attacks by neighbors—all these might seem like purposeless cruelty. However, these sufferings were a great stimulus in the children's spiritual transformation. They helped them pass beyond their childish spiritual lives, where they had spent most of their time at their own enjoyment, often devoting as little time as possible to prayer. In the two who died so young, we can clearly see characteristics of the illuminative and unitive ways.

The spiritual insights of the children overlap, but we can see a particular emphasis in each of them. In Francisco: The desire for God in prayer must have first place. In Jacinta: To keep in union with God in first place one must suffer, do penance, and deny self in reparation to God and for the salvation of poor sinners. In Lucia: Faithfulness to God is expressed in prayer and penance, and in being true to one's daily duties. Lucia has a special role as a continuing witness to the message of Our Mother in the world today.

As we have seen, the spiritual life is not always easy. Some have sought to enter the spiritual life at the illuminative way, or even at the unitive stage without proper purgation, not realizing that our spiritual transformation usually takes many years—our whole lifetime. They would jump into an advanced stage of union with God without developing the virtues, without accepting the cross which Christ said we all must carry daily if we would be worthy of Him and follow Him. Some have tried the spiritual life and acted scandalized at the crosses, which have appeared to them as obstacles to their holiness. In reality, it would be the carrying of those very crosses at which they are scandalized that would purify them, develop their Christ-like virtues, and admit them to the intimacy of the King.

The three children of Fatima carried out the design Heaven intended the world to follow: believe in God, love God, serve God. By following their example, we shall achieve the Heavenly reward which God intended for each of us when He created us.

8.
The Hearts of Jesus and Mary

The earliest written justification for devotion to the Immaculate Heart of Mary is found in the Gospel of St. Luke

> But Mary kept all these words, pondering them in her heart. (Lk. 2:19)
> And thy own soul a sword shall pierce, that, out of many hearts, thoughts may be revealed. (Lk. 2:35)
> And his mother kept all these words in her heart. (Lk 2:51)

St. Gertrude venerated the Heart of Mary. St. Bernardino of Siena, due to his Commentary on the Seven Words of Mary, merited the title of "Doctor of the Immaculate Heart of Mary." In the seventeenth century there surface others devoted to the Heart of Mary, such as St. Francis de Sales and St. John Eudes. As early as 1648, St. John Eudes had a Mass and Office in honor of Mary's Heart composed and celebrated for the first time.

In the seventeenth and eighteen centuries, the growing devotion to the Sacred Heart of Jesus, spread through St. Margaret Mary, had the indirect effect of promoting devotion to the Heart of Mary, for the two call attention to each other. In the seventeenth century and the beginning of the eighteenth, St. Louis Marie De Montfort (1673-1716) developed the practice of total consecration to Mary. In giving oneself entirely to Our Lady, one comes to belong entirely to Jesus Christ through her.

> We consecrate ourselves at one and the same time to the most holy Virgin and to Jesus Christ: to the most holy Virgin as to the perfect means which Jesus Christ has chosen whereby to unite Himself to us, and us to Him; and to Our Lord as to our Last End, to Whom as our Redeemer and our God, we owe all we are. (*True Devotion to Mary*)

While the saint does not mention the Heart of Mary, what he proposes is strikingly similar to the call of Fatima.

In the nineteenth century, St. Catherine Labouré (1806-1876) received from the Blessed Virgin in 1830 the command to coin the Miraculous Medal bearing the invocation: "O Mary, conceived without sin, pray for us who have recourse to thee!" The Hearts of Jesus and Mary appear inseparable on this medal. The definition of the dogma of the Immaculate Conception on December 8 of 1854, and four years later the words of Our Lady at Lourdes—"I am the Immaculate Conception"—contributed to the growing development of devotion to the Immaculate Heart of God's Mother. Moreover, St. Anthony Maria Claret (1807-1868), the first Archbishop of Cuba, was profoundly devoted to the Immaculate Heart of Mary.

A study of the words of the Angel who appeared three times to the Fatima children in 1916, and then the words of Our Lady at the Cova in 1917, shows that the essence of the message of Fatima is the same as that of Lourdes. At both places we were asked for prayer and penance. However, at Fatima are added the two elements of consecration and reparation to the Immaculate Heart.

On June 13 of 1917 Our Lady explicitly announced this devotion. She said to Lucia: "Jesus wishes to make use of you to make me known and loved. He wants to establish in the world devotion to my Immaculate Heart. I promise salvation to those who embrace it, and those souls will be loved by God like flowers placed by me to adorn His throne." The Hearts of Jesus and Mary are spoken of in the first apparition of the Angel: "The Hearts of Jesus and Mary are attentive to the voice of your supplications." At his second apparition, the Angel said, "The Hearts of Jesus and Mary have designs of mercy on you. . . ." And at the Angel's third apparition, the children were instructed to pray: "Most Holy Trinity. . . . And through the infinite merits of His [Our Lord's] Most Sacred Heart, and the Immaculate Heart of Mary, I beg the conversion of poor sinners."

It is the nature of good earthly mothers that the more their children are sick and in need, the more they bestow love on them. This would seem to indicate to us the reason why Our Heavenly Mother has reserved for these our times the strongest and clearest manifestation of the love of her Immaculate Heart.

It is significant that in Portugal, a country consecrated repeatedly to the Immaculate Heart of Mary, and a country where millions of people are dedicated to her Heart, "the dogma of the Faith will always be preserved." It follows. Devotion to the Immaculate Heart of Mary involves believing, living, and loving the Word of God as Mary our model did so well.

The Second Person of the Blessed Trinity, the Son, is called "the Word." The Son is the perfect image of the Father, and He has the same attributes as has the Father. God the Father is all-knowing, eternal, all-loving, etc—and so is God the Son. In somewhat the same way as a man expresses himself in his words, the Father expresses Himself, so to speak, in His Son. A man's words express the man's personality; the Son is the perfect expression of the Father, and so He is called "the Word," or "the Word of the Father." Yet the Word is Himself a Person, unlike the words which men speak.

When we say that "the Word was made flesh," we mean that the Son became man. Since He was still also "the Word," or the perfect expression of God the Father, He was able, just by being Himself, to show us what God the Father is like. And since He was (and still is) also human, He was able to become one of us and show us how we should love His Father, who is now also *our* Father. We also speak of the Scriptures as the "Word" of God; they too express to us what God is like.

Mary is that special spouse of the Holy Spirit, she who believed and loved the Word so perfectly that through this perfect correspondence of Her Heart, in virtue of the merits of Jesus Christ, she became the Mother of the Word. The Holy Spirit overshadowed her and the Word was made flesh. In conceiving and giving birth to the Head of the Church, Our Lady mothered the entire Church.

The early Church Fathers spoke of Mary as conceiving the word of God in her Heart before she conceived Him in her womb. The entire Trinity had, as it were, been born in Mary from the first moment of her Immaculate Conception through grace. The Son of God had spiritually dwelt in her from the very beginning of her life.

As it was revealed at Fatima that God wills our love for the Immaculate Heart of Mary, we see this as a call from Heaven to live—in faith, hope, love, adoration, and reparation—the Christian life as did Mary upon earth, choosing her as Mother and model of the Christian virtues. It is a call to recognize her as Mother of the Church since she is Mother of the Word made flesh, of Jesus who is the Church's Head. Our Lady's loving intercession with the Word of God, so that He may be conceived and grow in our hearts too, continues now in Heaven.

Mary's great faith and love for Christ Jesus while upon earth is testified to in Sacred Scripture itself. Conceived in grace perfectly joined in will to the inspirations of the Holy Spirit, the primary author of both the Old and New Testaments, Mary gained fruitful insights into God's Word more perfectly than any other Christian. She is the perfect model for the Christian faith and response to God's word. Being God in His very Person, Christ Jesus had no need for faith. He knew and understood the divine mysteries. It is Mary, therefore, who is the perfect model of Christian faith. Jesus Christ is, as He said and as the Bible records, "the Way, the Truth and the Life." The way of the Immaculate Heart of Mary is not a replacement of Jesus Christ, *the* Way; rather, we follow Our Lady in her perfect response to Christ.

What is remarkable about the revelations made at Fatima is that the basic message of the Heart of Mary, calling us in love and reparation to her Heart and ultimately to her Son, can be grasped by children or it can be explained and understood in scientific terms to please the theologian. Mary is truly a mother, and when she speaks to her children—and she desires to have all men as her children—her message is meaningful to the youngest child or to the most renowned of intellectual theologians, provided the virtue of humility is present.

As Jacinta insisted in so many ways, the Immaculate Heart is the way to heaven. Yes, like the children of Fatima, childlike souls without theological training may never be able to scientifically explain devotion to the Immaculat Heart of Mary, but they comprehend the message of Our Lady of Fatima in a simple way, efficacious to their souls and others. They venerate her Heart of flesh, because it is the Heart of God's Mother. But behind that Heart they see the total person of Mary and all that she is and stands for. Her goodness, her holiness, her compassion, her call to live the total Christian life in all its virtues, especially authentic love, the queen of virtues— such is the message of the Immaculate Heart of Mary.

The Reverend Cardinal Luigi Ciappi, O.P., theologian of the Vatican under Pope Paul VI, declared at a seminar at Fatima in August 1971:

> The Second Vatican Council has not contradicted in any way the theological substance of the message of Fatima, even though it has not expressly spoken of the devotion and of consecration to the Immaculate Heart of Mary. Rather, one may see a solemn, even though implicit, confirmation in the words with which the Constitution "Lumen Gentium" has exalted Mary for the charity with which she has cooperated in the

birth of the children of the Church.

Whatever is said in the Fatima message about Our Lady, as we keep insisting, must always be interpreted in terms of her Heart being inseparable from the Heart of her Son to whom she always points and leads us. Devotion to the Immaculate Heart of Mary was requested by Our Lady of Fatima as the Will of God.

St. John the Apostle, especially dear to Jesus because of his great purity, penetrated deeply into the love of Jesus' Heart. "Blessed are the clean of heart: for they shall see God" (Mt. 5:8). On the evening of the first Holy Mass ever offered, the beloved disciple reclined on the breast of Jesus. John witnessed Jesus' death on the cross, staying with Jesus and Mary unto the last. "But one of the soldiers with a spear opened His side, and immediately there came out blood and water" (Jn 19:34). It was to this same apostle of love that the Sacred Heart of Jesus from the cross confided the care of His Mother. The words "Behold your mother" were directed to men of the whole world until the end of time. No wonder that, burning with fervor, John wrote, "God is Love."

Other souls have contemplated the pierced side of Jesus, their thoughts going beyond the wounded side to the wound of love in His Divine Heart. During the thirteenth century, St. Gertrude was led by St. John to "the opening of the Divine Heart" whose beating filled her with ineffable joy. She asked John why he had not written of this directly in the Scriptures, and received the answer that this language of the love of the Sacred Heart was reserved for later times when the world would have grown cold to God's love.

More than three centuries after the mystical experiences of St. Gertrude, God chose to reveal His Heart at another place, Paray le Monial, in France. His modern apostle was St. Margaret Mary Alacoque, a humble nun. This privileged soul was entrusted "to the special care" of the Blessed Mother, so that she might guide her according to her own designs. At the age of four, without fully understanding what she was doing, Margaret made a vow of perpetual chastity. While she was yet a child, she found her greatest joy in praying to Jesus in the Most Blessed Sacrament. With God's Mother as her teacher from tender childhood, she was led to Jesus.

At a very young age she was stricken with an unknown disease and could not walk for four years. Margaret was finally cured by Our Lady when she made a solemn promise to one day become "one of her daughters." Though naturally attracted to the fine things of the world, Margaret gave them up. She loved poor little children and used to draw them to her by giving them her own property and teaching them catechism. Margaret had many opportunites for marriage and many confusing temptations against her vocation, but rejected them all to become a nun.

St. Margaret Mary had hardly entered the Visitation convent when she heard a voice say, "It is here that I want you." It was on December 27 of 1673, the Feast of St. John, that she was overcome by the Divine Presence while kneeling before the Blessed Sacrament, and was invited "to rest a long time on His Divine Breast"; Jesus revealed to her "the marvels of His love and the inexplicable secrets of His Sacred Heart."

From that day on, especially on First Fridays of the month, the Sacred Heart of Jesus continued to appear to St. Margaret Mary, at times "More radiant than the sun and as transparent as crystal," with its adorable wound visible, or again as a furnace or burning flames. Jesus asked her to make reparation, to receive Holy Communion on the First Friday of each month, to make the holy hour, and to honor the image of His Heart.

St. Margaret Mary was shown her own heart as a tiny atom consumed within the burning furnace of the great Heart of Jesus. A vision of fire played an important part at Fatima also. The sun, blazing and hurling itself upon the earth, was the supernatural sign that Heaven was bringing a message to us in the twentieth century. The message was again a message of love. As the Angel had said, "The Hearts of Jesus and Mary have designs of mercy on you."

To St. Margaret Mary, Jesus said,

My Divine Heart is so full of love for men, and for you in particular that, no longer able to contain within itself the flames of its burning charity, it must spread these flames by means of you, and it must manifest itself to men in order to enrich them with its precious treasures. I have chosen you to achieve this grand crusade of love.

This nun found her strength in the Blessed Sacrament and in Our Lady. One day while she was working in the little enclosure beside the chapel, the Heart of Jesus appeared to her surrounded by seraphim who associated her with them in singing the Divine Praises. This accords with Sacred Scripture, which tells us of angels adoring the God-Man. At Fatima we are informed that angels still adore Him in the Holy Eucharist, and they lead us to do the same. They carry out the desire of their Queen in leading us to adore our Eucharistic Lord.

Even before she entered the convent, and fifty years before St. Louis De Montfort, Margaret Mary consecrated herself to Mary: "[I] made myself her slave forever, asking her not to refuse me this role. I used to talk to her simply, like a child to a good Mother for whom I already felt a truly tender love." Margaret Mary was canonized on May 13, 1920, just three years to the day after Our Lady had revealed her Immaculate Heart at Fatima, calling us back to the love of the Sacred Heart.

The Sacred Heart of Jesus is now in Heaven, holding within Itself all God's love. By reason of a miracle of love, the Sacred Heart is also here, on this earth, in the Most Blessed Sacrament of the altar. We have God's love brought to earth and remaining with us. It was the love of the Sacred Heart for us that devised the plan to remain sacramentally in our midst. In the Holy Eucharist, Our Lord is really present; the Eucharist is the same Jesus, born of Mary, who suffered, died, rose and ascended.

It is the heart of a man which reacts to emotions and movements of love. All men of various cultures recognize the heart as the symbol of love and of the total person, and so it is the Heart of Jesus which was manifested to St. Margaret Mary in the late seventeenth century:

> Behold this heart which has so loved men that it has spared nothing, even to the point of spending itself and being consumed to prove Its love to them. And in return, I receive from most men only ingratitude because of their irreverences and sacrileges and the coldness and scorn they have for me in this Sacrament of love. But what offends Me most is that hearts consecrated to Me act in this way.

Devotion to the Immaculate Heart of Mary does not originate with Fatima, just as devotion to the Sacred Heart of Jesus does not originate with Paray. These devotions are based on faith and sound theology which existed in the Church long before the world heard of Paray or Fatima. Paray and Fatima, however, caused these two devotions to become more widely known and observed in a practical manner in the lives of the faithful.

There is a striking similarity between the two messages in that in both we are asked to make Eucharistic reparation. In our own century, the Immacualte Heart of Mary, Our Lady of the Holy Eucharist, has come to lead us back once again to adoration of the Sacred Heart of Jesus as found in the Most Blessed Sacrament in our tabernacles. The message of Paray and Fatima is that God's love for us is deep and *personal*. It is not cold and abstract; rather, it asks for a response: "love for love." Both can be summed up in the expression, "Eucharistic reparation." The Sacred Heart of the God-Man feels the effect of our sins and coldness. God has told us all this and the Bible records it in the accounts of the Good Shepherd, the weeping of Jesus over Jerusalem, the prodigal son, in John leaning his head on the breast of Jesus at the Last supper, and in His love poured out for us on the cross to the last drop of His Precious Blood as His Sacred Heart was pierced with a sword. Paray and Fatima reaffirm for us that God's loving designs of mercy on us have not changed now that Jesus has ascended into Heaven.

From eternity, before God became man, the Son of God was a pure, infinite spiritual Being, a bodiless Being. But on the day of the Annunciation, in Mary's body, the most holy blood of Mary's Immaculate Heart began to fashion, under the action of the Holy Spirit, a beautiful Body for the eternal Son of God. And beneath the Immaculate Heart of Mary there was soon beating another Heart, a little Divine Heart. There is only one Heart of God. That Sacred Heart, which was formed within the body of Mary by her consent and by the action of the Holy Spirit, brought to this earth and still holds within Itself all the love of God.

Jacinta was especially devoted to the Immaculate Heart of Mary, and she understood well the union between the Hearts of Jesus and Mary. Sister Lucia writes:

> A little while before going to the hospital, Jacinta said to me: "It will not be long now before I go to Heaven. You will remain here to make known that God wishes to establish in the world devotion to the Immaculate Heart of Mary. When you are to say this, don't go and hide. Tell everybody that God grants us graces through the Immaculate Heart of Mary; the people are to ask her for them; and that the Heart of Jesus wants the Immaculate Heart of Mary to be venerated at His side. Tell them also to pray to the Immaculate Heart of Mary for peace, since God has entrusted it to her. If I could only put into the hearts of all the fire that is burning within my own heart, and that makes me love the Hearts of Jesus and Mary so very much."

Jacinta is referring to the conversation with Our Lady on June 13, 1917:

> I would like to ask you to take us to Heaven.
> Yes. I will take Jacinta and Francisco soon. But you are to stay here some time longer. Jesus wishes to make use of you to mkae me known and loved. He wants to establish in the world devotion to my Immaculate Heart. I promise salvation to those who embrace it, and those souls will be loved by God like flowers placed by me to adorn His throne.
> Am I to stay here alone?
> No, my daughter. Are you suffering a great deal? Don't lose heart. I will never forsake you. My Immaculate Heart will be your refuge and the way that will lead you to God.

As St. Margaret Mary was left on earth to spread devotion to the Sacred Heart, even facing opposition from her community (which eventually joined her in honoring the image of the Sacred Heart), so Lucia was to be left on earth to spread devotion to the Immaculate Heart of Mary, a Heart inseparable from Jesus Christ.

Jesus has made Mary the treasurer of the gifts He gives to us; the Holy Spirit dispenses His graces to us through her hands. Her special relationship to each Person of the Most Blessed Trinity places her in a unique position as Mediatrix of all graces for her spiritual children. Our sins offend the Heart of Jesus; this is why He appeared to St. Margaret Mary with His Sacred Heart exposed, pierced by thorns, afire with love, speaking with sorrow of the irrevences, sacrileges, coldness, and scorn of men. But what offends the Heart of the Son offends the Heart of the Mother. Though she is not God or a goddess, Mary is still the Mother of God. She is the most delicate, sensitive, and grace-filled of all the human persons God has ever created.

Because Mary's relationship to Christ is so close—and a closer relationship to God is impossible to imagine, since she is the very Mother of God— their two Hearts are inseparable. The sins of mankind which wound the Sacred Heart of Jesus also wound the Immaculat Heart of His Mother. The thorns of sin penetrate the Sacred Heart of Jesus as Head of the Church, and they penetrate too the Immaculate Heart of Mary as Mother. But Christ Jesus and His Immaculate Mother are in heaven. How can they suffer, they who are removed from our vale of tears?

We know that our sins offend God (and also His Mother), even though we do not know exactly how this is. We can offend God by offending His creatures, but we can also offend Him directly. In fact, the first three Commandments of God deal with direct offenses against God, that is, with sins of false worship, sins of irreverence toward God, and with sins of neglect to worship Him.

Christ Jesus suffers in His Mystical Body, the Church; He is in a sense identified with His Church . Our Lord had already ascended into Heaven when He appeared to Saul and cried out, "Saul, Saul, why persecutest thou me?" (Acts 9:4), as Saul had been persecuting the Christians. Our Lord did not say, "Saul, Saul, why do you persecute *my followers*?" Rather, He identified Himself with His Church and said *"Me."*

In Sacred Scripture St. Paul tells us, "And if one member suffer anything, all the members suffer with it; or if one member receives glory, all the members rejoice with it" (I Cor. 12:26). In the same chapter the apostle says: "For as the body is one, and hath many members; and all the members of the body, whereas they are many, yet are one body, so also is Christ. For in one Spirit were we all baptized into one body" (I Cor. 12:12, 13).

"Now you are the body of Christ, and everyone of you is a member of it" (I Cor. 12:27).

We are familiar with Our Lord speaking of Himself as the Vine and of the members of His Church as the branches. The *head* of the Church is Christ Jesus. The *members* are the baptized believing members of the Church. The *Soul* of the Church is the Holy Spirit. The *Mother* of the Church is the ever-Virgin Mother of God, Mary, who is also the spouse of the Holy Spirit. Mary as Mother of the Head of the Church, the Vine, is also Mother of the members of the Church, the branches. The Holy Spirit, the Divine Life-Giver dwells in all the members of the Church who are in the state of sanctifying grace. This grace is a sharing in the life of God.

Jesus spoke to St. Paul of His persecution, even though He was already in Heaven. We can conclude that the suffering of the members of the Church, Christ's Mystical Body on earth, in some way has repercussions in Heaven. As the apostle outlines (in I Cor. 12), if any member of the human body is injured, all the other members suffer with it. Is this not also true of the Head?

The Church's doctrine of the Communion of Saints should be remembered. All sin is primarily and ultimately against God, but in Jesus Christ, God has united Himself to a Communion of Saints—the saints in Heaven, the souls in Purgatory, and the Church Militant on earth. In her July 13 apparition Mary told the children that "the good will be martyred, the Holy Father will have much to suffer. . . ." If the visible head of the Church, the Pope, suffers, and if other members of the Mystical Body on earth suffer for others' sins, surely the invisible Head of the Church, Christ, and our Mother Mary are not indifferent to our needs and sufferings.

It is not for us with our limited knowledge and lack of knowledge of the life of Heaven to analyze the sufferings of the Hearts of Jesus and Mary in a scientific manner so as to understand. Though Jesus and Mary are outside our time, since in heaven there is not time, still we can be most certain from Sacred Scripture and also from revelations such as those at Paray and Fatima, that they are not indifferent to the sins of God's children.

Pope Pius XI, in his encyclical entitled "Miserentissimus Redemptor" (1928), explains the Catholic teaching that the members of Christ's Mystical Body are called on to make reparation:

> Although the copious Redemption operated by Our Lord has superabundantly forgiven all sins, yet, through that admirable disposition of Divine Wisdom, there must be completed in us what is missing in Christ's sufferings on behalf of His Body, that is His Church (Col. 1:24). We can and we even must add to the homage and satisfaction (expiatory suffer-

ings) that Christ renders to God with our own homage and satisfactions, on behalf of sinners.

While men's malice incessantly increases, the breath of the Holy Spirit wonderfully multiplies the number of faithful who generously try to repair so many outrages made to the Divine Heart and they even do not hesitate in offering themselves to Christ as victims.

Pope Pius XII in "Mystici Corporis" (1953) said: "If ever we must unite our sufferings to those of our Divine Redeemer for salvation of souls, so much the more in these days!"

There has perhaps never been so much talk about love as in our own times. Movies, television, magazines are full of the concept of love. Often they are talking only about sexuality. Even catechetical series have sometimes confused authentic supernatural love for God and fellow man with a purely natural love devoid of true religion. One hears of youth who have fallen into mortal sin against purity speaking of their sin as "making love." How corrupted and profaned has the real meaning of "love" become.

God has given us His Mother, the perfect Mother and model of Christian love, to show us what authentic love is. True love requires sacrifice. True love does not count the cost in concern for others. Our Blessed Mother suffered because of her love for Jesus, as Simeon prophesied: "Behold this child is set for the fall, and for the resurrection of many in Israel, and for a sign which shall be contradicted; And thy own soul a sword shall pierce, that, out of many hearts, thoughts may be revealed" (Lk. 2:34-35).

The spirit of the times, which knows so little of authentic love, has thrown away the spirit of penance and reparation; these are even considered morose in some circles. The message of Fatima, the message of the Sorrowful and Immaculate Heart of Mary with its call to voluntary penance and Eucharistic Reparation, does not easily find a welcome in a world grown cold to true love. It is foolish to think that Mary's role as Mother of all mankind is only one of "honor." She is a *real* Mother of the living, having true maternal duties at the highest level of motherhood. She replaces Eve as the Mother of mankind; she is the new Eve who does not fail in her role. She has profound powers of intercession with God.

Our Lady knows what is needed for the present crisis—the loss of innumerable souls, and the spread of the errors of Russia—through which her family is passing. She has the means from God at her disposal for resolving the matter. Refusing the remedy, we must suffer the consequences. Without our prayers and sacrifices, many souls are lost, and without reparation on our part, Our Lady cannot obtain Russia's conversion and world peace. Yet only she can obtain it.

(Top) Jacinta, Lucia and Francisco as they looked at the time of the apparitions, taken in the Marto's garden; (bottom) the place of the apparitions at the Cova da Iria, with the three children.

(Top) Francisco, Lucia and
Jacinta during the apparition
of September 13, 1917;
(bottom) the crowds during
the miracle of the sun, October 13, 1917.

(Top) After the miracle of the sun, the crowds pressed so closely in upon Jacinta that a chauffer picked her up to keep her safe; (bottom) another photo of the three children taken at the parish church of Fatima a few hours after the July 13, 1917 apparition.

(Top, l to r) John Marto, Mrs. Marto and Mr. Marto (the parents of Jacinta and Francisco) in front of their home (taken in the 1940's); (bottom) the chapel of the apparitions at Fatima in 1935.

The Hospital of St. Augustine in Vila Nova de Ourém, where Jacinta was a patient for two months, July and August. Our Lady told Jacinta she would go to two hospitals and then die alone in Lisbon.

Reverend Father Manuel Marques Ferreira, parish priest at Fatima at the time of the apparitions, pastor from 1914 to 1919.

The first bishop of Leiria-Fatima with the third secret, which is now stored in the Vatican archives.

Dr. Eurico Lisboa, one of several physicians who treated Jacinta during her final illness.

Jacinta's and Francisco's father:
from the first he said, "My
children do not lie."

Jacinta and Francisco's mother:
harder to convince. Photos taken
in the 1950's.

Sr. Lucia at Fatima on the occasion of the Golden Jubilee of the apparitions. Her presence was requested by the Pope.

(Top) Lisbon's newspaper reported the miracle of the sun with reasonable objectivity, despite atheist control; (bottom) sculpture of the three children at the site of the angel's apparitions.

Sculpture of the angel as he appeared for the third time, with blood dripping from the Body of Christ into the chalice.

Pope Paul VI came to Fatima in 1967, saying "I come as
a pilgrim to pray for Peace."

This map shows the spread of Communism throughout the world, as of 1980. The black areas are under Communist control, the lined areas are under heavy Communist influence. Provided by Freedom House; the author makes no claims as to its complete accuracy.

(Top) The statue of Our Lady of Fatima is carried regularly in the processions at Fatima; (bottom) Cadets of Our Lady of Fatima from the United States start out on a hike in the countryside around Fatima, led by Fr. Fox.

(Top) Fr. Fox presents Pope John Paul II with a portrait of Jacinta in Rome; (bottom) Fr. Fox celebrates Mass for American youth in the garden at Pontevedra in Spain, where the Child Jesus appeared to Sister Lucia to request devotion to the Immaculate Heart of His Mother.

Isn't the problem today one of hard hearts, sinful hearts? Haven't our hearts grown cold with hate and violence? How can we melt these hearts which threaten to engulf the world with an "ice age" of sin, darkness, and wickedness? The answer was given at Fatima: devotion to our Mother's Heart. Isn't the heart of any mother the heart of the family? Though millions of women refuse to be mothers, and submit to abortion, the Immaculate Heart feels most keenly the hate and violence which her children offer one another. Could not that Heart, the Heart of our Heavenly Mother, which so desires peace for her children, give us a plan to bring peace and concord to the war-torn family?

In the message of Fatima Mary's Immaculate Heart has done just that. Her power of intercession is greater than that of all the angels and saints combined, and God has confided the peace of the world to her. For Mary, her great triumph would be that we permit her to solve the problem for us by responding to her requests.

This then is what delays the victory of the Immaculate: Mary cannot exercise the tremendous power at her disposal because the scales of justice will not permit it until enough of us make sufficient reparation. God always respects free will; we ourselves must desire peace and use the means to obtain it. If we do this we will then watch the world be flooded with the Divine graces and mercy which the Virgin Mary so wishes to lavish upon us. The source of all grace, of course, is her Son, but she is the powerful intercessor, the Mediatrix. We recall how Our Lady gave Jacinta the option of departing or remaining on earth longer in order to make more reparation to save more souls.

The sins committed against Mary's Immaculate Heart are the heart of the matter. The price of peace for the world is first to restore to the Mother the homage which mankind owes her. Then God in His mercy will bless the world with peace. Cardinal Cerejeira, the Cardinal Patriarch of Lisbon, some years ago summarized Fatima quite appropriately: "It is the manifestation of the Immaculate Heart of Mary in the world of today in order to save it."

The renowned scholar of Fatima, the late Dr. Joaquin Maria Alonso, C.M.F., director of *Ephemerides Mariologicae*, Madrid, with whom I was well acquainted, related the following:

At the end of the year 1935 on Christmas Day an exceptional document uniquely modified all the thought to date on the content of the message of Fatima. It was the publication of the first "Memoir" of Sister Lucia, which is, in reality, a wonderful biography of little Jacinta. The great surprise is the unexpected revelation of Jacinta's devotion to the Immaculate

Heart of Mary.

We cannot even briefly state all the relevance of this devotion of Jacinta to the Immaculate Heart of Mary. . . . Sister Lucia realizes that to speak
of Jacinta's devotion to the Immaculate Heart of Mary is already touching
the heart of the secret imparted by the Virgin. . . .

* * *

Already, from the theological point of view, it would be an error to
consider the theme "Immaculate Heart of Mary" *materially*, as "one more
devotion" to the Virgin which would be added to the "other" devotions.
The "Heart of Mary"—as well as the "Heart of Jesus"—symbolizes,
in agreement with the best theology of our time, *the expressed aspect of
the person* considered, showing her love by the "natural" symbol of the
Heart.

In Fatima it was the same. I would go so far as to say that this idea
showed itself there in a perfect catechistic way. It was not the "Heart"
of Our lady of Fatima that appeared; it was the Virgin herself, who finally called herself "Our Lady of the Rosary." At certain vital moments
of her appearances she showed, symbolically, her Heart to the seers, and
she made them take part in the hidden life of her Heart. We cannot speak
about the Immaculate Heart of Our Lady of Fatima except in a very material
sense, to indicate the specific way in which this Heart symbolically presents
itself at Fatima: without roses, without a sword, but surrounded by thorns.
. . . That, because all the "Our Ladies" have the same Heart, being the
same person. On the other hand, we can well say that the Virgin, in her
appearances at Fatima has shown her Heart and asked for a special devotion to her Immaculate and Sorrowful Heart.

This being said, in order to reply to possible objections, we affirm that
the Immaculate Heart of Mary is not a factor among others, but very much
the main factor of the message of Fatima by the position it occupies, and
it is both soul and spirit by the function it fulfills.

* * *

. . . Beyond history and time, Fatima projects itself into the future like
the untiring continuation of an apocalyptical struggle between the Woman
and the Serpent, as already spoken of in the Book of Genesis.

We could elaborate this thought and say something about the
"eschatological" meaning of Fatima, which is without doubt one of its
essential elements, but space does not allow. It is enough for us to point
out the final sentence of the secret (which is also the end of the third part
not revealed): "In the end my Immaculate Heart will triumph." It shows
that the message of Fatima is linked to the theme of the "Immaculate Heart
of Mary."

9.
Our Lady of Fatima as a Catechist

Every informed Catholic knows that the Mother of God is our spiritual Mother. Too seldom is Our Lady seen as Catechist, but that she is. In these times, when the depths of the Fatima apparitions are only beginning to be understood, Our Lady is catechizing her children through the Fatima message as never before.

Some find it surprising to hear God's Mother called a catechist. The role of catechist, however, is the natural consequence of being a mother. Every good mother is a teacher. The role of a mother is not simply to conceive a body and give birth. Rather, it embraces the whole child, and involves years of nourishing and caring for his body, and of teaching and forming his mind and heart.

During the Second Vatican Council, Pope Paul VI gave Mary the title "Mother of the Church," a title he asked us to use frequently. She is the model of everything the Church should be and hopes to become. The Church itself is spoken of as "Holy Mother Church," and its role is to teach and form us in Christ Jesus. The Mother of the Church, who perfectly images what the Church is destined to become in its final glory, is ever solicitous for her spiritual children, that each one be formed in her Son, Jesus Christ.

Much is made of Mary as the "Woman of Faith" in our day—and rightly so. But to see Mary only as the great "Woman of Faith," whose Scriptural image inspires us, while failing to see that her function in the plan of salvation continues in Heaven where she knows God not by faith, but rather by vision, is to be seriously ignorant of her continuing motherly love and concern for each member of her spiritual family.

The Second Vatican Council called us to imitate the virtues Mary manifested during her life on earth. But the Council Fathers also considered Mary's role in relationship to us in the here and now.

> This motherhood of Mary in the order of grace continues uninterruptedly from the consent which she loyally gave at the Annunciation and which she sustained without wavering beneath the cross, until the eternal fulfillment of all the elect. Taken up to Heaven she did not lay aside this saving office but by her manifold intercession continues to bring us the gifts of eternal salvation. By her maternal charity, she cares for the brethren of her Son, who still journey on earth surrounded by dangers and difficulties, until they are led into their blessed home. (Dogmatic Constitution on the Church, 62)

An authentic catechist teaches Christian doctrine. Similarly a good mother seeks to form the souls of her children reaching both their intellects and wills to instill knowledge and seek a response in love. This is exactly what Mary as Mother and as Catechist did at Fatima, beginning with the three shepherd children, and giving particular attention to little Jacinta.

We are living in times in which Catholic doctrines have been attacked, not only by outsiders, but also by Modernist theologians within the Church. Their opinions, so often destructive of true faith, have seeped into many modern religion textbooks and into our classrooms. Many of the over six million Catholic youths in the United States are being deprived of religious education by parents who refuse to expose their children to questionable religious teachings, or who simply neglect to provide religious instruction at all. Though good Catholic schools still do exist, many parents who send their children to Catholic schools or classes in religion are actually exposing them to false religious education, to the great detriment of their souls. This situation exists in many countries of the world.

I believe that Our Lady, as Catechist, foresaw all this at Fatima. No wonder her Heart was sorrowful. The errors and influences that are today destroying true Catholic faith were all present long ago, and our Popes have warned of them repeatedly. In 1907 St. Pius X, the Pope of the Catechism, issued *Lamentabili sane*, a syllabus condemning sixty-five Modernist errors. The Angel of Fatima came just nine years later, in 1916; Our Lady as Catechist followed the year after.

In his encyclical *Pascendi dominici gregis*, Pope St. Pius X called Modernism a "synthesis of all heresies." The roots of Modernism actually lie in the Protestant Reformation, and it has developed for centuries as an aggression against true religion. Forced underground by the vigorous conterattacks of the Popes, Modernism boldly reasserted itself in the aftermath of Vatican II, pretending to be the substance of what the Council taught and called for—much to the confusion of Catholics, including many of the clergy.

Some of the chief teachings of Modernists are: 1) the "Christ of Faith" is not the "Jesus of History"; 2) Jesus Christ did not personally establish the Catholic Church or its Sacraments—these are merely historical developments; 3) there should be freedom from religious authority and absolute autonomy of conscience; 4) everything modern is more perfect than what has gone before it; 5) there are no dogmas of Faith, no power in the Sacraments, no authority in the Scriptures. One can see then how Heaven intervened at Fatima to call us back to the authentic Faith by reaffirming the Church's dogmas and constant teachings. Pope Pius XII proclaimed that the apparitions presented us with a "Reaffirmation of the Gospels." But since Our Lady of Fatima said that in Portugal the dogma of the Faith would always be preserved, she implied its destruction in at least some other areas.

What informed Catholic is not aware of the confusion often evidenced in modern catechesis? There has been a denial of angels as personal spiritual beings. The Real presence of Our Lord's Body, Blood, Soul and Divinity in the Most Holy Eucharist has too often been explained away, and the Blessed Sacrament pushed into the background. Respect for the Church's authority, particularly of our Holy Father, has been destroyed in the hearts of millions. Sin is denied or made to seem real only when it obviously hurts our fellowman. "Community" is offered as a substitute for deep personal realtionship with God through the Heart of His Son.

Penance and reparation, essential to authentic Christian living, have been all but forgotten in modern catechesis, so that millions of Catholic youth do not even recognize the words, let alone practice the virtues. The Church's teaching on the suffering souls in Purgatory as part of the Communion of Saints, and her practice of praying for them, are forgotten and sometimes denied outright. The existence of Hell, even though mentioned by the Bible many times, is denied; or we are told that it should not be taught to children.

Sexual purity is a forgotten virtue. Catholic youth repeatedly claim that they have been taught that masturbation and fornication are not sinful, and can even be healthy and meaningful expressions of love. They have been taught such in the name of religion, even though Sacred Scripture and the Church have repeatedly condemned these serious sins.

The holiness and indissolubility of marriage are too often being ignored by modern catechesis as family life deteriorates. The fact that artificial birth control and abortive murder have become a common way of life in our time, spread from one country to another, is accepted with little objection. Modern denial of the very existence of God, and the growing worship of materialism, are passed over in silence.

All these major errors and defects of modern catechetical teaching were dealt with in one way or another at Fatima where Our Lady taught and spiritually formed Jacinta, Francisco, and Lucia, and gave the a message for the world. The Angel of Fatima came to the children as a young man of about fifteen years old. Why did he not appear as a mature adult? Perhaps he wanted to focus attention on our teenagers and the dangers to their Faith. In his first two apparitions the Angel immediately insisted on the existence of God and the Blessed Trinity, along with the need for reparation.

The Angel's third apparition was a witness to the Catholic dogma of the Real Presence of the Body, Blood, Soul and Divinity of Jesus Christ in the Most Blessed Sacrament. Above a chalice the Angel held a Host from which some drops of the Precious Blood fell. This provided a striking illustration of the doctrine of the Holy Eucharist as both Sacrament and Sacrifice. In this *Sacrament*, Jesus is really present; in this *Sacrifice* His very Blood is mystically shed.

In her very first visit at Fatima, Mary manifested her authentic role of drawing her spiritual children not to herself, but to God and to her Son Jesus in the Most Blessed Sacrament. As she pronounced the words, ''the grace of God,'' Our Lady opened her hands, streams of light came forth from them to penetrate the children's hearts and the innermost depths of their souls. It made them see themselves in God, who is light. Then, moved by an interior impulse communicated to them, they fell on their knees and prayed: *''Most Holy Trinity, I adore You. My God, my God, I love You in the Most Blessed Sacrament.''*

Many have forgotten Eucharistic reparation in recent years. Thousands upon thousands of Catholic youth have never witnessed Benediction of the Blessed Sacrament, or learned that Holy Mass perpetuates the Sacrifice of the Cross. All these are indicated simply but profoundly in the message of Fatima.

Too often modern catechetical teaching speaks only of this earth and omits all mention of the supernatural, but Our Lady explicitly told the three children that they would go to Heaven. From the very first apparition they longed for Heaven. By contrast, much of modern catechesis speaks little of the life God has promised us in the next world, and so leaves children with the impression that the promise of eternal life is not to be taken seriously.

The children were also shown a terrible vision of Hell, and for Jacinta this marked the beginning of a greater spiritual transformation and led to heroic sacrifices for the conversion of poor sinners. The doctrine of Purgatory is also contained in the Fatima message; Our Lady said that Amelia, an aquaintance of the children who had died at about eighteen or twenty years of age, would be in Purgatory until the end of the world. [A footnote of an early edition in Portugal of Lucia's *Memoirs* says that the statement "until the end of the world" admits of a conditional interpretation, as the book of Jonah teaches. Cf. also Exodus 32, 10 and Jeremiah 18, 7. Amelia will be in purgatory until the end of the world if nobody prays, makes sacrifices and offers Mass intentions for her, like many souls who go to Hell because they have no one to sacrifice and pray for them.]

In the Fatima accounts one also finds reaffirmed the Mysteries of the Most Blessed Trinity and the Providence of God directing the world in the events of salvation history. God is seen as knowing and foretelling future events. God is the rewarder of good deeds, but He is also a just God who punishes the evil deeds of His people. At the same time, His mercy towards the repentant sinner and His continuous work to bring back the prodigal son or daughter are strongly reaffirmed.

Our Lady as Catechist teaches us through Fatima that all, even children, are called to holiness, and that deep faith and response to this call is possible not only for adults but also for the very young. Perhaps we will soon witness the beatification and canonization of Jacinta, who, according to Sister Lucia, received and responded to singular graces. (Let us pray that the hopes for Jacinta's and Francisco's canonization may be realized before long.)

Our Lady as Catechist at Fatima teaches the reality of sin not only as a wound inflicted on our earthly community, but as an offense against God and even against the Communion of Saints, beginning with her own Immaculate Heart, which is inseparable from the Heart of Jesus. She teaches the consequences of sin in the punishment of the next life and in this life as well. Wars, hunger, the spread of Communism, the annihilation of nations, and persecutions of the Church and the Holy Father are foretold by Our Lady in 1917 if men "do not amend their lives."

Vatican II spoke of Mary as "Mediatrix," and said that "she is a Mother to us in the order of grace." Mary's apparitions at Fatima exemplify and confirm this teaching. As Mother of Grace her task is first of all to remove from us the obstacles to grace. We see her doing this when at Fatima she insisted on the essential role of penance and reparation in authentic Christianity. Without penance and the spirit of sacrifice, religion is incomplete and grace cannot endure or grow within us. Further gifts of grace are then not given, and faith itself cools and dies. Youth today are too rarely taught to sacrifice and do penance.

Another essential of a Christian life is of course prayer. Our Lady emphasized the importance of prayer, and she even identified herself as "Our Lady of the Rosary." She insisted that this prayer be prayed properly. Moreover, the sanctification of the family is called for not only in the last apparition which focused on the Holy Family, but also by the message given to Jacinta regarding the many marriages that are "not good." The call for loyalty to the Pope is seen in the predictions that the Holy Father will have much to suffer, and in the constant prayers and sacrifices the children were inspired to offer for him. These are but some of the profound and numerous doctrinal implications of the Fatima message. Our Lady not only taught doctrine, she also formed the souls of the children in sound doctrine.

In teaching children and teenagers, it is most effective to use Fatima not as a *source*, but to *reaffirm* Catholic doctrines. In this way Our Lady herself becomes the catechist. One who knows Fatima in depth can go through the catechism teaching the basics of the Catholic Faith effectively by relating them to the Fatima accounts. [The author has done this in *Catholic Truth for Youth*, a 448 page book available from Ave Maria Institute, Washington, N.J. 07882. The book is successfully used in many religious educational programs.]

The Bishop of Leiria-Fatima summarized the Gospel message contained in the Fatima message in these words:

> Fatima presents to our eyes the great and ineffable Christian dogmas, their power of suggestion and conviction taking hold of us: the Most Holy Trinity, the indwelling of God in the souls of the just by grace, the Mystery of the Redemption of Christ, the mystery of iniquity and sin, the sense of the solidarity of Christians in the Mystical Body of Christ making reparation, the interecession of the angels and saints, the ineffable Mystery of the Eucharist, the unique place of the Blessed Virgin, interceding for us, showing us the maternal solicitude of her Sorrowful and Immaculate Heart, the great dogmas of Heaven and Hell . . . we might go on forever. . . .
>
> Fatima is a summary of the Gospel.
>
> . . . We do not expect Fatima to be for us a theoretical course of Catholic Doctrine. No, Fatima is more than this. It is the whole of Christian dogma

in actual operation, the very bone and flesh of Christian life. Hence its power, its strong appeal to our generosity. Here is the explanation of the marvelous change produced in souls once they get into contact with the Cova da Iria and absorb its spirit. . . .

Now the fruits that Fatima produces are always and everywhere those that corresopnd to its own message, in perfect concord with the message of Christ and His Church.

The Gospel begins by reminding us of the need of doing penance and of being converted interiorly (Luke 3:3). In Fatima this message of penance is repeated with striking fidelity in the words of the Angel, in all the apparitions of Our Lady, in the wonderful spiritual transformation of the seers, in the penitential manifestations of the great crowds that come here unceasingly in ever greater numbers to visit the holy places.

In the Gospel, the Mystery of Redemption is realized by the insertion of Christ which makes sinful man in Himself, in that incomprehensible solidarity of innocence without stain and sin, which Christ assumes in His own flesh. In Fatima, innocence appears marvelously reflected in the Virgin, in the three little shepherds, in the primitive surroundings. There, innocence puts on the garment of severe mortification, thereby matching sin and grace in a great movement of reparation. Could we find perchance a more perfect formula than that proposed by the Angel—"Offer up everything you can as an act of reparation and sacrifice for the sins by which God is offended, and in supplication for the conversion of sinners. . . . But, above all, accept and bear patiently every suffering that God will send you"?

In the Gospel, Christ tells us that we must abide in Him, as the branches in the vine (John 15:4); He speaks of the necessity of continual prayer (Luke 18:1 and I Thess. 5:17); of abandonment to the providence of Him who makes the sun rise on the good and the bad . . . who sends the rain . . . who clothes the lilies of the field . . . who feeds the birds of the air (Luke 12:22 ff.). In Fatima one hears the purest echo of the basic teachings of the Christian life; prayer—the Rosary, assistance at Mass, the feasts of patron saints, the atmosphere of family life, respect for parents. . . .

The message of our Mother Teacher's Heart is all light; it is so profound and filled with the light of the Gospel that it draws us powerfully to the response of transforming love in Christ Jesus, our one Mediator and Savior. The message of her Heart is knowledge and love of Jesus and His Mystical Body which is the Church; she wants us to have a knowledge that leads to love through contemplation of the Word of God.

In a century that has produced much darkness and confusion, Our Lady as Catechist is teaching us again the full range of Divine truths first brought from Heaven to earth by her Son. The message of the Immaculate Heart is the message of the Gospels. Christ the Light of the World has sent the Lady of Light to renew our faith, hope, and love, transforming and leading us to a life of prayer and penance.

10.
Sister Lucia as Witness to the World

On June 13, 1917, Our Blessed Lady revealed to Lucia that she was being given a mission. As we have seen before, after Jacinta and Francisco were told they would soon be taken to Heaven, Mary told Lucia that she was "to stay here some time longer. Jesus wishes to make use of you to make me known and loved. He wants to establish in the world devotion to my Immaculate Heart."

Lucia, who is now Sister Lucia of the Immaculate Heart, admits that she has been gifted with a most keen memory. She has also said that when one has spiritual experiences such as the apparitions at Fatima in 1917, the words from Heaven burn themselves into the mind and heart of the recipient.

Sister Lucia clearly recalls her First Holy Communion. We recount the story as it tells us something about the personality of Our Lady's "witness." It is to be noted that at this time children were often not permitted to make their First Holy Communion until about the age of twelve. It was not until 1910 that Pope Pius X issued "Quam Singulari," which restored to children who have reached the use of reason the right to receive Holy Communion, and which advocated the frequent reception of the Sacrament.

Years after, Sister Lucia described how she made her First Communion at six years of age, on the Feast of the Sacred Heart of Jesus. The day before this, she made her first Confession. She recalled:

> After listening to me, the good priest said these few words:
> "My child, your soul is the temple of the Holy Spirit. Keep it always pure, so that He will be able to carry on His divine action within it."
> On hearing these words, I felt myself filled with respect from my interior, and asked the kind confessor what I ought to do.
> "Kneel down there before Our Lady and ask her, with great confidence, to take care of your heart, to prepare it to receive Her beloved Son worthily tomorrow, and to keep it for Him alone.
> . . . As I repeated this humble prayer over and over again, with my eyes fixed on the statue [of Our Lady of the Rosary], it seemed to me that she smiled and, with a loving look and kindly gesture, assured me that she would. My heart was overflowing with joy, and I could scarcely utter a single word. . . .
> The happy day dawned at last. . . .
> As the priest was coming down the altar steps, I felt as though my heart would leap from my breast. But he had no sooner placed the Divine Host on my tongue than I felt an unalterable serenity and peace. I felt myself bathed in such a supernatural atmosphere that the presence of Our dear Lord became as clearly perceptible to me as if I had seen and heard Him with my bodily senses. I then addressed my prayer to Him:
> "O Lord, make me a saint. Keep my heart always pure, for You alone."
> Then it seemed that in the depths of my heart, Our dear Lord distinctly spoke these words to me:
> "The grace granted to you this day will remain living in your soul, producing fruits of eternal life."
> . . . I don't know whether the facts I have related above about my First Communion were a reality or a little child's illusion. What I do know is that they always had, and still have today, a great influence in uniting me to God.

Thus Lucia's devotion to Our Lady of the Rosary began very early in her life. Our Lord enkindled in her heart devotion to Himself and to His Mother when she was still a child; it seems that He wished to preserve the purity of her soul for His own special designs of love.

One of Lucia's siters, Maria dos Anjos, has given her recollections of the events of 1917. The author of this book had an interview with Maria dos Anjos on a Sunday afternoon—August 5, 1979—in Aljustrel. She was about to celebrate her eighty-ninth birthday on August 13th, and she recalled that this was a Fatima anniversary—the day the children were in jail and could not keep their appointment with the Blessed Mother in the Cova. On this same day I met Maria dos Anjos' priest son, Father Joseph Valinho, who was at home for his mother's birthday.

During my visit in Aljustrel, Maria dos Anjos related to me the following:

> My mother did not want to believe that Our Lady was appearing to the three children, not to Lucia.
> She said, "If it is true that Our Lady is appearing it will spread all over the world".
> Mother believed Lucia was seeing the Lady only after the miracle of the sun.
> On the 13th, people would see a star coming from the East and going over the holm oak tree. I myself saw the star once and also the falling of the flowers [September 13th]. They were tiny little white flowers, like the flowers from the olive trees. People who had umbrellas tried to catch them but they never did. Everybody wanted to catch them with their hands but nobody did. They would disappear. They were always in the air. There were many flowers. I saw the raining of the flowers even better than the star. The star would come at mid-day. It would look like a night star. It was small. It would come and disappear in the direction of the tree. . . .Then my doubts whether Lucia was telling the truth began to disappear.

Lucia herself has begun her witness to the events of Fatima by trying to give some idea of the great beauty of Our Lady as the children saw her. As Jacinta exclaimed; "Oh, what a beautiful Lady!" While the appearance of the Blessed Virgin is not of the essence of the Fatima message, yet, in speaking of God's Mother, it would be remiss not to make some effort to describe this most glorious of all God's creatures. In a letter to the Bishop on May 13, 1937, Sister Lucia described Our Lady thus:

> In the pictures I have seen, Our Lady seems to be wearing two mantles. I think if I could paint, that I would not be able to depict her as she is, because I know that would not be possible, just as it is impossible for me to tell or describe. . . . I would only put one robe, the simplest and whitest possible, the mantle falling from the head to the hem of the robe; and as I could not paint the light and beauty that adorned her, I would suppress all the trimmings, with the exception of a little border of gold around the edge of the mantle. This would stand out as if it were a ray of light shining most intensely. This comparison is far less than the reality, but it is the best in which I can describe it.

When asked how old Our Lady appeared to be, Sister Lucia answered, "Perhaps seventeen."

"Did she always appear the same age?"

"Yes."

"Was she always sad?"

"She never smiled. She was pleasant but sad."

"What do you say of her beauty?"

"There are no words to express her beauty."

Our Lady would appear poised over the holm oak sapling, very close to the children, so near that the children "were bathed in the light that radiated from her person to a distance of about three feet," according to the description of Sister Lucia. "She was more brilliant than the sun, radiating a sparkling light." Yet the children never experienced fear at any of the apparitions, but only surprise. Sister Lucia said that the reported flashes of lightning which preceded Our Lady's visits were really not lightning, "but the reflected rays of a light which was approaching." In her *Memoirs*, Lucia wrote:

> It was because we saw the light that we sometimes said we saw Our Lady coming, but, properly speaking, we only perceived Our Lady in that light when she was already on the holm oak tree. The fact that we did not know how to explain this, and that we wished to avoid questions, caused us to say sometmies that we saw her coming and other times that we did not.

Sister Lucia added,

> When we said we saw her coming, we were referring to the approach of the light, which after all was herself. And when we said we did not see her coming we were referring to the fact that we really saw Our Lady only when she was on the holm oak.

At the June apparition, when Our Lady began to ascend toward Heaven, Lucia jumped to her feet and pointed to the East, crying: "There she goes! There she goes!" The small group of people gathered there looked in the direction she pointed out; they saw a little cloud rise slowly in the air, move away to the East, and finally disappear.

It was in the June apparition that Our Lady held in the front of the palm of her right hand a Heart encircled by piercing thorns. As she stood in this position with both her hands outstretched and Her Heart pierced with thorns in her right hand, she communicated to the children the rays of that imense light in which they saw themselves immersed in God.

In describing the apparition of God's Mother with her Immaculate Heart exposed, Lucia has said that the thorns in the Heart were the only part of the apparition not made of light. The thorns were simply burnt-out, brown, and natural looking. Of what significance is this? Our Lady was all light, as were her adornments, but that which represented the sins of mankind was not luminous.

In June there was also a disc as brilliant as the sun over her Heart. Some have speculated that this may have represented the Sacred Host, and it is true that the Fatima message centers largely on the Eucharistic Christ. Furthermore, in subsequent years, Sister received deep communications from Jesus Christ before the Tabernacle. Also on June 13th, Feast of St. Anthony (after whom the parish church at Fatima is named), there was a star with points of great brightness near the feet of Our Lady. Lucia never gave any indication as to the meaning of the star, though we know that traditionally Our Lady has been called the "Morning Star," "Ocean Star," etc. Some have interpreted the points of the star as the continents of the world, since Mary came as Queen to win the World to Jesus. This contrasts sharply with the red star of Russia which represents that nation's efforts to win the world to atheism. Though Sister Lucia could not remember the number of points on Our Lady's star, artists often represent it as a five-pointed star, like that of the Soviets, to symbolize her desire for the conversion of Russia. The little ball of light which hung from "two rays of sunlight" in the apparition is taken by many to symbolize the eventual triumph of Mary's Immaculate Heart over the entire world. Also, the message of Fatima is for the whole world, of which Mary is the Queen.

God's Mother spoke of sinners with sorrow in five of the six apparitions; the calling of sinners to salvation in the Eucharistic Jesus seems to have been a chief motive for her visits. It was in July that she asked that each decade of the Rosary be ended with the prayer, "O my Jesus, forgive us; save us from the fire of Hell; take all souls to Heaven, especially those most in need." Our Lady's concern for sinners on the way to perdition explains why she was almost always sorrowful at Fatima. In writing of the August apparition, Sister Lucia explicitly mentions this point: "Looking very sad, Our Lady said 'Pray, pray very much, and make sacrifices for sinners; for many souls go to Hell, because there are none to sacrifice themselves and to pray for them.' "

Father Thomas M. McGlynn, a Dominican priest known at the time of his death (September 3, 1977) as a priest, sculptor, playwright, and author, had the opportunity of interviewing Sister Lucia more than once. He had her assist him in sculpturing a statue of Our Lady of Fatima as she appeared when she revealed her Immaculate Heart. Father McGlynn's interviews and experiences with Sister Lucia tell us a good deal about the apparitions of

Our Lady of Fatima.

Sister Lucia told Father that Our Lady always had a star on her tunic and she always had a cord with a little ball of light. There was a pendant around her neck falling to about the waistline (not a cord and tassel as sometimes represented). Only two garments were visible: a simple tunic, and a long mantle or veil. There was no collar, no cuffs, no cincture, no sash around the waist—even though the tunic was drawn in at the waist. No hair was visible.

Sister Lucia also told Father McGlynn that Our Lady appeared as the Immaculate Heart only in June. Getting out her rosary, Sister Lucia draped it over the palm of her right hand and joined her hands in the attitude of prayer. "In June she appeared at first as in the other apparitions, then she opened her hands." Our Lady's right arm was extended, the forearm forward of the plane of her waist and elevated slightly above the horizontal. The hand gently arched, palm downward. Mary's left hand was upturned near the center and close to her body with the fingertips a little below the waist. Such were the minute descriptions given to Father McGlynn. He sculptured the Fatima statue of the Immaculate Heart as she appeared in the Cova, and he was later chosen to carve the large marble statue depicting these details for the front entrance of the Basilica of Fatima.

All was light in Our Lady. There were two waves of light, one on top of the other, to indicate the difference between mantle and tunic. Sister Lucia insisted that the garments on the statue must not be too smooth. The apparition of Our Lady had been very brilliant, with the light shining in waves, increasing and diminishing, thus giving the impression of folds.

Though Father McGlynn was attempting to be as exact as possible, Lucia told him, "No matter what you do, you won't give the impression of the reality." Referring to the line of gold on the mantle, Sister Lucia said: "It was like a ray of sunlight all around the mantle." The clothing of light was all white except for the cord holding the world and the star, which were of a more intense and yellow light. Sister Lucia said,

> She was all of light. The light had various tones, yellow and white and various other colors. It was more intense and less intense. It was by the different tones and by the differences of intensity that one saw what was hand and what was mantle and what was face and what was tunic.

The proportions of Our Lady's body were natural, not out of scale. She bent forward "because we were all small, below her feet." When Father McGlynn asked, "Did the face and hands and feet of Our Lady have the color of light or the color of flesh?" he received this answer from Sister

Lucia: "Flesh-colored light, light which took on the color of flesh." When asked about Our Lady's expression, Sister Lucia said, "Agradavel mas triste; doce mas triste; (Pleasing but sad; sweet but sad)."

Sister Lucia was most anxious to have Father McGlynn sculpt a statue of the Immaculate Heart of Mary as she appeared on June 13, 1917. She had even wished she could be a sculptress so as to make it herself. This indicates the great desire she felt in her heart to use every means to have devotion to the Immaculate Heart of Mary spread in the world. There is evidence that many experience a moral presence of Mary through her Fatima images.

The Bishop had some difficulty in choosing Father McGlynn's model for the Basilica, because the statue was different from the familiar image at the Chapel of the Apparitions. The following argument of Father McGlynn served to convince the bishop: The statue in the Capelinha, the one which is the focal point in the Sanctuary and is used on the 13th for the procession (Now also frequently placed on the pillar of apparitions), shows *how* Our Lady appeared at Fatima. But the smaller statue, sculptured under Lucia's watchful eye, declares *why* God's Mother appeared; in its gesture (as in the June apparition) it shows her call to penance, reparation, and salvation through devotion to her Immaculate Heart.

The United States of America can indeed be proud of the fact that an American was chosen by the Bishop of Leiria-Fatima to sculpt the statue for the eighteen-foot high niche over the main doorway of the Basilica in the Sanctuary in the Cova da Iria where God's Mother came with a message for the whole world.

At Fatima, the children were made to realize their nothingness in the presence of the all-good and all-powerful God. The Angel taught them to adore God in the Most Blessed Sacrament, and he also gave them Holy Communion. The light given by Mary was God, and it led the children to praise and worship the entire Blessed Trinity and Jesus in the Most Blessed Sacrament. This was a splendid manifestation of the Catholic teaching that devotion to Mary leads to Jesus Christ and to the entire Trinity.

Since Our Blessed Lady appeared so many times at Fatima, we may forget that there were manifestations of Our Lord also. If we study Lucia's accounts carefully, we learn that the children somehow saw Our Lord in the mysterious light of the June and July apparitions. And in October, the Child Jesus appeared with St. Joseph, and both blessed the world. In the same apparition Our Lord appeared as a man.

Sister Lucia of Francisco's great joy when she told him that in October Our Lord would come. Francisco said:

Oh, how good He Is! I've only seen Him twice, and I love Him so much! . . . Are there many days left till the 13th? I'm longing for that day to come, so that I can see Our Lord again. . . . But listen! Will he still be so sad? I am so sorry to see Him sad like that! I offer Him all the sacrifices I can think of.

The sadness Francisco noticed manifested the great desire of God for the conversion and salvation of sinners.

At times there were some visible manifestations to the people who began to come to the Cova da Iria on the 13th of each month. While people sometimes beheld a cloud, looking like a pillar of smoke, never did any except the three children see Our Lady.

At the various apparitions many people also noticed a dimming of the sunlight and a cooling of the air. Thousands would see a column of smoke enveloping the tree during the apparitions. On more than one occasion a shower of flowers was observed, the flowers fading away before touching the earth. This occurred again in October of 1924 when that month's pilgrimage was prohibited by the direct order of the government. Still, at least 150,000 pilgrims came to the Cova da Iria, and on that day the phenomenon of the shower of flowers was observed by many. It was actually photographed by Dr. Antonio Rebelo Martins, Vice Consul of the United State. He had a print of the photograph legally verified by witnesses before a notary public.

In June, only fifty people were at the Cova when Our Lady appeared a second time. The visible manifestations undoubtedly gave additional credibility to the apparitions and accounted for the crowds which grew rapidly month by month until there was a sea of humanity on October 13 of 1917. At this time travel was still very primitive; the roads leading to Fatima and the Cova lie on top of a mountain.

Sister Lucia told Father McGlynn that Our Lady had rested her feet on a tree, not on a cloud, but Lucia had seen none. Our Lady's feet rested lightly on the tops of the tree leaves. In his book entitled *Les Prophétes de Marie*, the French writer, Louis Pain, raised the question of why Mary appeared on a tree. He answers by explaining that the history of mankind is closely associated with trees—the tree of paradise and the tree of the Cross. He writes,

Like the tree in the Garden of Eden, so also the tree of Fatima is covered with dense foliage. The Most Blessed Virgin favors a component of the plant kingdom because the plants were the first to be created in the realm of life. With this, Mary indicates that she reigns over all created things.

It was the tree of the knowledge of good and evil that occasioned the fall of mankind into the state of original sin in which all are born yet today. But the tree of the Cross was the instrument for the New Adam to lift fallen mankind from its sinful state. Some therefore see in the tree of Fatima a symbol of the Cross beneath which the Sorrowful Mother, the New Even, stood—the cross on which Our Lord Merited our salvation. Fatima echoes the message of the Gospels, the message of the wood of the cross.

Our Lady's day of merit is over. In, with, and through Christ Jesus she has conquered sin. She is victorious with Christ. But her intercession continues, as the merits of Christ and Mary (in subordination to Christ) may still be drawn upon by the members of the Mystical Body of which Christ is the Head and Mary the Mother: "By the infinite merits of the Sacred Heart of Jesus, and the Immaculate Heart of Mary, I beg the conversion of poor sinners." (Angel's prayer before the Holy Eucharist.)

Sister Lucia has no literary ambition. However, by order of the Bishop, she wrote her reminiscences on four different occasions. They are known simply as the *First, Second, Third,* and *Fourth Memoir.*

The *First Memoir* was finished on Christmas Day of 1935. It was occasioned by a letter Sister Lucia wrote to the Bishop of Leiria in gratitude for a photograph he had sent her. This was a photograph of the face of Jacinta taken when her body was removed from Vila Nova de Ourem to Fatima. The casket had been opened, and Jacinta's face had appeared incorrupt. Sister Lucia thanked the Bishop for sending the photograph, and added that it brought back many memories of her cousin. This response moved the Bishop to order Lucia to write everything she could remember about Jacinta's life. Years after the apparitions, and even after the judgment of the Bishop that the apparitions were worthy of belief, the great depth of the revelations gradually unfolded. As the bishop and others became aware that there was more that had not been known or understood, Sister Lucia was commanded again and again to put into writing more of the events. One can see how the hand of God has worked in the Fatima events, making various aspects of the world-wide message known in God's good time.

Two years after the *First Memoir* was written, the Bishop of Leiria became convinced that the Fatima events of 1917 had to be studied more deeply. He ordered Sister Lucia to write the history of her own life and the apparitions just as they had happened. Always most conscious of the holy virtue of obedience, Sister Lucia obeyed and wrote the manuscript between the 7th and 21st of November in 1937.

What she wrote as the *Second Memoir* filled both the front and back of thirty-eight pages with close handwriting, and contained few corrections. It was in the *Second Memoir* that Sister Lucia first told of the apparitions of the Angel. This information came like a bombshell when this *Memoir* was first read.

On August 31, 1941, Sister Lucia wrote to her spiritual director regarding the *Third Memoir*.

> His Excellency the Bishop wrote me a letter and told me that the Rev. [Canon] Galamba [the author of the Preface to this book] will come to question me again. He ordered me to write everything else that I could remember related to Jacinta because they are going to publish a new edition of the book *Jacinta* [by Canon Galamba].
>
> This order fell into the bosom of my soul like a ray of light making me know that the time had arrived to reveal the first two parts of the secret and to add two chapters in the new edition of the book about Jacinta: one chapter about Hell and a second one about the Immaculate Heart of Mary.
>
> But my repugnancy in revealing these things is so great that I am in doubt about what to do. The writing is ready but I do not know if I am going to deliver it or rather put it into the fire. I know neither what to do nor what is more perfect.
>
> I have no doubt that both the revelation of Hell and the mercy of the Immaculate Heart of Mary, as well as the virtue that this moved Jacinta to practice, will do a great deal of good for souls.
>
> Can I even now keep silent about these things and only reveal the ones of less importance?
>
> I am afraid of the questions about Hell they are going to ask me. When your answer arrives probably what is going to be is already done. . . .

The *Third Memoir* was completed on August 31, 1941, and sent off immediately to the Bishop of Leiria. In it Sister Lucia reveals the first two parts of the Fatima secret which had never been told before: the vision of Hell, and the Immaculate Heart of Mary. Sister Lucia was asked by the Bishop to cooperate in an interview for use in a third edition of the book, *Jacinta*.

Many new facts and greater details emerged in the *Third Memoir*. Also, in it Sister Lucia wrote of the famous aurora borealis of January 25, 1938, which she interpreted as the sign preceding the outbreak of World War II, a sign which Our Lady had foretold on July 13, 1917.

Sister Lucia wrote in the *Third Memoir*:

> In my opinion, God and the Immaculate Heart of Mary would be pleased if, in the book *Jacinta*, one chapter would be devoted to the subject of

Hell and another to the Immaculate Heart of Mary. This suggestion may indeed seem very strange and nonsensical to you, but it is not my own, and God will show you that His glory and the salvation of souls is involved in it.

The *Fourth Memoir* is the longest of the four, and was again written not by the personal choice of Sister Lucia. On October 7, 1941, Feast of the Holy Rosary, Bishop José Alves Correia da Silva ordered her to write everything else she could remember about the events of Fatima. On December 8, 1941, Feast of the Immaculate Conception, Sister Lucia finished her final *Memoir*.

In this *Memoir*, Sister Lucia was asked to write down everything she could remember in connection with her cousin Francisco, just as she had already done with regard to his sister, Jacinta. She was asked to give further details of the apparitions, writing a new account of them, and to write any further recollections of Jacinta. She withheld only the third part of the secret; this she wrote down and gave to the Holy Father. It was opened by Pope John XXIII in 1960, but was not revealed to the world. The first act of Pope Paul VI as Pope was to ask to see the third part of the Fatima secret (according to information I was given from a reliable source at Fatima).

Referring to her silence in not revealing certain elements of the message before its proper time, Sister Lucia writes:

> I have always obeyed, and obedience deserves neither penalty nor punishment. First, I obeyed the interior inspiriations of the Holy Spirit, and secondly, I obeyed the commands of those who spoke to me in His Name. This very thing was the first order and counsel which God deigned to give me through Your Excellency.

When Dr. Galamba asked the Bishop to command Sister Lucia "to say everything, and to hide nothing," the Bishop replied, "No, I will not command that! I will have nothing to do with matter of secrets." Sister Lucia points out how clearly God has worked through His representatives, espcially the Bishop, in guiding her.

Jacinta was particularly taken up with the aspects of the Fatima message which comprise the first two parts of the secret: the terrible fact of Hell, and the role of the Immaculate Heart of Mary. Sometimes she would sit on the ground or on a rock and murmer, "Oh Hell! Oh Hell! How sorry I am for the souls that go there, who are burning in that fire!" Then she would kneel down trembling, join her hands, and repeat the prayer taught them by Our lady: "O my Jesus, forgive us; save us from the fire of Hell; take all souls to Heaven, especially those most in need."

Sister Lucia said that what she wrote about Hell only gave a vague idea of it. "I can't even find the exact words to explain its reality. What I say is nothing." In speaking of the first two parts of the secret, Sister Lucia noted that ordinarily God causes an interior and exact discernment of their meaning to accompany His revelations. "Jacinta seemed to have this discernment to an extremely high degree." That is why a study of her life is so important to a comprehension and appreciaiton of the message of Fatima.

The vision of Hell was so terrible that, Sister Lucia noted, if the children had not been promised that all three of them would go to Heaven, she does not think they could have handled it. Pictures taken on that July 13th after the vision show the children with their facial expressions as if frozen. It was a terrible ordeal, and yet it marked the beginning of a transformation to great spiritual heights. Sister Lucia was to note that it was one of the things that led Jacinta to a depth of spirituality uncommon even for adults advanced in virtue.

It was after the terrible vision of Hell that a deep transformation began to overtake the souls of the three Fatima seers. Jacinta wanted Our lady to show the same vision to all the people who were coming to the Cova. She wanted sinners to see what Hell was like and asked Lucia to ask Our Lady to show the vision to the people. If people could see what Hell is like, she thought, they would stop committing the sins which offend God and endanger their own salvation. But when the "beautiful Lady" came again, the children were so absorbed in her beauty and message that they would always forget to ask her to show the vision to others.

Lucia disagrees with those who might think she should have made known these things some time ago:

> For me, keeping silent has been a great grace. What would have happened had I described Hell? Being unable to find words which exactly express the reality—for what I say is nothing and gives only a feeble idea of it all—I would therefore have said now one thing, now another, wanting to explain but not succeeding in doing so. I might thus perhaps have caused such a confusion of ideas as even to spoil, who knows, the work of God. For this reason, I give thanks to the Lord, and I know that He does all things well.

Lucia was forcefully reminded of her mission by Jacinta. Knowing that she herself would soon die, Jacinta enjoined her cousin to be sure to tell people about the Immaculate Heart of Mary (which is the second part of the secret). Subsequent history will reveal the role of Jacinta, even after death, in making known this devotion. As we have seen before shortly before going to the hospital, she said to Lucia:

> You will remain here to announce that God wishes devotion to the Immaculate Heart to be established in the world. When you go to say that, do not hide yourself; tell everybody that God concedes us His graces through the Immaculate heart of Mary; that people should invoke her, that the Heart of Jesus wishes the heart of Mary to be venerated at His side. Let them ask for peace through the Immaculate Heart of Mary, for God has given it to her. Ah, if I could only put into people's hearts the fire that is burning within my own heart and that is making me love the Hearts of Jesus and Mary so much.

Aware of the different emphases suggested by different writers as the general motivation of the apparitions, Father McGlynn asked Sister Lucia to put into words what she considered to be the motivation. She replied, "In October, Our Lady said: 'Do not offend Our Lord any more; He is already much offended.'" When asked if that was addressed only to the three children or to the whole world, she answered, " I believe it was for the whole world." On one occasion, when asked about the devotions requested by Our Lady at Fatima, Sister Lucia replied: "The Rosary and Communions of Reparation." (She used the word "Terco," which is the Portuguese word for the five decade Rosary.) "In all the apparitions Our Lady mentioned the Rosary ("Terco"); in the third apparition she said she would come to ask for Communions of Reparation.

It is interesting that when Sister Lucia was asked what were the devotions recommended by Our Lady at Fatima, she did not answer, "Devotion to the Immaculate Heart of Mary." The Fatima scholar, Father Alonso, considered devotion to the Immaculate Heart to be so essential that it could not strictly be called a devotion, but rather in something much broader. Perhaps Sister Lucia felt the same way, since she answered the question on devotions by naming specific practices. When Father McGlynn asked if Our Lady had asked for the consecration of the world or of Russia, he received this answer: "No! Not the world! Russia! Russia ! Russia!"

Further questions by Fr. McGlynn and Sister Lucia's answers follow:

'When Our Lady said in 1917 that another and a worse war would begin in the next pontificate, did she use the words, "in the pontificate of Pius XI?"

"Yes, Pius XI."

"The great light that Our Lady spoke of—was it the aurora borealis of January 25-26, 1938?"

"Yes."

"What event, then, was considered the beginning of the war? Actual hostilities began with the invasion of Poland in September, 1939, Pius XII then being Pope.''

"For me the invasion of Austria was the beginning of the war. The Pope proclaimed it as such.''

"Would the consecration of Russia to the Immaculate Heart have prevented the last war?''

"According to the promise of Our Lady, if they had made it, I think so.''

"In 1927, it is said, Our Lord spoke to you from the tabernacle giving you permission to write all that Our Lady had revealed concerning devotion to the Immaculate Heart. Did this not include the consecration of Russia?''

"I think so. I wrote of it in 1929.''

"Was this wish made known to the Holy Father at that time?''

"I told my confessor; he informed the Bishop of Leiria. After a while my confessor said that the communication had been sent to the Holy Father.''

"It seems from the words of Our Lady in 1917 that the war of 1939-1945 was threatened as punishment for sin. But the warning was not known generally until 1942, after the punishment had begun. How is this explained?''

"This had all been said in 1917, that is, that men must amend their lives, that they must not offend God, that He was already much offended.''

According to Father McGlynn, Sister Lucia explained that Our Lady told her in 1917 that part of the secret was not to be revealed until 1927; the threat of punishment was included in this part. When asked about the fact that this had not been published, she replied, "After all, this was not for the Bishop to publish since the communication had been made to the Pope. The part necessary for the people to know was already known since 1917.''

"Can you give an explanation of why the portions of the secret now revealed had to remain secret? They seem to include docrines always known: that sinners are punished eternally in Hell, and that through the interecession of Our Lady sinners can be saved. The only thing not known is the wish of Our Lady that Russia be consecrated to her Immaculate Heart.''

"I explain this by saying that that is what Our Lady wanted. The Bishop says it was providential, because it did more good at the time it was revealed.''

Notice that the simple but profound faith of Sister Lucia comes through again and again. There is no effort to draw attention to herself. She was asked: "Is the promise that Russia will be converted (Our Lady's message of July 13, 1917) conditional or absolute?''

"In the end, absolute."

There has been speculation that Our Lady's message at Fatima was not only for Catholics, but for everyone. Sister Lucia was asked,

"Does Our lady request that every Catholic recite the Rosary every day?"

"She didn't express anyone in particular, but everyone in general."

Sister Lucia explained that Our Lady used the word "Terco" in asking that everyone in general say the Rosary, but when in October she told who she was, she said, "I am the Lady of the Rosary"("*Rosário*").

Sister Lucia has written many letters in the fulfillment of her mission. She has written these from the convent, as her vocation was to become a nun. Given the circumstances of her youth, the Dorothean Order was the one Lucia had been able to join. However, she had long been drawn to the Order of Our Lady of Mt. Carmel, whom she had seen at the apparition of October 13, 1917. In addition, she considered the brown scapular of the Carmelites as an external sign of consecration to the Immaculate Heart of Mary. Lucia was eventually able to become a Carmelite, though the Dorotheans were sorry to have her leave them.

Sister Lucia now lives in the Carmelite Monastery of St. Therese, where the author has repeatedly had the privilege of offering the Sacrifice of the Mass with Sister Lucia participating from behind the grille. She has confined herself behind the walls of this strict contemplative Carmelite Order where individuals have been able to visit her only on rare occasions, and then only with the permission of the Pope.

Nevertheless, Sister Lucia has kept in touch with the outside world, so to speak, through her correspondence. Her letters give us her own spiritual insights. Regarding certain happenings in the world on January 21, 1940, She wrote: "When Our Lord wants me to know something, He takes it upon Himself to let me in on it. He has many ways of doing this." On April 24, 1940, she wrote from Tuy:

To punish the world He [Our Lord] will let it go slowly. His justice, provoked by our sins, wants it that way. Sometimes He becomes annoyed not only at grave sins, but also at our laxity and negligence in attending to His requests. . . . He's right, there are many crimes, but above all there is much more negligence now on the part of the souls whom He expected to do His work with fervor. The number of souls with whom he communicates is very limited. The worst part is that I'm in the group of lukewarm people, after the efforts that He has made to incorporate me in the group of those more fervent. . . .

From Tuy, August 18, 1940:

How I wish I could satisfy this burning desire to His Divine Heart. But unfortunately I often correspond to inspirations of His grace with many infidelities. Now more than ever He needs souls that will give themselves to Him without reserve; and how small this number is! In this respect pray for me. I really need it. . . .

Despite what some may conclude from the fact that Heaven has chosen Sister Lucia for a very extraordinary mission, it is to be noted that she has an absolutely normal personality. Those who know her personally and have interrogated her through the years notice nothing to suggest physical or mental imbalance. There is no indication of a morbid temperament or excessive sensitivity. There has been unanimous agreement on this by all who have known her, and her superiors testify that her daily life exhibits nothing singular; all appears ordinary.

Sister Lucia has retained the simplicity of the country folk of the Serra de Aire region where she grew up. They speak a tongue that is blunt and graphic and has no affectations; they are refreshingly honest and direct in their speech. Their language is alive, though translation into English loses much of this. Nevertheless, even in translation Sister Lucia's words exhibit common sense, as well as a distinct absence of emotionalism and fantasy.

Father John De Marchi lived for some years in Fatima. He made detailed studies of witnesses living at the time of the apparitions, and wrote extensively of his findings. He states:

My ministry in the priesthood has more than once afforded an opportunity for the study of pseudo-mysticism and I can affirm, with all confidence, that my impression of Sister Lucia is entirely contrary to that received from false mystics.

Father De Marchi added:

It is true to say that the initial impression of almost everyone who sees the seer for the first time is one of disappointment, so ready are we to presuppose certain characteristics in connection with the supernatural.

The very commonness of Sister Lucia testifies to her psychological balance and to a mentality free from any neurotic tendencies. God chose a mentally healthy person to be the witness for the Immaculate Heart of His Mother. The humility of Sister Lucia is revealed in her letters as she writes openly and honestly to her spiritual director, and shares her fears of being mistaken and of deceiving Mother Church.

The humility of Sister Lucia again came out in a letter of May 18, 1941, which she was asked to write:

> I have already written the letter to His Excellency the Bishop. Our Lord asked me to tell some things which have cost me very much. What I mean is the same thing you suggested, to continue the reparation and prayer. I hope the Bishop does not read it in public. I am so ashamed, O my God! Now is the time to answer what you ask me.

Sister Lucia then repeated the information given about First Saturdays. Also:

> The request about Russia. In my opinion it was in June 1930 on the night of Thursday-Friday, 12-13, between 10 p.m. and midnight. . . .
> The exact words of the prayer—*"O my Jesus, forgive us; save us from the fire of Hell; take all souls to Heaven, especially those most in need."* They interpreted it, making the last petition for the souls of Purgatory because they said they didn't understand the meaning of the last words. But I believe that Our Lady referred to the souls who are in the most danger of being condemned. This was the impression I got and maybe you feel the same after reading the part I wrote about the secret. As you know, she taught us the prayer at the time of the third apparition in July, immediately after the secret.

Bishop Venancio once told the author a story which shows that Lucia is a person of great simplicity and also that she is very intelligent.

> I will give you an example of her intelligence. One day a theologian went to see her. He said, "Sister Lucia, I do not believe that the Angel should have said that prayer to the Holy Trinity." And she replied, "I don't know about that. I do know that the Angel has said this prayer, in this way. I don't know whether the Angel was a theologian or not."

The prayer alluded to:

> Most holy Trinity I adore You! My God, my God, I love You in the Most Blessed Sacrament . . . Most Holy Trinity, Father, Son and Holy Spirit, I adore Thee profoundly. I offer Thee the most precious Body, Blood, Soul and Divinity of Jesus Christ, present in all the Tabernacles of the world, in reparation for the outrages, sacrileges and indifference by which He is offended. By the infinite merits of the Sacred Heart of Jesus, and the Immaculate Heart of Mary, I beg the conversion of poor sinners.

The Angel's prayers indicate that angels as well as men adore God in the Holy Eucharist, in Eucharistic reparation.

On one occasion, Sister Lucia's spiritual director (whom she called "Father Superior") came to see her, but unfortunately was not able to do so. She was told that he had been at the entrance hall of the convent, but at such a bad hour that due to the fact that they have only one locutory, it was impossible for her to speak to him then. At that moment the family of a postulant coming in had just arrived. The priest was not able to come back later. Just as Lucia had experienced sorrow years before at the separation from her mother, and had offered it all in reparation, so she wrote to her "Father Superior," offering her sorrow over having missed him when at long last he came to her convent:

> I would also have liked to say good-bye, since you are going so far away. But our immolation must be complete, that all our steps be marked with the sign of the Lamb's Cross. Saint John says that he saw in heaven a multitude that followed the Lamb everywhere. I believe that on earth the Lamb has a similar procession that follows Him waving the banner of the Cross for His love, until they are incorporated into the eternal procession, singing the hymn of victory.
>
> I don't know if you were ever in a Carmelite's cell. Too bad you did not come on one of those occasions when the Cardinals come in and let others come in as well. You would see then what its best ornament is— one big single wooden Cross covering the white of the main wall. When I had the good fortune of entering the Carmelite Order, I was led to the cell, and as I was entering it I fixed my eyes on the big stripped Cross that opened its arms to me. Our Reverend Mother Prioress asked me: "Do you know why this Cross has no statue?" and without giving me time to answer she added: "It is so that you may crucify yourself on it." What a beautiful ideal to be crucified with Christ! That He may inebriate me with the gladness of the Cross. Here lies the secret of my happiness—not to want or to wish for more than to love and suffer for love. . . .

On December 29, 1955, Sister Lucia wrote of the difficulties that grow everywhere,

> and that is why we need the help of the divine grace in order to obtain something that is good. May Our Lady as a loving mother watch over us and help us all. The multitude of letters that arrive here from all over the world bears witness to this. They do little more than complain about the miseries that flood mankind. In view of this I become convinced that only myself and the little group, who as myself had the good fortune of consecrating themselves to our Lord, are the only happy people on earth.

It is not that one does not live without a Cross, because this is part of being the chosen people. But if it is carried with love, it becomes a treasure of appreciable value, which in fact none of those who follow Christ wants to lose. . . .

Under obedience to the Supreme Pontiff, Sister Lucia came out of her cloistered convent on May 13, 1967, when Pope Paul VI came a as humble pilgrim to Fatima to pray for peace in the world and in the Church. On that occasion, without thousands of journalists from different parts of the world present, and with the television cameras of the world focused upon the Vicar of Jesus Christ upon earth, the Pope led Sister Lucia forth and presented her to the world. It was the one time her witness role was visibly demonstrated to the world, and it was the Pope of the universal Church who called her forth for this demonstration.

Bishop John Venancio, who at that time was the Bishop and administrator of the diocese of Leiria-Fatima which hosted the Pope's pilgrimage to Fatima, interpreted the Pope's gesture for me in this manner: "By coming in 1967 to Fatima and presenting Sister Lucia to the world, the Pope was saying, 'I stand behind what she represents.'" Pope Paul VI's gesture was papal recognition of the role given Sister Lucia by the Mother of God on June 13, 1917, fifty years earlier. Our Lady had said, "Jesus wishes to make use of you to make me known and loved. He wants to establish in the world devotion to my Immaculate Heart. . . ." Lucia has carried out this mission through her letters, her memoirs, and through her prayers and sacrifices. In studying the letters and documents of Sister Lucia one can see that she constantly pursues the vocation given her by Our Lady. She was left in the world to spread reparatory devotion to the Immaculate Heart of God's Mother, because God wills this.

False rumors have often circulated about Sister Lucia, such as the one which arose in 1975 when the Communists were openly struggling to take over Portugal. The press carried reports that Sister Lucia had secretly left Coimbra for an undesignated place in Spain. The author of this book inquired of the International President of the Fatima Apostolate and found this to be a totally false report. Sister Lucia remained in her Carmelite convent in Coimbra, praying and sacrificing for peace. Likewise, reports were issued that Sister Lucia would not accept the New Rite of the Mass; however, she has more than once participated at New Rite Masses I have offered at her Coimbra convent.

Following is an excerpt from a letter written to Dr. Alcino on December 27, 1969. It indicates not only Sister lucia's awareness of the disobedience among some Church members in the Church after Vatican II, but also her undivided loyalty to the Holy Father:

> We ask the Child Jesus to compensate you with a holy and happy New Year of 1970. That it may be to you a year of grace, of an increase of firm faith in God and his Church, in His representatives that remain united to the supreme chief that is Pope Paul VI. There is no other that is true or chosen by God to be the Head of His Mystic Body on earth. He is the guide of his people. People of God, who form the militant Church, of which we have the fortune to be members, we need to remain faithful, firm in Faith, Hope and Charity, united to the representatives of Christ on earth, following His doctrines, His teachings, His directorates—If somebody tells you differnt, don't believe him, because he is in error; those are the ones Our Lord speaks of in His gospel: The branches which, separated from the vine, wither, dry up and are only good to be thrown into the fire to burn. We remain united to the grapevine, in order that the divine sap may run into our souls and save us. . . .

Sister Lucia of the Immaculate Heart has not been forsaken. While the public apparitions—those from May to October 13 in 1917—have ended, the letters and other documents written by her bear testimony to the constant contact she has had with the Hearts of Jesus and Mary.

Sister Lucia has spoken of her "field of action" as "sacrifice and prayer," and has added, "I hope that the Sacred Hearts of Jesus and Mary will accept them from the conversion of sinners." As she has grown older one can see that the basic formation given her by Our lady of Fatima has always stayed with her. Sister Lucia continues to call the world to the hearts of Jesus and Mary, and only Heaven knows the favors her prayers and sacrifices have won for the world.

11.
Fatima's Call to Prayer

"Pray! Pray a great deal!"—Angel of Fatima, 1916

"Pray, pray very much. . . ."—Our Lady of Fatima, 1917

The Fatima message, like that of Lourdes, is frequently summarized with this simple sentence: "It was a call to prayer and penance." In this chapter we explore the aspect of prayer in order to gain, hopefully, a deeper appreciation of the meaning and urgency expressed in Heaven's call to prayer in our own times.

The first words of the Angel of Peace, after calming the children's surprise and amazement, were: "Pray with me." Thus the very first words of Heaven's message at Fatima were a call to prayer.

Prayer is frequently defined as a "lifting of the mind and heart to God." This shows that both the intellect and will are involved in prayer. Through grace, we know God with our intellects, and with our wills we respond to Him in love. In this way we grow in union with God. The depth of this union varies according to the intensity of our love, which is a supernatural love—not simply a natural love.

It is possible to have a natural love for God—that is, a merely human love for Him. One could be in the state of mortal sin and yet love Him in this way. There are souls living in the state of mortal sin, attached to sensual sins which they refuse to give up, and who try to justify themselves by saying, "I love God." But to have a supernatural love of God, to be in the state of sanctifying grace and thereby share in the very life of God within the human soul, requires that we be free from serious sin. If a person is not in the state of God's grace, he is a dead branch on the Vine and is cut off from God and the other members of Christ's Mystical Body. This is true even of a person with a kind and loving personality. It is true even of a person who might have a natural love for God.

One falling frequently into mortal sin, which is the death of supernatural life in the soul, and who refuses repentance and Confession with a firm purpose of amendment but who still says, "I love God," may still have the gift of faith, but this is only a dead faith. He or she is certainly not loving God supernaturally with the divine love, with divine hope, with the very love of God which exists in Jesus Christ in its fullness. A person who dies in the state of mortal sin will go to Hell; in order to enter Heaven we must have God's life in us through sanctifying grace. Our Savior said, "If you love Me, keep My commandments" (John 14:15).

With sanctifying grace comes the indwelling of the Most Blessed Trinity. God the Father, God the son, and God the Holy Spirit dwell by grace in the soul, and within the soul can thus be adored. When we are in the state of grace we can grow in union with God through prayer. Of course, sinners in the state of mortal sin should pray also; they should ask God for the grace of repentance, and for pardon and the return of grace.

Men without lives of prayer will not become close to God. People who lose their faith are people whose faith was weakened or never built up, because they did not remain or become people of prayer. Perhaps this began with carelessness in participating in Holy Mass. In the August apparition, Our lady looked very sad and then said: "Pray, pray very much, and make sacrifices for sinners; for many souls go to Hell, because there are none to sacrifice themselves and to pray for them." Through the years, Sister Lucia has maintained the great need for prayer in our times. Significant among her writings is a letter she wrote on April 13, 1971 to her priest nephew, Father José dos Santos Valinho, S.D.B., superior of the Salesians at Ludlow, U.S.A.:

> I saw from your letter how you are preoccupied with the confusions of the present times. It is indeed to be lamented that so many allow themselves to be dominated by the diabolic wave that enslaves the world and they are so blind as not to see the error. But the main error lies in the fact that they have given up prayer, and so become separated from God; and without God they lack everything " . . . for without Me you

can do nothing" (John 15:5).

Therefore, what I recommend to you most is to go to the Tabernacle and pray. There you will get the light, strength, and grace you require to keep youself holy and to give holiness to others; to give it humbly and sweetly and at the same time firmly, for above all, Superiors have the duty to keep truth in its proper place, acting with calmness, justice, and charity.

To effect this well requires that you pray more and more in order to bring yourself closer to God, and to present all subjects to God before you present them to men. Follow these means and you will see how at the Tabernacle you will find more knowledge, more light , more strength, more grace and more virtue, which you will never find in books, in studies, nor from any creature.

Do not ever think that the time spent in prayer is lost, and you will see how God gives you light, strength, and grace needed to do everything that God wishes you to do . This is the most important for us; to do the Will of God, to be where He wants us to be, and do what He asks us to do, but always with the spirit of humility, convinced that by ourselves we are nothing and that it is God who must work in us and use us for everything that He wills. For this purpose we must all intensify much our inner life in union with God, and this is realized through prayer. When you pray even though time is insufficient for everything else, you will later find how much more is done in less time.

Everyone, but especially a Superior, who does not pray or who habitually sacrifices prayer for doing material things, is like a hollow and split bamboo which only serves to beat the egg whites and raise castles of froth. Without sugar to sustain them these castles soon break up and turn into foul water. Therefore Jesus said: You are the salt of the earth, but if the salt loses its flavor, it is good for nothing except to be thrown out. We can receive our strength from God alone. We must get close to Him for Him to communicate it to us. We can only realize this closeness through prayer because it is in prayer that the soul encounters direct contact with God.

The above letter written by Sister Lucia after many years in the convent, many years after the apparitions, shows how her spirituality has continued to grow on the same Eucharistic foundation given at Fatima.

We can best interpret the message of Fatima, where Our Lady of Light and of Hope called the world back to her Son, by studying the lives of the children of Fatima. They lived the message intensely. Their lives demonstrate that the call to prayer, which Heaven gave us in the present century, was a call to "pray always" as Jesus told us in the Scriptures. Rather than being one department of their lives, the prayer-lives of the three children spilled over into their daily activities. At Fatima, Heaven called us to a *total* response in a spirit of prayer in every aspect of our lives, sanctifying everything—our studies, our work, our family life, our recreation, and our civic responsibilities—in addition to the time spent in formal prayer.

But in order to "pray always," we must first be sure to set aside time daily for prayer. Without doing this, how can we maintain a spirit of union with God throughout the day? Our union with God cannot spill over into our daily duties, as from a reservoir, unless we have allowed the reservoir to be come filled through daily and persevering prayer. When we pray, we may not feel the reservoir being filled, so to speak, but we know by faith that this is happening.

All aspects of life must center on Jesus in the Most Blessed Sacrament. Jesus in the Holy Eucharist must always be the focal point of our spirituality, and of our prayer life in word and in deed, in thought and action. Sadly, the years after Vatican II have seen misrepresentations of the beautiful call to spiritual renewal by the Council Fathers acting under the inspiration of the Holy Spirit. There are some churches in which one has to hunt for Our Lord in the Blessed Sacrament. Misrepresentations of Vatican II have downplayed the Virgin Mother's role and then that of her Eucharistic Son.

It is with profound sorrow that we learn of abuses of the Most Blessed Sacrament. There have been cases of Yoga bread used instead of hosts, with Offertory processions in the Yoga style; in place of God's own Word in Sacred Scriptures, there have been secular readings, fables, readings from Yoga books. Interpretative dances by dancers in scanty dress have occurred in front of the main altar during the divine liturgy which perpetuates the Sacrifice of the Cross. One thinks of the great sufferings endured by Jacinta when she observed people visiting with each other in front of the Most Blessed Sacrament. One thinks of Francisco who spent all day in front of the Tabernacle, at times with his elbows on the altar, as close as he could possibly get to the Tabernacle. There he would go in the morning hours and be found yet in late afternoon. How the Fatima children were saddened when after finding peace in prayerful adoration before their Eucharistic King in the parish church, they were interrupted by curious interrogators coming into the church to disrupt their prayer.

But on the other hand, thousands of Eucharistic prayer cells have been formed throughout the world by those in the Fatima apostolate. They meet in the presence of our Eucharistic Lord in their parish churches whenever possible, or else in their homes, turning their thoughts to the nearest Catholic church, where Jesus Christ is present in the Most Blessed Sacrament.

In more recent years a Fatima youth apostolate has been founded and is spreading throughout the world. Youth who enter more fully into this apostolate are known as Blue Army Cadets of Our Lady of Fatima (founded by the author in 1975); they meet bimonthly, or in accordance with local circumsatnces, adoring Jesus in the Most Blessed Sacrament. Members range in age from six to nineteen, although in a few cases parents have adapted the program in their families even for pre-schoolers. Remember the very young age of all three Fatima children and especially of Jacinta, who was hardly six years of age when the Angel of the Holy Eucharist began appearing.

St. Peter Julian Eymard, the Apostle of the Holy Eucharist, was a saint who deeply revered and loved Our Eucharistic Lord. He wrote,

> Our Lord has ascended a throne; He can be seen and is radiant. We no longer have an excuse. If we forsake Our Lord, if we pass by Him without amending our lives, Our Lord will go away, and we shall be done forever. Serve Our Lord, therefore, and console Him; light the fire of His love wherever it is not yet burning; work at the establishment of His reign of love. *Adveniat regnum tuum, regnum amoris* [May Thy kingdom come, Thy kingdom of love].
>
> The mere presence of Jesus lessens the power of demons and prevents them from lording it over men as they did before the Incarnation. It is a fact that since Our Savior's coming, there have been relatively few cases of possession by the devil; pagan lands have many more than Christian lands. The reign of the devil returns in proportion to the lessening of faith in the Eucharist. . . . Jesus is then with us; and as long as there is an adorer on earth, Jesus will be with him and protect him. This is the secret of the longevity of the Church. People often fear the enemies of the Church; that comes from a lack of faith. But we must honor and serve Our Lord in His Sacrament. What would a father do if he were despised and outraged by his children? He would leave them. Let us take good care of Jesus and we shall have nothing to fear.

It should come as no surprise that the same period in the United States and abroad that has seen a lessening of Eucharistic adoration and prayer life, a lack of faith in the real presence of the Lord Jesus Christ in the Holy Eucharist, a tragic falloff in Mass participation by Catholics, churches locked all day long, hiding of Tabernacles, and youth growing up in ignorance of Catholic faith in the Eucharist—the same period has seen the spread of devil worship, and Satan distributes his own "bible."

When asked about the devotions requested by Our Lady at Fatima, Sister Lucia replied: "The Rosary and Communions of Reparation." Our Lady asked for the Rosary at each visit, but she did not ask simply for the *body* of the Rosary, that is, not just for the mechanics of so many Our Fathers, Hail Marys, etc. She insisted that the children pray the Rosary *properly*. Praying the Rosary properly is devotion to the Immaculate Heart of Mary. Sacred Scripture tells us more than once that Mary pondered the mysteries of Christ's life in her heart. That is what the soul of the Rosary is essentially about.

When asked about the importance of the Rosary, Sister Lucia said:

My impression is that the Rosary is of greatest value not only according to the words of Our Lady at Fatima, but according to the effects of the Rosary one sees throughout history. My impression is that Our Lady wanted to give ordinary people, who might not know how to pray, this simple method of getting closer to God.

On September 16, 1970, Sister Lucia wrote to a former companion in the Order of St. Dorothy concerning the Rosary:

Regarding what you said about the prayer of the Rosary, it is a pity because the prayer of the Rosary, or five decades of it, after the Holy Liturgy of the Eucharist, is what most unites us with God by the richness of prayers that compose it.

All of them came from heaven dictated by the Father, by the Son and by the Holy Spirit.

The "Glory" we pray between the decades was dictated by the Father to the Angels when He sent them to sing it close to His Word, the newborn Child. It is also a hymn to the Trinity. "Our Father" was dictated by the Son and it is a prayer to the Father.

The "Hail Mary" is all impregnated with Trinitarian and Eucharistic sense. The first words are dictated by the Father to the angel when He sent him to announce the mystery of the Incarnation of the Word.

It is interesting that Sister Lucia sees in the "Hail Mary" these central Christian mysteries, the mysteries of the Holy Trinity and the Holy Eucharist. This indicates the depth of her penetration into the prayers and doctrines of holy Church. The mysteries of the Rosary, all fifteen of them, can in fact be meditated upon in terms of the Blessed Trinity and/or the Holy Eucharist. The Rosary is then sometimes called the "Eucharistic Rosary."

Sister Lucia continues:

"Hail Mary, full of grace; the Lord is with thee"; you are full of grace because in you dwells the fountain of grace, and it is by the union with the most Holy Trinity that you are full of grace. Moved by the Holy Spirit, St. Elizabeth said, "Blessed art Thou among women, and blessed is the fruit of thy womb, Jesus."

The Church, also moved by the Holy Spirit, added, "Holy Mary, Mother of God, pray for us sinners now and at the hour of our death."

This is also a prayer to the Father through Mary. Because you are Mother of God, pray for us. It is a Trinitarian prayer because Mary was the first life temple of the Most Holy Trinity. "The Holy Spirit will come upon you. The power of the Most High will overshadow you. And so the Child to be born will be called the Son of the Most High."

The Rosary is an exciting prayer if it is prayed properly. The author of this book has taken hundreds of youth to Fatima on pilgrimages, and although the Holy Eucharist and the Scriptural word of God are central to the spiritual life of the pilgrimage, the Rosary meditated becomes a popular form of prayer for the youth who, their parents tell me, continue with this prayer after they return home.

People who have never learned to love the Rosary have doubtlessly never learned to pray it as a Gospel prayer. Without meditation on the mysteries of Christ, the Rosary is lifeless. Pope Paul VI in an Apostolic Exhortation to the world entitled *Marialis Cultus*, put it this way:

> Without this [contemplation] the Rosary is a body without a soul, and its recitation is in danger of becoming a mechanical repetition of formulas and of going counter to the warning of Christ: "And in praying do not heap up empty phrases as the Gentiles do; for they think that they will be heard for their many words" (Mt. 6:7).

Simply reciting fifty Hail Marys, with the Our Father and Glory Be between the decades is *not* praying the Rosary properly. It is not the way parents should teach their children in the home.

The comparison is well made that the reciting or chanting of the Hail Marys is like soft music in the background, while in the foreground are our thoughts and movements of the heart as we join ourselves in spirit with one of the fifteen Mysteries of our salvation. We imitate Mary; as the Scriptures tell us: "But Mary kept all these words, pondering them in her heart."

The Rosary is Christ-centered. There are fifteen chief Mysteries to it: the Joyful, Sorrowful, and Glorious Mysteries. These center on the chief events of the life of Jesus Christ from His virginal conception, through the Mysteries of His Childhood, to the culminating moments of the Passover. The Blessed Passion and the glorious Resurrection of Jesus Christ are meditated on, as are the effects of these events on the infant Church at

Pentecost. The Ascension of Our Lord into Heaven and the Assumption of the Virgin Mary are also included.

Pope Paul VI has said that the Rosary, "by means of devout contemplation, recalls these same Mysteries [of Christ's life] to the mind of the person praying and stimulates the will to draw from them the norms of living." Thus we see that praying the Rosary properly involves not only our minds, but also our wills, to the very core of the person which we call the heart. From the various mysteries we become familiar with Our Lord's and Our Lady's outlook on life, and can see how they practiced the virtues while on earth. Thus we can discover how to live these virtues in our own lives.

We do not need to *feel* devout or to experience spiritual consolations in order to pray the Rosary well. It is the strength of our faith and the perseverance of our love for God in continuing to pray—even when we feel bored, distracted, or tired—which count. The Hearts of Jesus and Mary are honored, and the whole Mystical Body of Christ is helped, when we persevere in this prayer. As Sister Lucia has said, only through prayer can we be closely united with God. He increases our love for Him and for Our Blessed Mother when we pray.

On Feb. 18, 1981 I visited the Stigmatist, Brother Gino Burresi, O.M.V. at San Vittorino, near Rome. Brother Gino shared the fruit of his meditation when he had been lying abed in sickness and pain. He said that Jesus had taught the Apostles how to pray. They could not get it. Only when they were in the Cenacle with Mary, awaiting the coming of the Holy Spirit did they learn how to pray. Mary taught them. She who pondered the Word so well in her heart.

Mary successfully instructed the Apostles how to pray in the Cenacle. They could not pray properly before because they did not have the Heart of Mary in their own hearts. Only her Immaculate Heart could receive the Holy Spirit perfectly so that He might pray in them with "inexpressible groanings". In the Cenacle the Church waited with Mary's own Heart to receive the Holy Spirit and thus the Church learned to pray. Wherever the Church, or an individual Catholic, lacks Mary's Heart, then there is no prayer. We cannot pray unaided with our own hearts. They are neither pure nor humble of themselves. Only Mary's Heart is perfectly pure and humble. Only her faith among the early members of the Church, including the Apostles, was perfect. We can pray only when our hearts become like hers through the intercession of her Heart as Mediatrix of all grace. This grace she obtains for the indwelling of the Holy Spirit to take place within us.

Devotion to Mary's Immaculate Heart will lead one to learn to pray properly. It will lead one to open oneself to the action of the Holy Spirit within one. Mary who is the Spouse of the Holy Spirit thus as she pray with us.

Even without speaking of Fatima, one can see Pope John Paul II reinforcing the prayer traditions of the Church which were reaffirmed at Fatima. The Vicar of Christ called the Rosary his "favorite prayer," after the Eucharistic Sacrifice of the Mass and the Liturgy of the Hours. His predecessor, Pope John XXIII, prayed the entire fifteen decades daily. For many years, Vatican Radio has been airing a twelve-minute broadcast of the Rosary in Latin between evening news and information programs. Then one night in March of 1979, less than a half year after his election, regulars who prayed along with this Vatican program heard the voice of Pope John Paul II leading the Rosary. The Plan appeared to be that the Pope would continue to do this regularly on the First Saturday of each month.

Pope John Paul II's aim in leading the radio Rosary is "to make known his wish that Catholic faimlies join him" in that prayer. It is a call to parents to their duty of Christianizing their families. The Pope's backing of the Rosary in such a public gesture also has the kind of flare that can counter the trend with regards Our Lady as an embarrassment in this post-Vatican II era of ecumenism. The Pope's leadership of the radio Rosary was reported as an encouragement of the Rosary's use in evangelization. Our Lady would certainly be pleased with this, as she is so concerned for the conversion of souls.

Prayer is esential to the message of Fatima. At each of her six apparitions, Our Lady told the children to pray the Rosary, in particular for the intention of world peace. This is especially important at a time when many nations of the world are enslaved under Communism, an evil system which continues to spread, to the detriment of true peace and of religion.

In drawing us to Jesus and Mary, prayer strengthens us to carry out the sacrifice of doing our daily duty out of love for them. It is this which we shall explore in the next chapter.

12.
Fatima's Call to Daily Duty

In his second appearance, the Angel told the children not only to "Pray! Pray a great deal!" but also to "Offer up prayers and sacrifices to the Most High." He said,

Make everything you do a sacrifice, and offer it as an act of reparation for sins by which He is offended, and in supplication for the conversion of sinners. Bring peace to your country in this way. . . . Above all, accept and bear with submission the sufferings sent you by the Lord.

Our Lady came the next year, and in her very first apparition asked the children: "Do you wish to offer up to God all the sufferings He desires to send you in reparation for the sins by which He is offended, and in supplication for the conversion of sinners?"

The spirituality that developed in the three Fatima children and has continued through the years in the case of Sister Lucia was by no means a selfish spirituality, concerned only with personal salvation. Lucia wrote of her visit to Jacinta in her first stay in the hospital at Vila Nova de Ourem: "I found her as happy as ever, suffering for the love of God and the Immaculate Heart of Mary, for sinners and the Holy Father. She was living her ideal and it was of this that she spoke." Lucia asked: "Do you suffer much, Jacinta?"

"Yes, but I offer it all for the conversion of sinners and the Holy Father. I love to suffer for the love of Jesus and Mary. They love people who suffer for the conversion of sinners. . . ."

Everything about our personal lives can be offered as sacrifice in reparation to God and for the salvation of souls. It is climaxed in the Sacrifice of the Cross perpetuated in Holy mass where Jesus Christ is offered and to which we join the sacrifice of our personal lives. At Fatima we received a call to sanctify every moment, every action of every day, but these everyday sacrifices have value only in virtue of the Sacrifice of the Son of God become Man who is inseparable from His Church.

What kind of sacrifice does Heaven want? On August 18, 1940, Sister Lucia wrote to her spiritual director:

> I feel that it would be good to impress on people, as well as a great amount of confidence in the mercy of Our good Lord and in the protection of the Immaculate Heart of Mary, the need for prayer accompanied by sacrifice—especially that one needs to avoid sin. . . .

On May 4, 1943, Sister Lucia wrote: "He [God] wishes that it be made clear to the souls that the true penance He now wants and requires consists first of all of the sacrifice that each one must make to fulfill his own religious and daily duties. . . ." Sister Lucia had been reported as saying that the sacrifice requested was merely the sacrifice required for the fulfillment of duty, so she was asked: "When Our Lady asked for sacrifice, did she ask merely for the observance of the commandments?" Sister Lucia answered: "The meaning we took was that she wanted voluntary sacrifices, of course, after keeping the commandments, because, if we started making voluntary sacrifices without keeping the commandments, it wouldn't be much good." Sister Lucia explained that in 1917 Our Lady asked for penance and sacrifice and the children had understood this to mean voluntary sacrifice. But, "In 1940 she asked again for penance and sacrifice, but the penance and sacrifice necessary for fulfilling religious duties and the duties of one's state." When asked if Our Lady had mitigated her earlier request, Sister Lucia simply replied, "Our Lady did not explain that to me."

In further explanations brought forth by the interpretations of those inquiring and listening, Sister Lucia added, "Obviously she wanted more than the fulfillment of duty because she had already asked us not to offend God, that means doing one's duty, then she went on to ask for sacrifice and penance." Lucia added, "But they don't do their duty! If they did Our Lord would be more content." In a letter written by Sister Lucia to the Bishop of Gurza, made public on April 20, 1946, she wrote:

> The good God has shown me His contentment at the act [of consecration], although incomplete according to His desire, of the Holy Father and several Bishops. In exchange, He promises to end the war soon, but the conversion of Russia will not yet take place. If the Bishops of Spain accede to the wishes of Our Lord and undertake a real reform of the people and the clergy, good, but if not it will once again be the enemy with which God will punish them.
>
> The good God is allowing Himself to be appeased, but He bitterly and sorrowfully complains of the limited number of people in the state of grace willing to renounce what the observance of His law exacts of them.
>
> The penance which God now asks is this: the sacrifice which each person has to impose on himself in order to lead a life of justice in the observance of His law. He wishes this way to be made known to souls with clearness, for many consider the meaning of the word "penance" to be great austerities, and, not feeling strength or generosity for such, become discouraged and remain in a life of tepidity and sin.
>
> Between Thursday and Friday, at 12 o'clock at night, being in the chapel with the permission of my Mother Superior, Our Lord said to me: "The sacrifice of each one requires the fulfillment of duty and the fulfillment of My law; this is the penance that I now ask and exact."

Years ago when Sister Lucia was asked to help draw up a short and practical formula that would outline the fulfillment of the Fatima message, at least as a minimum, she desired to include mention of the sacrifices one may encounter every day in the performance of one's daily duty according to one's state in life. This resulted in the Fatima pledge:

> Dear Queen and Mother, who promised at Fatima to convert Russia and bring peace to all mankind, in reparation to your Immaculate Heart for my sins and the sins of the whole world, I solemnly promise: 1) To offer up every day the sacrifices demanded by my daily duty; 2) To say part of the Rosary (five decades) daily while meditating on the Mysteries; 3) To wear the Scapular of Mt. Carmel as profession of this promise and as an act of consecration to you. I shall renew this promise often, especially in moments of temptation.

The most important part of the Fatima message is not simply praying the Rosary every day. Sister Lucia has indicated more than once that the most important part of living the Fatima message is being true to the duties of one's state in life. This means as a husband-father, wife-mother, child, student, etc. It means that Christians in public positions must integrate the principles of God-given truth and the laws of God into society.

In the Fatima pledge we see how prayer and penance are linked together. By prayer we directly honor God. In addition, prayer is necessary in order to remain true to one's state in life, performing one's daily duty. In announcing that he prays the Rosary to help him in making major decisions, Pope John Paul II clearly shows us the importance of the Rosary as a means of obtaining spiritual strength for the fulfillment of one's call to daily duty.

The wars and the persecutions so rampant in the twentieth century are ultimately the result of many not fulfilling the duties of their state in life. It is claimed that no age since the flood has suffered more because of its sins than the twentieth century. Millions of people have been killed in wars and in Communist suppressions. The faithful fulfillment of daily duty as required by each one's state in life is what God calls for to bring peace to the world and the conversion of Russia. Man's abandonment of his daily duty has been the cause of his drift from God and of so much unhappiness and suffering in the world. An understanding of the Chuch as Christ's Mystical Body reveals that the sins of mankind cause sufferings in the whole Body.

The world praises heroic acts and sacrifices that are of short duration. But the faithful fulfillment of daily duty, year after year, in the single, married, priestly, or religious life requires much heroism too. God has promised sufficient grace for those who will cooperate with His Holy Will.

The couple who desire children but are given none and must remain childless have a real sacrifice to offer in accepting their daily duty. They are often given time for works of charity which parents of large families do not have. The person who had hopes of a certain work in life but was not given the necessary talent, the couple expecting another child soon after the birth of their last child, the priest or religious who faces rejection when preaching or living the word of God authentically in imitation of the great Woman of Faith and of Love—all these and others are asked to offer the sacrifice required in the performance of their daily duty. It is the sacrifice which God is now asking of each one of us.

Fulfillment of daily duty was practiced by Lucia's eldest sister on the occasion of the translation of the relics of Jacinta. Maria dos Anjos and others were working in the fields as the funeral procession passed. When they learned that it was the translation of Jacinta's remains, they longed to join the procession. But their training in honesty and obedience to God's law, given so strictly by their mother, showed through. Maria dos Anjos related that they were being paid by their employer for that hour's work, and it would not have been honest to have left the fields. So they stayed.

God is pleased with sacrifices which involve very ordinary things. Many people have the opportunity to offer up the tensions of their work, the worries and uncertainties connected with raising children, the pain of dental work, the common annoyance of driving in heavy traffic, or the lack of courtesy of other people. Children often have the opportunity to offer their sufferings from unkind teasing by classmates, to offer the sacrifice of doing their homework carefully when it would be much easier to rush through it and then spend the time playing, or to cheerfully eat what is given them even if they do not like it. All these sacrifices can be offered up in answer to Fatima's call for loving fulfillment of our daily duties. They can be "the sufferings sent you by Our Lord."

The Angel also told the three children: "Make of everything you do a sacrifice." Even very little things can be offered up. Lucia recalls one occasion when she and Jacinta were chasing butterflies, but were making the sacrifice of letting them fly away as soon as they were caught. In July, Our Lady told the children: "Sacrifice yourselves for sinners, and say many times, especially whenever you make some sacrifice: *'O my Jesus, it is for love of You, in reparation for the offenses commited against the Immaculate Heart of Mary, and for the conversion of poor sinners.'* " Of the August apparition, Lucia has written that, looking very sad, Our Lady said: "Pray, pray very much, and make sacrifices for sinners; for many souls go to Hell, because there are none to sacrifice themselves and to pray for them."

It is also true that there is a relationship between repentance and spiritual insight. To a person not living a life of repentance and prayer, the presence of Jesus in our very midst, in the Tabernacle, in the Sacrifice of the Mass, may seem a hollow shell. Similarly, 2000 years ago John the Baptist tried to open men's eyes and hearts by preaching repentance. Yet some never opened their hearts, and so they remained blind and never did recognize Christ as more than just another man. Furthermore, He bothered their consciences so much that they tried to destroy Him by crucifixion. How often do guilty consciences act that way? Instead of facing truth, accepting it—which often requires an inner change of heart, some seek to destroy truth. They think that they will thereby justify themselves. But truth always resurrects itself, just as in the end the Sacred Heart and the Immaculate Heart will triumph, for Jesus is Truth and Mary is inseparable from Him.

When Our Lady appeared as Our Lady of Mt. Carmel on October 13, 1917, she held the brown scapular of Mt. Carmel down to the world. Sister Lucia has been asked why Our Lady did this. She answered: "Because she wants everyone to wear the scapular. . . . Because it is our sign of consecration to her Immaculate Heart." And Pope Pius XII said of those who wear the brown scapular: "May it be to them a sign of their consecration to the Most Sacred Heart of the Immaculate Virgin." Sister Lucia has also said: "The scapular and the Rosary are inseparable." This simple "garment," composed of two small rectangular pieces of brown wool cloth held together by cord and placed over the head so that it is worn with one piece of cloth in front and one in back, is an abbreviated form of the large scapular which is part of the Carmelite habit.

Those who live their consecration to the Immaculate Heart of Mary should wear the brown scapular as a sign of this. When a person wears the scapular he is saying to Mary: You are my mother, and I want to please your Heart. A person who lives the Fatima message, the "reaffirmation of the Gospels," is true to his daily duty in the living out of his vocation. The scapular is a reminder to oneself, as well as a sign to others, that one is striving to be true to his consecration, to prayer and daily duty.

The history of the brown scapular is closely tied in with the history of the Carmelite order. In February of 1981, the author of this book visited Mt. Carmel in the Holy Land, and was privileged to visit the large church constructed by the Carmelites over a grotto in which Elijah was said to have lived. There, with the assistance of one of the Carmelite Fathers, he renewed his enrollment in the brown scapular of Our Lady of Mt. Carmel.

The Carmelites are a group of religious of the Catholic Church who derive their name from Mt. Carmel, where their order had its origin. Toward the end of the 12th century, a number of Crusaders, desirous of imitating Elijah the Prophet, settled on the western slopes of Mt. Carmel to live a hermit-like life in the grottos of the mountain. Sometime between 1206 and 1214, their prior, St. Brocard, solicited a written rule of life from the Patriarch of Jerusalem, St. Albert. This act incorporated them into the diocese of Jerusalem and began the history of what was to become the Carmelite order. The following centuries saw their spread to Europe, as well as varied persecutions. At any rate, a group of hermits who believed themselves to be the spiritual sons of Elijah the Prophet, and who lived on Mt. Carmel in the Holy Land, pondered the Word of God and developed a deep devotion to the Mother of God.

St. Simon Stock became the new superior general of the Carmelite Order in 1246 at Aylesford, England. At this time, it was feared that the order would come to an end because it was having so many problems. Then Our Blessed Mother appeared to St. Simon Stock and gave him the scapular of the Carmelite order. She said: "This shall be a sign to you and to all Carmelites: Whosoever dies clothed in this shall not suffer eternal fire." Thus, to receive this promise, a person must first be enrolled in the brown scapular by an authorized priest. This enrollment incorporates one into the confraternity of Mt. Carmel; he is then affiliated with the Carmelite order.

Catholic authorities have interpreted Our Lady's wonderful promise to mean that those enrolled persons who die wearing the scapular will be granted at the moment of death, the grace of final perseverance in sanctifying grace or the grace of repentance. The scapular is not, of course, a magic guarantee of salvation to a person who would wear it but continue to live a sinful life in disregard of God's will. Such presumption would be an abuse of the scapular. And it is quite certan that a person who sins continually with the idea that he will be saved by the scapular regardless, will not die wearing the scapular.

The cloth has no power in itself. Rather, the scapular's efficacy, as that of all sacramental, comes from the intercession of the Church and the devotion which it excites in us. The "power of the scapular" is the intercessory power of God's Holy Mother. Wearing the scapular is like a constant, silent prayer to her. It is a sign of our dedication, devotion to, and trust in Mary.

When visiting the church built above the traditional cave of Elijah, one can see a beautiful statue of Our Lady of Mt. Carmel; this statue is over Elijah's cave and also over the high altar. The head of the statue is the work of Caraventa of Genoa (1820) and was crowned in the Vatican, in the presence of Pope Pius VII, in 1823. About a hundred years later, a body was sculptured of Cedar of Lebanon wood by Riedi, and the statue was blessed by Pope Pius XI before being sent back to the Holy Land.

The paintings in the dome were executed by Brother Luigi Poggi, a lay brother of the monastery. These show Elijah elevated in his chariot of fire, Kind David laying his harp, the saints of the order, and the Prophets Isaiah, Ezekiel, and Daniel, as well as the Holy Family. Below them are depicted the four Evangelists. The base of the cupola bears two texts from the Old Testament used in the Mass of Our Lady of Mt. Carmel. The stained-glass windows portray Elijah in the desert and his ascent in the fiery chariot.

Visiting the traditional cave of Elijah with all these beautiful furnishings brought the author to meditation on the continuity of our holy Catholic Faith from the Old to the New Testament. It also brought to mind the reaffirmation which Our Lady gave to all this at Fatima when she held the brown scapular, which is a sign of our pesonal consecration to her Immaculate Heart as we live our duties according to our state in life.

Mt. Carmel was always renowned in the Holy Land as the scene of contest between monotheism and paganism, as it was there that the Prophet Elijah challenged the priests of Baal; he confounded them, as their incantations failed while his own prayer brought down fire from heaven (Kings 18). Our

Lady of Fatima came to earth to urge Christians to combat the errors of paganism and atheism, so it is not surprising that in the 20th century she should appear robed as Our Lady of Mt. Carmel, named after that famous mountain which has forever been known as a symbol of the contest between faith in one God, and belief in no God or in false gods. By expressing our devotion to Our Lady through wearing her scapular, we also express our faith in God, who is her Son.

When Pope Paul VI in his Apostolic Constitution *Poenitemini Agite* of 1966 called the world to renewed penance, he stated: "All the members of the Church are called to participate in the work of Christ and so, to participate in His expiation, too." The American Bishops responded with a pastoral statement on Penitential Observance for the Liturgical Year. (November 18, 1966).

In the Bishops' four-page, single-space implementation directive, they said:

> We ask, urgently and prayerfully, that we, as people of God, make of the entire Lenten Season a period of special penitential observance. . . . We strongly recommend participation in daily Mass and a self-imposed observance of fasting. . . . We also recommend spiritual studies, beginning with the Scriptures as well as the traditional Lenten Devotions (sermons, Stations of the Cross and the Rosary) and all the self-denial summed up in the Christian concept of "mortification". . . .
>
> Friday should be in each week something of what Lent is in the entire year. For this reason we urge alk to prepare for that weekly Easter that comes with each Sunday by freely making of every Friday a day of self-denial and mortification in prayerful remembrance of the passion of Jesus. . . .

While the bishop terminated the traditional law of abstinence every Friday, binding under pain of sin, they added, "We give first place to abstinence from flesh meat. We do so in the hope that the Catholic community will ordinarily continue to abstain from meat by free choice as formerly we did in obedience to Church law." They asked that we continue to do penance on all the Fridays of the year "out of love for Christ Crucified."

Finally our Bishops said,

> In summary, let it not be said that by this action, implementing the spirit of renewal coming out of the Council, we have abolished Friday, repudiated the holy traditions of our fathers, or diminished the insistence of the Church on the fact of sin and the need for penance. Rather, let it be proved by the spirit in which we enter upon prayer and penance, not excluding fast

and abstinence freely chosen, that these present decisions and recommen-
dations of this Conference of Bishops will herald a new birth of living
faith and more profound penitential conversion by both of which we
become one with Christ, mature sons of God and servants of God's people.

It is well known how the official instructions of the hierarchy were
misrepresented and then disregarded, and the spirit of penance which they
asked to be "intensified" was all too often forgotten.

Faithfulness to one's duties can be very difficult, and can involve either
large or small matters. We know what has happened in the United States.
The Supreme Court in America, which has considered itself a Christian land,
has legalized the murder of unborn babies. Over a million abortive murders
are performed per year in the United States. Pornography is commonplace.
Movies and television are often immoral. Movies have been produced portraying Christ Jesus Himself as guilty of sexual immorality, and portraying
the Passover as only a plot, a deception on the part of Jesus.

Artificial birth control has become the mentality of the land, not only
in the United States, but in other countries as well. This mentality has led
to the abortive mentality. The legalization of abortion was quickly followed by attempts to introduce euthanasia. Attempts have been made to legalize
and dignify unnatural sex. All this has led to the breakdown of family life,
with the divorce rate nearing 50 percent and millions living in sinful marriages. A drug-sex culture took over the youth of the land, as alcohol was
too often the master of many adults in their social lives.

Not Christ as King, but permissiveness came to reign. Unbelievable
as it is rather, than working to correct all this, Christians—sometimes even
clergy and religious—under the influence of Modernistic theologians, have
advocated adapting the teachings of the Church so as to put her blessing
upon such falsehood and immorality.

For decades before such a sad state of affairs came about, popes had
been saying: Mankind is losing its sense of sin. Fifty and more years ago
such statements on the part of the papacy may have seemed extreme to some.
Now we can more fully realize tha the popes accurately saw the trends of
the world situation. Our Lady of Fatima also alerted the world at the beginning of the present century to the direction in which it was headed. She came
to give light and hope to a world headed for darkness and despair.

Gradually Christians were led into the spirit of secularism. Rulers said
there should be no meddling of religion into the affairs of the state or of
society. Religion was something very private, a personal matter between
the individual and his God, not something to affect one's public or social
life. Some public figures saw no contradiction in being atheistic in business,

in society, and in legal and governmental decisions while claiming to be religious in their private lives.

First, society—including our schools—became de-Christianized. Christ ceased to be King over the land publicly. Then it developed that Christ was no longer recognized as king in million of homes which make up society. Parents too often gave up their authority in the home, and the father frequently did not recognize his role as the representative of Christ in the family in unity with his wife.

Years ago it was seldom if ever heard that a Catholic was divorced. But at this writing, it is reported that divorce among Catholics is almost as common as among non-Catholics. But the law of God is still the same. *Marriage lasts until death.* Where there has been a real consummated sacramental marriage between two baptized Christians, there is no possibility of a second marriage in Christ while both spouses still live on this earth.

People have become so removed from the spirit of sacrifice in observing the duties of their state in life that when obstacles come, they run away from them, rather than facing reality and accepting the burden in love of God and neighbor. In the case of marriage, this means carrying the burden together, husband and wife. But the spirit of the times is to seek comfort and to avoid pain, effort, and penance in order to escape whatever is difficult.

What has happened in so many marriages? Self-control is needed at times to preserve the virtue of purity, but modern technology says we have the scientific means whereby you can have pleasure unlimited without need for sacrifice at any time. Many couples have fallen for non-Christian principles. That which could unity and strengthen their marriage as they do penance together, instead serves to drive the couple apart.

Religion has become so departmentalized, relegated to the four walls of the parish church and to the religion classroom, that many parents no longer bother to teach the true Faith to their own children. Family prayer and formation in the practical living of the Faith have left our homes. Millions of parents still send their children to a CCD class once a week for twenty-six to thirty weeks of the year. But how can one expect the children to learn everything during those twenty-six or so hours each year? Parents have complained that children are not taught their prayers during those hours, which amount to little more in a year than the span of hours in one day. Little formation is given at home. Parents have acted this way because education and formation of children are thought no longer to be parental duty. Millions have begun keeping their children home from religion classes and do not even participate in the Sacrifice of the Mass on the Lord's Day.

When Pope Paul VI's encyclical *Humanae vitae* ("Of Human Life") was issued in 1968 it was a call to daily duty for husbands and wives. The subject of this encyclical was marriage doctrine and morality and it upheld the dignity of human life. Unfortunatley, this teaching was misrepresented and disobeyed, causing a crisis in the Church. The disregard spread from the Church's teachings on sexual ethics to many other aspects of faith and morals. The Pope's encyclical condemning artificial birth control was framed in the manner of traditional teaching and of statements made by the Second Vatican Council, e.g., ". . . Each and every marriage act (*quidlibet matrimonii usus*) must remain open to the transmission of life" (Art. 11).

The Pope declared that his teaching in *Humanae vitae* was authoritative and required the assent and obedience of Catholics. The Second Vatican Council had also stated that when the Pope speaks in such an authoritative manner, Catholics must give their assent. However, it is well known that even before the encyclical could be read, much less studied, so-called theologians took to the airwaves calling for protests. What they were calling for was for married people not to remain faithful to their daily duty of obeying the Pope who speaks for Christ on faith and morals, and not to be true to their daily duty in the married state. Confusion resulted as millions reportedly disobeyed the highest authority in the Church. Yet time has proven Pope Paul VI a prophet, as disobedience to God's laws as interpreted by the Church has resulted in legalized abortive murders of unborn babies, a great increase in divorces even among Catholics, and many happy marriages, as people were unfaithful to their daily duty.

Heaven saw all this happening and spreading more than a half century ago. Failure to be true to the duties of one's state in life has at times reached even those in the Church called to the priesthood and religious life. Indeed, it is obvious that what has been happening in the Church is not merely the lack of education. Married adults who have rejected their marriage vows have not all been uneducated in the Faith. Certainly priests and religious who left their calling wre not lacking education in the Faith.

Pope John Paul II, in a letter addressed "to all the priests of the Church on the occasion of Holy Thursday 1979," called for their loyalty to the duties of their state in life. Laicization is a papal dispensation freeing a priest from his priestly duties. However, he is still a priest, for, once ordained, the indelible priestly character of Jesus Christ will remain upon his soul for all eternity. The Pope indicated that emphasis must be placed on lifelong fidelity to the priestly vocation. He urged priests to call on their resources of faith and prayer in moments of crisis "and not have recourse to a dispensation"—from their duties.

As mentioned earlier in this chapter, fulfillment of daily duty is an obligation for government and institutions as well as for individuals. It is interesting to hear Sister Lucia quote Our Lord and King as saying, "My justice will fall most heavily on those who want to destroy My reign in souls." Our heavenly Mother and Queen came at Fatima to call the world back to the reign of her Son as King over the entire world and over individual souls. The Fatima message is a call to nations as well as individuals back to recognizing Christ in word and in deed as King. This means the living of the social doctrines of the Church.

The popes with their world-wide vision realized long ago that society, even among so-called "Christian countries," was becoming less and less Christian in mentality and in action. Nevertheless, when Pope Pius XI issued his encyclical letter on Christ the King on December 11, 1925, he pointed out that people are instructed in the truths of Faith far more effectively by the annual celebration of the Sacred Mysteries than by any pronouncement, however weighty, of the teaching of the Church. The Pope was most anxious to reach the average Christian, one and all, with the message of Christ the King who should rule over nations and individual souls instead of sin and therefore Satan reigning.

But this must begin in individual hearts and lives, through the humble practice of the duties of each one's state—whether lofty or lowly. And supernaturally speaking, such offerings to God out of love for Him are beautiful and glorious. We can understand this to some extent now, but only in Heaven will we realize what glory and consolation was thus given to the Hearts of Jesus and Mary, as well as how many souls have come closer to God—or have been saved—through our loving practice of our daily duties.

13.
The Errors of Russia

Sister Lucia has described the terrible vision of Hell which the Fatima children were shown on July 13, 1917:

The rays of light seemed to penetrate the earth, and we saw as it were a sea of fire. Plunged in this fire were demons and souls in human form, like transparent burning embers, all blackened or burnished bronze, floating about in the conflagration, now raised into the air by the flames that issued from within themselves together with great clouds of smoke, now falling back on every side like sparks in huge fires, without weight or equilibrium, and shrieks and groans of pain and despair, which horrified us and made us tremble with fear. (It must have been this sight which caused me to cry out, as people say they heard me.) The demons could be distinguished by their terrifying and repellent likeness to frightful and unknown animals, black and transparent like burning coals. Terrified and as if to plead for succour, we looked up at Our Lady, who said to us, so kindly and so sadly: "You have seen Hell where the souls of poor sinners go. In order to save them, God wishes to establish in the world devotion to my Immaculate Heart. If you do what I tell you, many souls will be saved, and there will be peace. The war will end, but if men do not cease offending God, another and more terrible war will break out during the pontificate of Pius XI. When you see a night lit up by an unknown light, know that it is the sign God gives you that He is about to punish the world for its crimes by means of war, hunger, and persecution of the Church and the Holy Father.

"In order to prevent this, I shall come to ask for the consecration of Russia to my Immaculate Heart, and the Communion of reparation on the First Saturdays. If my wishes are fulfilled, Russia will be converted and there will be peace. If not, Russia will spread her errors throughout the world, promoting wars and persecution of the Church. The good will be martyred, the Holy Father will have much to suffer, and various nations will be annihilated. But in the end, my Immaculate Heart will triumph. The Holy Father will consecrate Russia to me and it will be converted, and a time of peace will be conceded to the world. In Portugal the dogma of the Faith will always be preserved. . . ."

Notice that Our Lady mentions the "errors of Russia" in the same breath, so to speak, with her words about Hell. It is significant that the Fatima children witnessed the vision of Hell, with its demons and lost souls, during the very time when Lenin and Trotsky, both of whom had turned to the spirit of Satanism, were lanuching a violent revolution in Russia.

The "errors of Russia" clearly refer to Communism. Communism is essentially an atheistic, materialist system which plans to conquer the entire world. Even while Our Lady was speaking at Fatima, the forces of atheism and materialism were beginning this program within Russia. To accomplish their planned world conquest, the communists wish to gain control of the Catholic Church, of all other Christian churches, and even of non-Christian religions, such as Islam. Their ideas have become popular in almost all parts of the world; the heresy of our times is the spirit of atheism. But the message of Fatima from beginning to end is just the opposite of the message of Communist materialism.

Basic to the philosophy of Communism is denial of God and of the immortality of man's soul. Communism denies any moral order or human rights, including the rights to life, liberty, justice, self-determination, free speech and ownership of property. Communists do not hesitate at mass murder to achieve their goals; millions in China have suffered this fate. The battle against the "errors of Russia" is not always clearly defined; one does not always recognize the enemy with ease. Communism is not always clearly labeled with the hammer and sickle and the red star, although it is true that at times the communists have openly displayed their symbols.

While a formally Communist government may not actually be in control of a specific country, nevertheless, the spirit of atheism and materialism have already spread to many nations. This spirit leads to Hell. The devil uses every agency he can to achieve his goal. The fact that even some priests and laity within the Church cannot recognize the evils of Communism, and have attempted to collaborate with Marxism, is testimony to the cleverness of materialistic ideas—whether from Moscow, Peking, or from evil angelic intellects. Though Communism manifests itself at times under the sign of the red flag, Satan never makes himself visible with a red suit and pitchfork.

In 1917, Our Lady seemed to be saying that the greatest evils today are epitomized in Communism as it was then sprouting in Russia. What did she mean?

Communism is atheistic, materialistic, and deterministic as it continues today to follow the theory of Karl Marx. Its nature and goals have never changed. On the political level, it teaches that the social order evolves through economic struggles between classes in the direction of a violent revolution, followed by the substitution of a society where all things are owned in common, or "nationalized" (owned by the Communist state). But more importantly, atheistic Communism denies God's existence, the immortality of the human soul, and the rights of the individual. Marriage and the family are considered to be artificial institutions which the government is free to manipulate. The primary responsibility for the education of children is taken away from the parents and given to the state.

Before the Communists took over Russia, the Orthodox Church had over one hundred million members. By 1961, so many churches had been closed that the figure had dropped by more than 80,000,000, and more churches have been closed since 1961. When it takes over, Communism promises freedom of religion, but in truth it is dedicated to the *destruction* of religion. But though it seeks to destroy all religions—especially Catholicism—it is itself a false religion, and not just a political, economic, or military system. Any traditional idea of God is out of the question under Marxism, and is replaced by empty promises of a heaven on earth at some undetermined future time when political forces shall have sufficiently evolved.

Joseph Cardinal Hoffner, Archbishop of Cologne in West Germany, is one of the Catholic Church's most outstanding spokesmen today. According to Cardinal Hoffner, since 1917,

> Tens of thousands of priests, religious, and faithful in the Soviet Union have been murdered for their Faith. Of the 79,767 churches and chapels counted in Russia in 1914, there remained only 7,500 in 1973. In the capital of Moscow, only 26 churches are open. They are shown to tourists. Of 57 diocesan seminaries of the Orthodox Church, only three are left. Of the numerous Catholic seminaries in Russia, Estonia, Latvia and Lithuania before World War I, only one exists still in Lithuania.

The Cardinal Archbishop wrote: "Pope Paul VI spoke of a 'drama of fidelity to Christ.' Numerous believers, simply because they were Christian and Catholic, were systematically and violently oppressed, 'a persecution of Christians which is camouflaged with general declarations of human rights.' " He continued:

> The adversaries of religion, according to the Vatican II Council, wherever they have come to power, have fought religion violently, and have propagated atheism, especially in education of youth, using the pressure which is so readily available to those in power. In China, Christians are terribly persecuted, and are pushed into going underground. Cruelty and persecution rage in Albania. Most of the churches and mosques have been run down or are being used for secular purposes. In 1972, the Catholic priest Stephan Kurti was shot for baptizing a child in a concentration camp at the request of its mother. In the whole of Albania in 1973, only fourteen Catholic priests were alive—thirteen of them in concentration camps.

Cardinal Hoffner said that in Communist East Europe the situation differs from country to country, but that everywhere, Christians, regardless of whether they are Orthodox, Protestant, or Catholic, are in a deep pool of common suffering; they are persecuted and oppressed. The terror in Prague, Czechoslavakia has been especially bad, and the pastoral activity of the Church has been choked by all kind of administrative chicanery.

> Even in Poland, where the great majority clings faithfully to the Catholic Faith, where vocations both secular and religious are more numerous than in any other country of the world; even here, the Church is under hard pressure by the Communist authorities. The Primate of Poland, Cardinal Wyszynski, said to tens of thousands of Catholics that it is incredible how government "mobilizes a political battle against the Church" in order to wipe out religion.

The Church is under heavy pressure in North Korea and in South and North Vietnam. In Cambodia and Laos, where the saintly Dr. Tom Dooley labored, the Church is practically destroyed. Catholic priests there have either been expelled or murdered. The Church suffers under Communist oppression in several countries of Africa. Who remembers to pray for these people and how many are keeping these facts before public opinion and calling for justice and the end of persecutions?

Cardinal Hoffner said that the situation in East Germany is well-known. Christian parents are urged to take their children out of religious instruction classes. The Lutheran Bishop D. Albrecht Schonherr pointed out in April of 1976 that the state party was enforcing atheism upon the whole population. He said: "Freedom of conscience and belief is not guaranteed for all those who cannot accept the ideology of Marxism-Leninism."

And the Cardinal added: "In sixty years the model and pace-maker for persecution of Christians remains the Soviet Union. The founder of the Soviet Union, Lenin, has changed the Marxist formula of religion, 'opiate of the people,' to 'Religion is spoiled liquor.' "

Cardinals Beran, Trochta, Mindszenty, Slipyj, and Wyszynski, Bishop Walsh, and others have spent a large portion of their lives as bishops in concentration camps and prisons, suffering under Communist tyranny. Not since Jesus Christ was born has the blood of so many Christian martyrs been shed as during the present century—a time ironically, when so much emphasis has been placed on human rights.

In his pastoral letter, Cardinal Hoffner pleads:

> Brethren and Sisters! You will ask: what can we do? Are we not powerless? I give you three suggestions:
>
> First: help to form public opinion; call the persecution of Christians, "persecution of Christians"; call injustice, "injustice," and violence, "violence." Public opinion has its impact upon the persecutors of Christians.
>
> Second: do not forget the persecuted Church! Do we really suffer with them? A bishop from Slovakia who spent many years in prison asks us, "Why do we venerate the martyrs of the first centuries and forget the martyrs of the 20th century? Why do we hush up today's witnesses for the Faith? Why do you call the Church whose members they are, falsely, the "Church of silence," although she doesn't keep silence at all, but cries with a loud voice for help and support?
>
> Third: include the persecuted Christians and their persecutors in our prayers. We pray also for their persecutors, that some of them might turn from a Saul into a Paul.

How very close Communism has come to taking over Italy! What does the future hold, as many even in Italy are turned against the Church, and the Communists bide their time? Rev. Peter N. Kurguz, O.P., Ph.D., in an article entitled *Why is Communism Intrinsically Evil? Rome Is the Big Prize* (published by the Catholic Russian Center), points out that if they should gain control in Italy, we can look for the following to happen:

> 1. Communist civil authority could make a formal declaration that the Vatican is no longer considered an independent nation and its territory

is now part of Italy and falls aunder the Communist civil authority of Rome.

2. All Church property would be confiscated.

3. Income from Vatican investments would be part of the confiscation. Without funds, it is difficult to run an organization.

4. And just as the authority under Lenin hindered the pastoral office of Patriarch Tikhon, so too the Pope would be hindered; perhaps jailed or murdered.

5. All foreign clergy and nuns in Italy would be expelled.

6. The Vatican museum would be declared a public museum.

7. The Basilica of St. Peter's and the Sistine Chapel would be declared public museums, and closed to religious services; just as the enormous and beautiful cathedral of the Russian Orthodox Church in Leningrad, or St. Basil's in Moscow.

8. Most of the office buildings would become either offices for the government or housing for Communist government officials.

9. Many monasteries, seminaries, priories or convents of religious orders and congregations would become housing for the poor, and many other means would be used to stop the work of those religious orders and congregations.

10. The Church would be considered "counter-revolutionary," and everything COUNTER-REVOLUTIONARY MUST BE DESTROYED.

In such terrible circumstances, it can be concluded that if the clergy remaining in the Vatican wanted to eat, they would have to get jobs approved by the government, change their thinking, and become quiet citizens of the communist state.

It is known that every Communist country has very strict entry and exit scrutiny with special visas required for entrance. No visas would be issued to clergy; the Vatican's contact with Bishops, maintaining the unity of the Church throughout the world with the Pope as visible head, would be curtailed. While Christ promised that the Church would never be destroyed, we know that it can be cruelly persecuted, hindered, and that it can disappear among large numbers of people in various parts of the world.

This chapter on atheistic Communism will doubtlessly be called extreme and ridiculous, *and that is exactly what the Communists would desire*. In Italy before the election in which the Communists made an ucomfortably good showing, I heard the claim that "the kind of Communism being promoted in Italy is not like that of Russia." Communists encourage this misguidedly optimistic view. The truth is that regardless of shades of difference, Marxist-Leninist—Maoist philosophy today dominates one-half of the world's population.

The Communists have also had a program to destroy the Catholic Church in Cuba. A manifesto was printed in China; it contained the following quotations, quoted from Fr. Kurguz's article:

*If the People's democracies are to continue . . . they must first and foremost put an end to the influence of the Catholic Church and of its activities.

*When the political struggle and the productive forces have reached a certain level, we shall then be in a position to destroy the Church.

*The first line of action to be followed consists in educationg, persuading, convincing the Catholics to participate in study-circles and political activities.

*We shall progressively replace the religious element by the Marxist element.

*The Church must not be allowed to preserve its supra-national character. . . .

*By making the Church subject to the processes of democratic centralism, we open the way, via the masses, to patriotic measures that will weaken the Church and undermine its prestige.

*The next step is to destroy the link existing between the Church and the Vatican.

*Once the separation of the Church from the Vatican is complete, we can proceed to the consecration of Church dignitaries chosen by ourselves.

*It is notorious that when the practice of religion has simply become a matter left to the individual's sense of responsibility, it is gradually forgotten.

*The rising generations will succeed the older, and religion will become merely an episode of the past.

There have been many events in the past decade which have caused concerned Christians of the free world to ask if we are in the process of losing our Christian civilization. In his 1937 encyclical entitled *Atheistic Communism*, Pope Pius XI said that "the all too imminent danger" of our own days is "Bolshevistic and atheistic Communism, which aims at upsetting the social order and at undermining the very foundation of Christian civilization." The same Pope said of Communism that its propaganda is

so truly diabolical that the world perhaps never witnessed its like before . . . [and that it is directed] from one common center. . . . It is shrewdly adapted to the varying conditions of diverse people. It has at its disposal great financial resources, gigantic organizations, international congresses, and countless trained workers. It makes use of pamphlets and reviews, of cinema, theatre and radio, of schools and even universities.

Politicians who have attempted to deal with the Communists have often been unmindful that it is not a mere matter of dealing with another political system, with another economic ideology. They are dealing with a system that believes in no morals. To the authentic Communist, truth is whatever will help his cause, even if it is a lie. Some Christians also have not understood the Satanic nature of Communism, and have thought they could Christianize Marxism.

Liberation theology is a system of collaboration with Marxism, in hopes that Marxist principles may be the guiding lines for the future of the Church. In the years immediately following World War II, when the Catholic Church was looked upon as the greatest enemy of Communism, it would have been unbelievable that some theologians would actulay call for this collaboration. Although liberation theology is being preached in not a few pulpits in the United States and in other countries, never are words said or prayers offered in these places for the persecuted behind the Iron, Bamboo, or other curtains. On the occasion of Mao's death, his soul was remembered in the Prayer of the Faithful in some parishes. We know that it is good to pray for the dead; however, not a word was mentioned about the millions in China who were killed as that Communist murderer took over, or about the countless millions in China who have suffered and are still suffering because of him. Who remembers to pray for the persecuted Church?

The Communists have so succeeded in brainwashing people of the United States of America, which Lenin described as "the last bastion of capitalism," that it has become unpopular to speak of Communism as a danger to our country or Church. Christians and even clergymen flirt with Marxism. In France, when the Soviet Union was celebrating the 60th anniversary of communism, 182 French worker-priests stated that the view of Marxism and Christian Faith as incompatible was "an error of perspective." They even parroted the Communist line in saying:

> Taking our place in the struggle of the working class for its liberation, belonging to various organizations whose references are not exclusively Marxist, we all practice Marxism more or less in our analyses and in our action as do a good number of militants with whom we act and dialogue daily.

The trick of the Communists is to get Christianity wedded to Marxism in order to form a "Christian Marxism" which sees material prosperity as the goal of man's existence. Today there is much watering down of supernatural faith in Catholic educational circles, and even in many major seminaries all over the world. How ideal the time is in many countries for Communism's final success, now that the free world is in a stage of cultural, economic, and social revolution, when confusion reigns among Christians, and when Church leaders have often been lacking in strength of leadership.

In their desire to sow even more confusion, Communists like to spread the idea that the Church has compromised with Communism. Communists are particularly adept at exploiting and inciting all sorts of conflict; they would love to be able to preach that the Roman Catholic Church has helped atheistic Communism. Many articles have already appeared in magazines and newspapers in various parts of the world, criticizing and blaming the Church for the spread of Communism. On May 19, 1976, Rome's *Il Tempo* had on its front page: "Also in Italy the Church of Silence?". On May 25, 1976, *Panorama* carried a caricature of a Bishop crying "hammer and sickle" tears with the lead article: "From Christ to Marx."

When it was decided that Vatican Council II would issue no new condemnation of atheistic Communism, and when the post-Conciliar policy of dialogue followed, this was seen by some as official acceptance of Communism by the Catholic Church. However, the Church has long been the great foe of Communism. Pope Leo XIII (1878-1903) instructed and warned Christendom in clear and profound encyclicals against the dangerous errors of the time. He also encouraged sacred learning and attracted the hearts of men by his apostolic dignity, charity, and mildness. In 1878 he defined Communism this way: "The fatal plague which insinuates itself into the marrow of human society, only to bring about its ruin." Two years before the *Communist Manifesto* was published, Pope Pius IX in 1846 solemnly condemned "that infamous doctrine of so-called Communism, which is absolutely contrary to the natural law, and even society itself."

Pope Pius XI's encyclical letter entitled *Atheistic Communism* (March 19, 1937) was issued just twenty years after Our Lady of Fatima had mentioned Russia by name and had said that if Heaven's requests were not granted, "Russia will spread her errors throughout the world, promoting wars and persecution of the Church." Pope Pius XI instructed Bishops of the world in this fashion:

> See to it, Venerable Brethren, that the faithful do not allow themselves to be deceived! Communism is instrinsically evil, and no one who would save Christian civilization may collaborate with it in any undertaking whatsoever.

He spoke of the "conspiracy of silence" on the part of the press throughout the world concerning the true character of Communism and its techniques. Regarding the international Communist conspiracy, Cardinal Cushing stated:

"Courage, persistence, and intelligent knowledge of our foe are required."

Pope Pius XI issued *Divini Redemptoris* on Communism in 1937, and in 1949 the Sacred Congregation of the Holy Office decreed that the penalty of excommuncation is automatically incurred by a Catholic who voluntarily professes, defends, or spreads Communism. Pope Paul VI has said: "There can be no reconciliation with the forces that speak of man's respect for man but of ignoring God."

In 1977 a Bishop stood up at a national meeting of the hierarchy in the United States and stated that Communism has invaded the Church in this country. Julio R. Cardinal Rosales, Archbishop of Cebu in the Philippines, issued a pastoral letter on Our Lady of Fatima for the 60th anniversary of the apparitions. In this letter of May 13, 1977, he summarized his message: "We have said all this about Communsim, my beloved clergy, sisters and faithful, because you have to be warned against the subtle propaganda and infiltration of the Communists even in the work of the Church." The Kremlin cleverly uses religion to advance its power. An East Berlin summit meeting of Europe's twenty-nine Communist parties passed a resolution to encourage religious groups to help Communism. The Kremlin planned an enormous world conference in Moscow for July 1977 to promote peace, Communist style. The idea was to use bishops, priests, and nuns—whether they realize they are being used or not. Communists set no limits to their tricks to divide and destroy the Church and its administration.

But how many of our schools teach anything at all concerning the real nature of Communsim? When I was in Portugal in 1974, I witnessed the Communist activity which was quite visible in that country at that time. Upon returning to the United States, I decided to question American youth about their knowledge of Communism. I discovered that many I questioned knew nothing about the nature or terror of atheistic Communism. Evern American soldiers returning from military duty often know little about Communism.

Christianity has always taught that man, after the angels, is the crown of God's creation, with man being man in God's own image and likeness and destined for eternal union with Him. Until Marx developed his philosophy which considers man a mere economic entity whose needs are primarily those of his belly, no other philosophic system had so degraded him. Marx denigrates love, marriage, and all the finer things of life. Religion, science, art, and philosophy are all considered super-structure. The only determining fact is the belly. Thus Marx rejoiced over Darwinism which taught evolution from lower forms of life and the brute survival of the fittest. This seemed to disprove the divine origin of man and the immortality of the human soul.

In accord with their low esteem for individual human life, the Soviets have murdered sixty million men in half a century. Red China has murdered another sixty million. One-third of the Cambodian people were murdered by the Communists in the 1970's after the American pull-out from Vietnam. Lenin said that Communism must destroy all religion. It aims to silence moral authority and thus to enslave the world. Lenin said: "Militant materialism should carry on untiring atheist propaganda and struggle. . .

It is essential to give the masses the greatest variety of atheistic propaganda material."

Communists still spread the idea, using every available means of propaganda, that belief in God makes the people stupid and dull, and that those who believe in God are, therefore, "spitting" on themselves. Followers of Lenin still regard all churches and religious institutions as reactionary, as instruments of slaveholders, feudal lords and capitalists, and thus as part of a superstructure to be phased out as soon as possible. The struggle against religion is inherent in atheistic Marxism. Yet Marxism continues to spread, bringing about the annihilation of nations. Its goal is still, more than ever, world-wide domination. Moscow is still pulling the strings and directing this effort. We need to be wise as serpents. But how many visit Moscow, a show place to conceal the reality of Russia's sad state, only to return to the free world singing its praises?

Communists use an "Aesopian" language in order to further their aims among non-Communists. They have succeeded at times in deceiving even priests and religious. In Aesopian language, one uses ordinary words, but these words mean something other than what they seem to mean. For example, "peace" refers to the end of opposition to Communism. Lenin first used and spoke of this trick. It is embedded in Communist history and practice and has fooled many politicans into selling out to Communist causes. One can never assume that a word means the same to a Communist as it does to the rest of the world.

From the time of Marx's earliest writings, the Communits have always proclaimed the ideal of an eventual stateless society, to be accomplished by the "withering away" of the state after the proletarian revolution. Only when the capitalist establishment is liquidated can the "withering away of the state" begin; in the meantime, the Soviet Union must be powerful. Lenin's 1923 plan for world conquest is as follows: "First we will take Eastern Europe, then the masses of Asia; then we will encircle the United States, which will be the last bastion of capitalism. We will not have to attack. It will fall like over-ripe fruit into our hands." True to the Communist plan, this is being accomplished by brainwashing people into accepting no morals; the method is that of infiltration. But, of course, the Communists have simply needed to encourage the degenerative materialism caused by our own spiritual irresponsibility. Much of the modern West is indeed "over-ripe fruit," now rotting on the ground, for we have perhaps already fallen under the weight of our unrepented sins.

The philosophy of Communism requires systematic and untiring efforts to destroy organized religion and prevent religious worship and education. Members of the Young Communist League must make an official pledge to atheism. However, Communism is very subtle, and its attack is not always so direct. More often it secretly infiltrates the clergy and church-related organizations, as well as the press, radio, and television. When it takes over a country it enforces strict censorship of the news. University students are sometimes deceived into thinking: "We'll try Communism. If it doesn't work we can try something else." Little do they realize how it works; their freedom once lost, Communism would enslave them permanently.

On November 7, 1977, the Soviet Union celebrated sixty years of Communism with the traditional parade in Red Square. Slightly before that date, Soviet President Leonid I. Brezhnev had boasted that there was hardly a corner of the globe that was outside Soviet interest and influence. The Associated Press in the United States of America stated: "He and his Kremlin colleagues believe in the triumph of Communism as inevitable everywhere." About half the world is now under the diabolic hammer and sickle. It is more than a theory of politics or economy that murders leading churchmen, imprisons and tortures them, and destroys and desecrates churches attempting to force millions to accept atheism.

We have designed this chapter to stimulate our readers to greater understanding of the grave situation, as the prophecies of Our Lady of Fatima are being more and more fulfilled. Russia plays a crucial role in the future of the world, and its errors daily enslave more of the world's population. Yet many do not recognize this. But spread of Communist principles is not limited to countries where Moscow-style Marxism-Leninism or any other style of Communism have officially taken over governments. The "errors of Russia" surely include the spirit of atheism which has filtered into the United States of America and throughout the world bringing a crisis of faith.

Why are catechisms appearing which ignore the immortality of the soul and speak only on the natural plane, seeking a perfect order here below, with little or no mention of Heaven or of the supernatural life of grace? Why was the Vatican document on *Sexual Ethics* ridiculed by theologians even within some Catholic educational circles, and why is it still largely ignored in classrooms?

One would have to be totally blind not to recognize the internal corruption of our country, the falling away from Christian principles: the breakup of family life, divorce, abortion, and sexual suicide while calling virtuous what God's word clearly calls "sin unto death"—pornography, immodesty in dress and actions, corruption of the entertainment media, drug abuse, desecration of the Lord's Day. The list seems endless.

Who would dare say that none of what has happened and continues to happen is due to the spirit of atheism spreading over the world? One can see, amidst the economic and governmental struggles and sins of society, how far our own country has leaned—intentionally or not, by infiltration or not—to Communistic principles. Parents have less and less control over the education of their children. Family life and respect for human life itself are unbelievably low, such as we would not have imagined even fifteen years ago. Confusion reigns among Catholics regarding authority in the Church and the solid doctrines of Catholicism.

The Fifth World Synod of Bishops dealing with religious instruction, especially among children and youth, witnessed speakers in October of 1977 declaring the "reality" of Marxism. They warned that the young must be taught during catechesis how to cope with aggressive anti-Christian and anti-spiritual ideologies coming from this sector. Obviously, it is present throughout the world. Those acquainted with the serious faults in modern catechetics will see much in the words of the Communist, Hess, who spoke in religious terms, but did not believe in God. He wrote: "Our god is nothing more than the human race united in love." This statement points to a basic failure in much of modern catechetics; natural love, centered on this earth has become the goal. Little wonder then that Our Lady of Fatima came as a Catechist teaching the supernatural. The spiritual combat between Mary and the forces of atheistic Communism is illustrated by an incident regarding the Pilgrim Virgin statue of Our Lady of Fatima.

In May of 1978 in Poland, a Catholic country under Communist control, the Communists knew that a plane named "Queen of the World" and carrying 175 pilgrims and six crew members was bringing the Pilgrim Virgin statue to Poland. When it landed in Warsaw, a Communist officer refused to allow the people to deplane. The Communists permited only Louis Kaczmarek, the escort for the statue, to leave the plane. Carrying Our Lady's International Pilgrim Virgin statue encased in its blue traveling bag, he was led, following the Communist officer and some armed soldiers, into a special van which had been parked alongside the plane.

Louis was told to remove the statue from the case. Having done so, he was asked, "Who is she?" He replied, "the Mother of God!" The officer then told the soldiers to take Louis and the statue into another van. After some time, the Communists permitted the passengers of the jet to deplane, but the famous statue had to be kept on the plane at Warsaw for the next three days while the Fatima pilgrims were in Poland. Louis Kaczmarek said, "The thought struck me: How powerful the Communists are and yet they fear this little thirty-three-pound statue of Our Lady."

Father Strumski, the spiritual leader of the around-the-world pilgrimage, worked tirelessly, going through all channels—the Polish authorities and ultimately Cardinal Wyzsinski—seeking permission for Our Lady's statue to deplane. According to Father Strumski it was in vain, as the Communists were determined that the statue would never leave the plane. The statue was locked in the cabin of the plane and there guarded by Communists.

Polish priests then told Father Strumski about an ingenious plan they had developed. With wire, they made an outline figure of Our Lady of Fatima with lettering at the bottom: "Our Mother Never Leaves Us." Below that line were listed four most Marian cities of Poland: Warsaw, Cracow, Czestochowa, Niepolkolona (Father Maximilian Kolbe's City of the Immaculata). With this wire outline, they traveled over 500 miles, visiting the four cities. Each time, they placed the wire outline on the main altar and held devotions, in which they apologized to Our Lady for the treatment her image had received at the airport in Warsaw.

The Poles across the land were aware of what had happened. Father Strumski spoke to them in Polish, telling them what the Communists had done. As he spoke, priests and laity, especially at Czestochowa, fought to hold back the tears. When Father Strumski completed his rousing talk, the Poles shouted in unison: "Long live Poland; praise be to the Mother of God." As the Fatima pilgrims left Poland, they left the wire outline of Our Lady of Fatima with a Monsignor from the chancery office. The Monsignor said he would take charge of the project; this wire outline was going to travel daily from one church of Poland to another.

Shortly thereafter, and before the election of Cardinal Wojtyla as the successor St. Peter, the Communists in Poland, publicly embarrassed, were willing to negotiate terms for the Pilgrim Virgin's tour of Poland perhaps the following year. Cardinal Wyzsinski, not to be outwitted by the Communists, at the same time managed to negotiate the building of some churches which had long been forbidden—and in areas where the people had to hold services outside a church, at times even in the open air. Through her image, Our Lady had succeeded in having temples for her Eucharistc Son built in Communist Poland.

The beginning of the decade of the 1980's saw unrest and violent acts of terrorism and revolution in central America, especially El Salvador and neighboring countries. Authorities in the United Staes feared such terrorism and revolution could spread and eventually reach the U.S.A., "the last bastion." At the same time similar acts of violence, terrorism, the killing of innocent victims was reported around the world.

Our Lady said that the "errors of Russia" would spread to the annihilation of nations, unless men returned to God, to prayer, to sacrifice. However, she also promised the ultimate triumph of her Immaculate Heart, which means that Christ the King will rule in the hearts of men and in society. Our Lady and Communism: both are striving for world conquest. We have an absolute promise from Heaven that in the end Our Lady will succeed. How long it takes depends upon us, upon our resonse to her requests. This is the greatest hope for the world.

As this book goes to press in 1983 the Polish Marian Pope from a communist dominated country continues to travel the world, leading it back to Christ through the intercession of the Mother of God. "Totus Tuus" (totally yours) expresses his personal consecration to Mary's Immaculate Heart as a bishop and now as the Pope of the Universal Church. Future history will tell whether the defeat of communism and the triumph of Mary's Immaculate Heart will come under Pope John Paul II. The events in Poland in 1980, 1981, 1982, and 1983, with the unrest of the laboring class and the farmers focussing world attention on Poland while thousands of Russian soldiers encamped near the Polish borders threatening invasion, give evidence to the need for increased prayer and sacrifice to save Poland and bring the triumph of Mary's Immaculate Heart. Her triumph has surely *begun* under the great Marian Pope who has arisen from the communist controlled countries of eastern Europe. Indeed, the communists of Poland have referred to the Church in Poland and that means to the faith of Poland's people as a "bomb."

14.
The Origins of the "Errors Out of Russia"

Fatima and Communism were born at the same time—one for faith and love, the other for atheism and hatred. If we are to get a deeper insight into the diabolic spread of atheistic Communism we would do well to study the men who conceived it and first put it into operation.

Karl Marx and Frederick Engels are responsible for formulating the basic Communist philosophy. Richard Wurmbrand made a study entitled *Was Karl Marx a Satanist?* Although the author clearly admits that he has not proven conclusively that Marx belonged to a sect of devil-worshippers, he brings forth evidence that Karl Marx was a Jew who hated Jews, a Christian who turned on Christianity and even on God Himself, but who continued to believe in God while honoring the devil. I have drawn from the information in Wurmbrand's book in preparing this chapter.

After being a Christian in his youth, Marx later spoke as favorably of Satan as he had written of Christ Jesus in *The Union of the Faithful with Christ*, Marx's first extant work.

Through love of Christ we turn our hearts at the same time toward our brethren who are inwardly bound to us and for whom He gave Himself in sacrifice. . . . Union with Christ could give an inner elevation, comfort in sorrow, calm trust, and a heart susceptible to human love, to everything noble and great, not for the sake of ambition and glory, but only for the sake of Christ.

The author of these words it the Christian Marx. His secondary school certificate states: "His knowledge of the Christian faith and morals is fairly clear and well grounded. He knows also to some extent the history of the Christian church."

Though he was later to write Satanic words that raise the serious question of whether he had made a pact with Satan, early in life he wrote a thesis entitled "Considerations of a Young Man on Choosing His Career." It includes the following:

Religion itself teaches us that the Ideal toward which all strive sacrifices Himself for humanity, and who shall dare contradict such claims? If we have chosen the position in which we can accomplish the most for Him, then we can never be crushed by burdens, because they are only sacrifices made for the sake of all.

But having moved away from such ideals, Karl Marx came to write of violence in hatred, and to admire the French revolutionary, Babeuf, who had written: "The love toward revolution killed in me any other love and made me cruel like the devil." Indeed, from his earliest writings in praise of Christ and Christianity, Marx soon changed his attitude to the following: "I wish to avenge myself against the One who rules above." This indicates faith in God. In a poem entitled "Invocation of One in Despair," he wrote:

So a god has snatched from me my all
In the curse and rack of destiny.
All his words are gone beyond recall!
Nothing but revenge is left to me!

I shall build my throne high overhead,
Cold, tremendous shall its summit be.
For its bulwark—superstitious dread.
For its Marshall—blackest agony.

Who looks on it with a healthy eye,
Shall turn back, deathly pale and dumb,
Clutched by blind and chill mortality.
May his happiness prepare its tomb.

While he was a student, Marx wrote a drama entitled *Oulanem*. Now the word "Oulanem" is an inversion of the Biblical word "Emmanuel" which in Hebrew means "God with us." Such inversions take place in black magic. And in his poem entitled "The Player," Marx wrote:

> The hellish vapors rise and fill the brain,
> Till I go mad and my heart is utterly changed.
> See this sword?
> The prince of darkness
> Sold it to me.
> For me beats the time and gives the signs.
> Ever more boldly I play the dance of death.

How interesting this is in light of the fact that in high initiation rites of the Satanist cult, a sword is sold to the new member. The sword guarantees success; to pay for it the candidate signs a covenant with blood from his wrists stating that his soul will belong to Satan after death. One thus in pact with Satan spends his time on this earth in success. With this in mind, listen to *Oulanem*:

> And they are also Oulanem, Oulanem.
> The name rings forth like death, rings forth
> Until it dies away in a wretched crawl.
> Stop, I've got it now! It rises from my soul
> As clear as air, as strong as my own bones.
> * * *
> Yet I have power within my youthful arms
> To clench and crush you [i.e., personified humanity] with tempestuous
> force,
> While for us both the abyss yawns in darkness.
> You will sink down and I shall follow laughing,
> Whispering in your ears, "Descend, come with me, friend."

At his death, Oulanem says:

> Ruined, ruined. My time has clean run out.
> The clock has stopped, the pygmy house has crumbled,
> Soon I shall embrace eternity to my breast, and soon
> I shall howl gigantic curses on mankind.

In *Oulanem*, Marx also writes of eternity:

> Ha! Eternity! She is our eternal grief,

An indescribable and immeasurable Death,
Vile artificiality conceived to scorn us,
Ourselves being clockwork, blindly mechanical,
Made to be the fool-calendars of Time and Space,
Having no purpose save to happen, to be ruined,
So that there shall be something to ruin.

Young manhood is usually a time for idealism, but Marx was only eighteen when he ended *Oulanem* this way:

If there is a Something which devours,
I'll leap within it, though I bring the world to ruins—
The world which bulks between me and the abyss
I will smash to pieces with my enduring curses.

I'll throw my arms around its harsh reality:
Embracing me, the world will dumbly pass away,
And then sink down to utter nothingness,
Perished, with no existence—that would be really living.

Correspondence shows concern from Karl Marx's father. On November
10, 1837, the son wrote: "A curtain had fallen. My holy of holies was rent
asunder and new gods had to be installed." Earlier that same year, on March
2, Marx's father had written to his son that his [Karl's] advancement and
fame were not the things which would make him happy; rather, he wrote
to Karl: "Only if your heart remains pure and beats humanly and if no demon
will be able to alienate your heart from better feelings, only then will I be
happy."
       According to Richard Wurmbrand,

   Two years after his father's expressed concern, in 1839, the young Marx
   wrote *The Difference Between Democritus' and Epicurus' Philosophy of
   Nature*, in the preface of which he aligns himself with the declaration of
   Aeschylus, "I harbor hatred against all gods." This he qualifies by stating
   that he is against all gods on earth and in heaven that do not recognize
   human self-consciousness as the supreme god-head.

I quote from another of Karl Marx's poems, "The Pale Maiden":

Thus heaven I've forfeited,
I know it full well.
My soul, once true to God,
Is chosen for hell.

According to Wurmbrand, "Marx adopted Satanism after an inner fight. The poems were ended in a period of severe illness, the result of this tempest within his heart. He writes at that time about his vexation at having to make an idol of a view he detests. He feels sick."

Marx's family life reveals something about the nature of this man who, along with his collaborator, Engels, conceived the philosophy of Communism. Marx's daughter, Eleanor, told about story time with her father. One story was about Hans Röckle; it took months to tell. Hans was a witch who owned a toy shop but had many debts. The toys were sold one by one to the devil with whom Hans had made a pact. A biographer of Marx concludes that there can be little doubt that these stories were autobiographical, and that Marx saw the world from the devil's point of view and had the devil's malignity.

Three of Marx's children died of malnutrtion. His daughter Laura married the socialist Laforgue, buried three of her children, and then she and her husband committed suicide. Marx's daughter Eleanor decided on suicide along with her husband. While her husband backed out at the last minute, Eleanor died.

Marx rejoiced when his uncle died, leaving him money; he had looked forward to the death of "the dog." Even his own mother's death apparently left him untroubled, for he wrote to Engels in December of 1863 in this manner:

> Two hours ago a telegram arrived to say that my mother is dead. Fate needed to take one member of the family. I already had one foot in the grave. Under the circumstances I am needed more than the old woman. I have to go to Trier about their inheritance.

While Marx and Engels had a high level of intelligence, their correspondence is replete with obscenities. Satanic cults are secretive in nature so it is difficult to obtain precise documentation that Marx actually belonged, yet his attitude, revealed in his life and writings, show Satanic characteristics. He approved of his daughter Eleanor marrying Edward Aveling, who lectured on the "wickedness of God" and the right to blaspheme.

In *The Communist Manifesto*, Marx advocates the abolishing of all religion, yet his wife speaks of Marx as "high priest and bishop of souls," when she writes to him of his "last pastoral letter" which "has again given quiet rest and peace to your poor sheep." It is strange that Marx, supposedly an atheist, would write "pastoral" letters, for Marx was not motivated by love of society or sympathy for the poverty of the working class. He spoke of the proletarians as "nuts." He spoke with contempt of Germans, of the Jews (though he himself was Jewish), and even in contempt of his own comrades in the fight for Communist domination. Richard Wurmbrand cites Arnold Künzli's *Karl Marx, A Psychogram*: "Mazzini, who had known him [Marx] well, wrote that he had 'a destructive spirit. His heart bursts with hatred rather than with love toward men.' " In his poems Marx never pretended to help the world, but expressed a desire to destroy, rather than reform or revolutionize it. In "Human Pride," he wrote:

> With disdain I will throw my gauntlet
> Full in the face of the world,
> And see the collapse of this pygmy giant
> Whose fall will not stifle my ardour.
>
> Then will I wander godlike and victorious
> Through the ruins of the world
> And, giving my words an active force,
> I will feel equal to the Creator.

Mikhail Bakunin, an associate of Marx in the First International, wrote: "In this revolution we will have to awaken the devil in people, to stir up the basest passions."

The hair style and beard of Marx were not typical of his time. Rather, his appearance was characteristic of the followers of a Satanic priestess, Joanna Southcott. Bakunin tells us that a friend of Marx, Proudhon, worshipped Satan. Wurmbrand's conclusions on Marx's life and work follow:

> Marx did not hate religion because it stood in the way of the happiness of mankind. On the contrary, he wished to make mankind unhappy here and throughout eternity. He proclaimed this as his ideal. His aim was the destruction of religion. Socialism, concern for the proletariat, humanism— these were only pretexts . . . Marx believed in hell and his program was to send man to hell.

Frederick Engels was Marx's collaborator in drawing up the Communist philosophy. Engels, too, was a former Christian who as a young man wrote so beautifully of the "Lord Jesus Christ, God's only Son" that he could have stirred the heart of any good Christian mother whose son wrote half as well:

> Lord Jesus Christ, God's only son,
> O step down from Thy heavenly throne
> And save my soul for me.

Come down in all Thy blessedness,
Light of Thy Father's holiness,
Grant that I may choose Thee.
Lovely, splendid, without sorrow is the
    joy with which we raise,
Saviour, unto Thee our praise.

And when I draw my dying breath
And must endure the pangs of death,
Firm to Thee may I hold;
That when my eyes with dark are filled
And when my beating heart is stilled,
In Thee shall I grow cold.
Up in Heaven shall my spirit praise
    Thy name eternally,
Since it lieth safe in Thee.

Engels not only collaborated with Marx in writing, but also contributed financially to Marx's support. Marx refused to support his own family, and even let some of them die from lack of necessities.

How did Engels begin to doubt the Christian faith? It happened after reading the book of Bruno Bauer, a liberal theologian. Engels wrote that he prayed much for truth, in anguish, when he felt the doubts, but ended by joining Marx whom he had called "the monster possessed by ten thousand devils."

The following quotation, taken from Bruno Bauer's writing of December 6, 1841, should give some idea of the kind of theologian he was:

> I deliver lectures here at the university before a large audience. I don't recognize myself when I pronounce my blasphemies from the pulpit. They are so great that these children, whom nobody should offend, have their hair standing on end. While delivering the blasphemies, I remember how I work piously at home writing an apology of the holy Scriptures and of the Revelation. In any case, it is a very bad demon that possesses me as often as I ascend the pulpit, and I am so weak that I am compelled to yield to him. . . . My spirit of blasphemy will be satisfied only if I am authorized to preach openly as professor of the atheistic system.

A realization of what liberal theology did to the formerly devout young Engels raises the question of what liberal theologians are doing today to youth regarding the teachings of the Church on the Real Eucharistic Presence of Our Lord, on prayer and penance, on abortion, contraception, and personal purity. We have repeatedly heard of youth, sometimes in Catholic schools and even universities, being taught not only permissiveness, but vice as virtue—and it is all explained away in the sweetest sounding terms. It must cause those in the devil's cause "to follow laughing," as their aim is to draw all mankind into the abyss.

Moses Hess, who converted Marx and Engels to the Socialist ideal, wrote the *Red Catechism for the German People* in which he used some Christian language in order to win believers to his religion of socialist revolution. The technique of Aesopian language among leading Communists has never changed. Hess, credited with being the founder of modern socialism, founded a diabolic type of Zionism. Its purpose was to destroy the Zionism of love, understanding, and harmony with surrounding states.

In *Was Karl Marx a Satanist*, Wurmbrand notes that

> Hess speaks persistently in religious terms but he does not believe in God. He writes that "our God is nothing more than the human race united in love."
>
> Hess was not only the original source of Marxism and the man who attempted to create an anti-God Zionism, but also the predecessor of the theology of revolution current in the World Council of Churches, and of the new tendencies in Catholicism which speak about salvation [on earth]. One and the same man, who is almost unknown, has been the mouthpiece of three Satanic movements: Communism, a racist, hateful brand of Zionism, and the theology of revolution.

Vladimir Lenin put into practice the Communist theory which Marx and Engels had drawn up. Lenin laid down the principle that the Communist party would become the ruling dictatorial party by remaining in a small group. This group would manipulate the thinking and actions of the masses through infiltration. Since destruction of all religions and all morals was a prime goal, infiltration in a religion must be a prime effort. There have been extraordinary efforts to destroy faith, morals, and authority from within the Church in recent decades. Yet Lenin's own despair is expressed in his words: "I hope we will be hanged on a stinking rope. And I did not lose the hope that this would happen, because we cannot condemn this dirty bureaucracy. If this happens, it will be well done."

Lenin died in 1924. After Lenin's death, a deep rivalry arose between the two leading Communists, Stalin and Trotsky. Trotsky had been a co-leader with Lenin in the "October Revolution" of 1917 at the same time that Our lady of Fatima was calling for a spiritual reovlution in—or rather renewal of—faith and morals. Stalin had Trotsky exiled, and finally assassinated on August 26, 1940. The act was organized, directed, and carried out by the Soviet secret police from American soil.

Leon Trotsky was a great collector of pronographic pictures already at the age of eight. Pornography was not then on most of the newsstands as today in the permissive United States of America, and an eight-year-old boy filled with lust was hardly an ordinary situation. It is interesting that Stalin first wrote under the pseudonym of "Demonoshvili." Translated from the Georgian language, this means something like "the Demoniac." He also wrote under "Besoshvili," which means "the Devilish."

Bukharin was the Secretary General of the Communist International, and an important Marxist. He read the last book of the Bible at age twelve and wanted to be Antichrist—so much so, that he wanted his own mother to say that she had been a harlot, so that he could fit the Apocalyptic description of Antichrist. It was this Communist leader who described Stalin as "not a man, but a devil." Bukharin became a victim of the diabolic system he had helped create and which killed millions. He himself was arrested and executed.

Mao-Tse-Tung, the great Chinese Communist leader who took over China with the murder of missions, wrote: "From the age of eight I hated Confucius. In our village there was a Confucianist temple. With all my heart, I wished only one thing: to destroy it to its very foundations." It is strange that a small child would have such a passionate hatred for his religion.

Communists have sought to destroy all religions, and especially Christianity; the clergy of all Christian faiths have been persecuted. But Communists have not stopped with closing churches and persecuting believers; rather, they have often shown a violent hatred for God. Catholic clergy have been forced to offer the Sacrifice of the Mass in circumstances and in disgusting surroundings that can only suggest demonic influences. It appears that Satan recognizes the Real Presence of Jesus Christ in the Catholic Holy Eucharist. Some of the perversions of religious rites forced upon Christians are almost too terrible to put into print. Such Satanic orgies have been carried out during Communist persecutions.

Baptism is another sacrament the Communists hate. Children in many Communist countries must be baptized secretly, and parents risk persecution if they are discovered. Both Catholic and Protestant pastors have been arrested for baptizing people. Catholics believe Baptism washes all sin from the soul, and the one baptized becomes a temple of the Holy Spirit. He then shares in the life of God, called grace. Is it not strange that Communists, to whom baptism supposedly means nothing, would have such a hatred for this sacrament?

Satanism, however, is not confined to Communist countries. Thousands on our own continent have substituted Satan for Almightly God. Satanists actually go through rituals of worship which are almost unimaginable to a Christian with a clean heart. In Satanism, darkness replaces light. Hate replaces love. Young people are often lured into Satan through the use of sex and drugs, or through the use of ouiji boards. By the end of the 1970's, popular hit songs of youth in the United States were glorifying Satan in the very lyrics of crude music. Satanists admit, however, that they can have no effect over Christians who sincerely believe and practice their holy faith in love.

Reports of Satanism have been widespread in the United States of America. A former Satanic priest, who found his way back to Christ years ago, wrote a letter to the bishops in the United States begging them not to approve of Communion in the hand because this would make it easier for members of Satanic cults to obtain consecrated Hosts from Catholic churches for desecration in devilish worship. Satanists are careful to obtain consecrated Hosts from *Catholic* churches. If there is a lessening of faith among some Catholics today in the Real Presence of the Body, Blood, Soul and Divinty of Jesus Christ in the Holy Eucharist, this is not true of Satanists.

Someone put into the hands of the author of this book the *Satanic Bible*. This 272-page book by Anton Szandor LaVey is all too real. It deals with Satanic worship which brings spiritual death to souls. LaVey has been called "the Black Pope" by many of his followers. He considers himself a high priest of the church of Satan. He seriously sees the need for a church that would recapture man's body and his carnal desires as objects of celebration. He encourages worship of fleshy things, impure desires and actions.

Also in circulation are pornographic literature and pictures displaying our Crucified Saviour, the Blessed Virgin Mary, the Little Flower, and the Vicar of Jesus Christ in highly immoral poses—almost enough to make one's heart stand still. There are pictures and descriptions of sexual orgies, and addresses for actual experiences. Such are sold on the newsstands in our cities. In the third degree initiation into Satanism one takes this oath' "I will do always *only what I will*." In the seventh degree, one swears: "Nothing is true and everything is permitted." The permissiveness which dominates American society must be very pleasing to Satan.

I have devoted these two chapters to stimulating readers to awareness of the grave situation in the world as the prophecies of Our Lady of Fatima are being more and more fulfilled. Russia plays a crucial role in the future of the world, and her errors are enslaving and corrupting more and more people. Yet many do not recognize the fulfillment of Our Lady's words. The story of Fatima does not end with the deaths of Jacinta and Francisco and with the retirement of Lucia to a convent. Rather, it is the story of the world's history in these our times—a great drama of Heaven versus Hell. But we know we are not helpless against the evil in our own lives and in the world. Immaculate Mary is even now doing battle against sin and the devil. As powerful as the devil is, the All-holy God is much more powerful—infinitely more powerful—and Satan is terrified of Our Lady.

As clever as he is, the devil must be taking great pains to discourage and distract Christians from their daily duties, from prayer, and from sacrifices of reparation. He knows that the evil monster of Communism—which is such a great tool for the damnation of souls—could be utterly destroyed with the spiritual weapons Our Lady has given us. Let us be wise enough to use them, as Satan is so vigilant in working to seduce souls. The "little ones" of Our Lady, who resond to her plea for prayer, penance, reparation—as Jacinta and Francisco did so generously—can move mountains through their faith, love, and humility, and through the intercession of the Immaculate Heart of Mary.

15.
The Triumph of the
Immaculate Heart of Mary

The first two parts of the Fatima secret are the vision of Hell, and the devotion to the Immaculate Heart of Mary. We recall again Our Lady's words immediately after the terrifying vision:

You have seen Hell where the souls of poor sinners go. To save them, God wishes to establish in the world devotion to my Immaculate Heart. If what I say to you is done, many souls will be saved and there will be peace. The war is going to end; but if people do not cease offending God, a worse one will break out during the pontificate of Pius XI. When you see a night illumined by an unknown light, know that this is the great sign given you by God that He is about to punish the world for its crimes, by means of war, famine, and persecutions of the Church and of the Holy Father.

To prevent this, I shall come to ask for the consecration of Russia to my Immaculate Heart, and the communion of Reparation on the First Saturdays. If my requests are heeded, Russia will be converted, and there will be peace; if not, she will spread her error throughout the world, causing wars and persecutions of the Church. The good will be martyred, the Holy

Father will have much to suffer, various nations will be annihilated. In the end, my Immaculate Heart will triumph. The Holy Father will consecrate Russia to me, and she will be converted, and a period will be granted to the world.

Note well what Our Lady said: "If my wishes are fulfilled, Russia will be converted and there will be peace. If not . . ." We should ask, "What wishes?" Obviously, the consecration of Russia and the First Saturdays.

On December 10 of 1925 the Mother of God appeared to Sister Lucia in her convent at Pontevedra, Spain. The Child Jesus was by her side and they were elevated on a cloud of light. In one hand Our Lady held a heart surrounded by sharp thorns. The Child Jesus spoke first: "Have pity on the Heart of your Most Holy Mother. It is covered with the thorns with which ungrateful men pierce it at every moment, and there is no one to remove them with an act of reparation."

It was then that Our Lady spoke, saying,

My daughter, look at my Heart surrounded with thorns with which ungrateful men pierce it at every moment by their blasphemies and ingratitude. You, at least, try to console me, and say that I promise to assist at the hour of death, with all the graces necessary for salvation, all those who, on the first Saturday of five consecutive months, go to confession and receive Holy Communion, recite five decades of the Rosary and keep me company for a quarter of an hour while meditating on the mysteries of the Rosary, with the intention of making reparation to me.

The importance of the First Saturday devotion in reparation to the Immaculate Heart of Mary cannot be overlooked. Our Lord Himself came to introduce this devotion. His Mother then announced it, while exposing her Sorrowful and Immaculate Heart.

The Child Jesus returned to Sister Lucia—this time alone—on February 15 of 1926, and asked if the devotion had been propagated. His appearance as a child rather than as an adult in these two apparitions has special meaning. It suggests the disposition which we should have in carrying out this devotion, that is, the attitude of a child in relation to his mother.

In response to His question, Sister Lucia told the Child Jesus of the difficulties which the confessor pointed out. Although the Mother Superior strongly desired to propagate the devotion, the confessor warned her that she could do nothing by herself alone. Our Divine Lord answered, "It is true that your superior alone can do nothing, but with My grace she can do all."

Then Sister Lucia spoke of the difficulty which some people had in confessing on First Saturday, and she asked if they might be allowed eight days in which to fulfill this part of Our Lady's request. Jesus replied, "Yes, even more time still, as long as they receive Me in the state of grace and have the intention of making reparation to the Immaculate Heart of Mary."

When Sister Lucia asked, "My Jesus, what about those who forget to make this intention?" Jesus answered, "They can do so at their next Confession, taking advantage of their first opportunity to go to Confession."

Sister Lucia tells us that on May 29-30, 1930, during that night, Our Lord informed her of the reason for *five* First Saturdays, rather than some other number, like *nine* for the nine First Fridays, or *seven* for the Seven Sorrows. Our Lord said:

> My daughter, the motive is simple. There are five kinds of offenses and blasphemies uttered against the Immaculate Heart of Mary: 1) Blasphemies against the Immaculate Conception. 2) Blasphemies against her virginity. 3) Blasphemies against her divine maternity and at the same time refusal to recognize her as Mother of men. 4) Blasphemies of those who openly seek to foster in the hearts of children indifference or contempt and even hatred for this Immaculate Mother. 5) The offenses of those who directly outrage her in her holy images.
>
> Here then, my daughter, is the reason why the Immaculate Heart of Mary has inspired Me to ask this small reparation, the effect of which will be that I will show compassion by forgiving those souls who have had the misfortune to offend her. As for you, strive without ceasing by your prayers and sacrifices to move Me to compassion toward these poor souls.

In studying these words, we should also think back to what Our Lady announced on July 13 of 1917. At that time she predicted that she would come requesting the consecration of Russia and the First Saturday Communions of Reparation, and this for the conversion of Russia and for peace. Thus the primary reason for the Communions of Reparation on the five First Saturdays concerns the whole world. However, through the power of her intercession, Our Lady also promised a bonus for those who make the five First Saturdays. She promised her assistance at the hour of death with all the graces necessary for salvation.

Sister Lucia wrote to her mother about this devotion. She spoke of the pain existing in her mother's heart at being separated from her daughter, and she advised her mother to offer the pain in reparation. Then she spoke directly of her great concern:

I would appreciate it also if you would give me the consolation of embracing a devotion that I know God is pleased with and that has been asked by our lovely Heavenly Mother. As soon as I knew it, I decided to embrace it and to do my best so that all other people may embrace it as well. Therefore I hope that you will answer me saying you are practicing it and doing your best so that all those people coming to your house may embrace it too. You could never give me a greater consolation than this.

To restore the right order between themselves and their Heavenly Mother, and ultimately between themselves and God the Father, the wayward offspring must repair their damaged relationship by reparation. Heaven has told us specifically how to do so. If not all, at least a representative number can work to restore the proper relationship by making reparation, especially on First Saturdays.

In practicing the First Saturday reparation, one takes into account Heaven, Hell, and the salvation of other souls as well as of oneself. One's vision even becomes worldwide as he performs sacrifices for the conversion of Russia. In making the First Saturdays one sacrifices for those who are persecuted for their Faith, those who are at war or in danger of war, and for the Holy Father who suffers because of all these sins.

What is more, learning to meditate on the Mysteries of the Rosary will bring us to the very heart of the word of God, for these mysteries review the chief events of our salvation. In fulfilling the five First Saturday requests we are also incorporated more fully into the sacramental life of the Church.

It is important to remember that all the elements of the five First Saturdays are to be performed with the intention of *reparation*: Confession, Holy Communion, and praying the Rosary while meditating on the Mysteries for fifteen minutes. Notice that Our Lord instructed Sister Lucia that those who went to Communion but forgot about the spirit of reparation could take advantage of their first opportunity to go to Confession, at which time they could make the intention of reparation to the Immaculate Heart of Mary. Parents should assist younger members of the family in remembering to form the intention of reparation regarding each element of the First Saturday devotion.

On more than one occasion it has been the author's privilege to interview Bishop Venancio, formerly Bishop of Leiria-Fatima, while he was International President of the Blue Army of Our Lady of Fatima. I asked him about First Saturdays. "Are the five First Saturdays officially approved by the Church?"

The Bishop answered: "The First Saturdays have been approved by the Church for centuries. The *five* First Saturdays began with the appearance of Our lady and the Christ Child at Pontevedra, December 10, 1925. This was approved by the competent Bishop, the Bishop of the Diocese of Leiria-Fatima.''

"In other words, the Pope has not approved of the *five* First Saturdays?''

"No. But *implicit* papal approval was given by Pope Paul VI by coming to Fatima in 1967 and presenting Sister Lucia to the world, which said that he stands behind what she represents.''

Bishop Venancio pointed out how on the occasion of his visit and pilgrimage to Fatima the Pope had called the Carmelite nun out from her convent at Coimbra; with millions of people before him, including three thousand journalists from all over the world, and with the television cameras of the world aimed at both, the Pope led Sister Lucia of the Immaculate Heart forth and with a gesture of the hand presented her to the world. This was saying: What she stands for, I stand behind.

I next asked Bishop Venancio, "May a bishop any place in the world promulgate in his own diocese the *five* First Saturdays since the Pope has not *explicitly* done so?'' He answered: "It is not yet opportune for the Pope to propagate it [explicitly] for the whole world, it appears. . . . Any Bishop in the world can propagate the five First Saturdays if he wants to do so.''

There has been a question regarding the conditions for fulfilment of the First Saturday requests, and so I quizzed the Bishop on a point that has been much discussed: Is the fifteen-minute meditation on the Mysteries of the Rosary to be done *in addition* to the meditation one does while praying the Rosary?

Some have held that Mary requested an *extra* fifteen-minute meditation. They have interpreted this as meaning that Our Lady dfeinitely wants us to get into the habit of meditation. Because of the discussions that have taken place on this point, in the presence of a national meeting of Fatima leaders, I questioned Bishop Venancio most carefully several times.

The Bishop answered:

> The *first* Bishop of Fatima said we can say the Rosary, the five decades, meditating at the same time. I myself meditate on a Mystery five minutes. That is, in a quarter of an hour I have meditated on three Mysteries. I then continue meditating on more Mysteries, one or two, so that I have meditated for perhaps a half hour. But the first bishop said that one can pray the decades and meditate on the Mysteries together to fulfill the conditions.

At this point, the audience was not satisfied that Bishop Venancio had answered my question sufficiently, and so he was questioned again. "May we feel secure spending fifteen minutes praying the Hail Marys and meditating on the Mysteries of the Rosary *at the same time* and thus fulfill the conditions for First Saturdays?'' The bishop answered: ''According to the first Bishop of Fatima, *that is sufficient.*''

The questioning continued: ''We realize that our question is not about the *ideal* way, that is, an additional fifteen minutes after the Rosary is completed, but we desire answers for practical questions which may come up.'' Bishop Venancio answered: ''According to the first Bishop of Fatima, that would be sufficient—fifteen minutes of meditating and the Hail Marys together.''

In addition to the First Saturday devotion, Our Lady asked for the consecration of Russia to her Immaculate Heart by the Pope united with all the Bishops. Sister Lucia's many letters state firmly that the First Saturday reparation is firmly linked with the consecration of Russia to her Heart; the two are joined as a unit.

On June 13, of 1929, the Blessed Mother spoke to Lucia. Lucia describes the apparition:

I had sought and obtained permission from my superiors and confessor to make a Holy Hour from eleven o'clock until midnight, every Thursday to Friday night. Being alone one night, I knelt near the altar rails in the middle of the chapel and, prostrate, I prayed the prayers of the Angel. Feeling tired, I then stood up and continued to say the prayers with my arms in the form of a Cross. The only light was that of the sanctuary lamp. Suddenly the whole chapel was illumined by a supernatural light, and above the altar appeared a Cross of light, reaching to the ceiling. In a brighter light on the upper part of the Cross, could be seen the face of a man and his body as far as the waist; upon his breast was a dove of light; nailed to the Cross was the body of another man. A little below the waist, I could see a chalice and a large Host suspended in the air, onto which drops of blood were falling from the Face of Jesus Crucified and from the wound in His side. These drops ran down onto the Host and fell into the chalice. Beneath the right arm of the Cross was Our Lady and in her hand was her Immaculate Heart. (It was Our Lady of Fatima, with her Immaculate Heart in her left hand, without sword or roses, but with a crown of thorns and flames.) Under the left arm of the Cross, large letters, as if of crystal clear water which ran down upon the altar, formed these words: ''Grace and Mercy.''

I understood that it was the Mystery of the Most Holy Trinity which was shown to me, and I received lights about this mystery which I am not permitted to reveal.

Our Lady then said to me:

''The moment has come in which God asks the Holy Father, in union with all the Bishops of the world, to make the consecration of Russia to my Immaculate Heart, promising to save it by this means. There are so many souls whom the Justice of God condemns for sins committed against me, that I have come to ask reparation: sacrifice yourself for this intention and pray.''

I gave an account of this to the confessor, who ordered me to write down what Our Lady wanted done.

Later, in an intimate communication, Our Lord complained to me saying:

''They did not wish to heed My request. Like the King of France, they will repent and do it, but it will be late. Russia will have already spread her errors throughout the world, provoking wars, and persecutions of the Church; the Holy Father will have much to suffer.''

Do we want peace? Do we want to save the souls of poor sinners who would otherwise go to Hell? Do we desire to save the world from punishment by means of war, hunger, and persecution of the Church and the Holy Father? Do we want the conversion of Russia? *Then we must make the First Saturdays* in reparation to Mary's Heart. Most certainly we all want the bonus, the graces necessary for our own salvation at the hour of death. But let us not focus only on that.

If a person, as an individual, can merit through this devotion the conversion of a sinner, then cannot the Church earn the graces for the conversion of an entire nation? It is fair to assume that the Church, as the body of Christ and united with Him as its Head, possesses a far greater potential of conversion by means of this devotion than any one of its members can exercise. For whatever power the Church exercises in her members as individuals, she possesses in a far superior way and to a higher degree as the Mystical Body of Christ. This is why it is desired that more and more bishops will promulgate the First Saturday devotions.

The members of the Christian community must serve and honor their Mother and must offer Eucharistic reparation to the Most Blessed Trinity before they can receive and deserve the great gifts of peace and of unity in one Faith. Our good and heavenly Mother has been calling us back to her Son through the First Saturdays, but even Catholics have largely ignored her requests.

That the Mother of the Church desires the return of individuals and nations we know without a doubt. To secure this end she has offered us a sure means, simple to perform and demanding very little of us. The demands are faith, love, reparation as expressed in the devotions of the First Saturdays. Her Heart must be served; her Heart leads us to the Divine Heart.

Regarding Sister Lucia's letter to her confessor written shortly after Our Lady appeared in 1929 to ask for the consecration of Russia, Father Alonso wrote:

> We knew already that in July, 1917, the relation between Russia and the Immaculate Heart of Mary concerned not only consecration but also devotion of reparation. What is now explicitly indicated in this document [Lucia's letter] is this: the devotion of reparation has not only the purpose of conversion of Russia but the avoidance of the evils which result from her non-conversion. We see therefore that logically the practice of this devotion is the means for obtaining the conversion of Russia through the consecration of Russia.

If we study carefully what Sister Lucia has been saying and what Our Lady has been telling her, it is this: We cannot have the end without the means. The end is peace, an end of persecution of the Holy Father and the Church, the triumph of the Hearts of Jesus and Mary. The means are the First Saturday reparation to Our Lady's Heart by a sufficient number of people, and the consecration of Russia.

When the Virgin Mary first appeared in 1917, she had already experienced the loss of many spiritual children. She knew very well that their numbers would increase greatly throughout the remainder of the century. She must have foreseen that very shortly, merely a few weeks after the Miracle of the Sun on October 13, 1917, Russia would be taken over by atheistic Communism. Could she not also foresee that the atheistic government of Russia would move many other nations to follow its example in departing from the Mother whom God has given to be our life, our sweetness, and our hope? Many nations have fallen under the hammer and sickle. Let no one be deceived; the Communist control of Poland, Hungary, etc. is master-minded from Moscow, as have been the Communist efforts in Portugal.

When enough loyal sons and daughters of Mary have truly served her Heart through the Communion of reparation on First Saturdays, they can win the return of other children to that sorrowing Mother's Heart. These in turn will pray for the grace of the conversion of Russia, and then, of course, for the conversion of all the other nations that have been seduced by Russia's errors. Only by such a change in that country can the chains of slavery of many other nations be broken.

In the 1930's Sister Lucia desired to reach the Holy Father with the message that the time had arrived for him, *in union with all the Bishops of the world,* to consecrate Russia to the Immaculate Heart of Mary.

The official historian of the Fatima documents, Father Joaquin Maria

Alonso, C.M.F., reported that even after Pope Pius XII had seemingly honored Our Lady's request by consecrating the world (1942) and then Russia (1952) to Mary's Immaculate Heart, Sister Lucia stated in a letter that she was grieved because the consecration of Russia had not yet been carried out as Our Lady had asked on June 13, 1929.

Repeatedly through the years Sister Lucia has written that the Holy Father—not alone, but in union with "all the Bishops of the world"—was to consecrate Russia to the Immaculate Heart. She has said that the Pope could order all the Bishops to do so. She wrote this from Tuy, Spain, on May 29, 1930, and again on June 12, 1930, in answer to six questions put to her by the Reverend Father José Bernardo Gonzalves.

In May of 1936, Sister Lucia wrote the following concerning the consecration of Russia: "Intimately I have spoken to Our Lord about the subject, and not too long ago I asked Him why He would not convert Russia without the Holy Father making that consecration." Sister Lucia said that Our Lord answered her this way: "Because I want My whole Church to acknowledge that consecration is a triumph of the Immaculate Heart of Mary, so that it may extend its cult later on, and put the devotion to this Immaculate Heart beside the devotion to My Sacred Heart." Lucia continued, "But my God, the Holy Father probably won't believe me, unless You Yourself move him with a special inspiration." Jesus answered, "The Holy Father. Pray very much for the Holy Father. He will do it, but it will be very late. Nevertheless the Immaculate Heart of Mary will save Russia. It has been entrusted to her."

In autumn of 1940, Sister Lucia was asked by her director as well as by the Bishop of Gurza to write a letter to the Pope, Pius XII. First a copy was sent to the Bishop of Leiria-Fatima, who asked Lucia to modify it somewhat. The Bishop sketched a better beginning and conclusion to her letter; Sister Lucia's first draft had not mentioned herself as "the only survivor of the children to whom Our Lady appeared in Fatima." The Bishop asked her to include the thoughts we find in the first two paragraphs and in the last paragraph.

In reading this letter, note how Sister Lucia has always requested not simply that *the Pope* consecrate Russia, but that it be done *in union with all the Bishops of the world*. Her letter to the Pope from Tuy, Spain, December 2, 1940 follows:

> Most Holy Father,
> Humbly prostrated at your feet, I come as the last sheep of the fold entrusted to you to open my heart, by order of my spiritual director.
> I am the only survivor of the children to whom Our Lady appeared

in Fatima (Portugal) from the 13th of May to the 13th of October 1917. The Blessed Virgin has granted me many graces the greatest of all being my admission to the Institute of Saint Dorothy.

I come, Most Holy Father, to renew a request that has already been brought to you several times. The request, Most Holy Father, is from Our Lord and our good Mother in Heaven.

In 1917, in the portion of the apparition that we have designated "the secret," the Blessed Virgin revealed the end of the war that was then afflicting Europe, and predicted another forthcoming, saying that to prevent it she would come and ask the consecration of Russia to her Immaculate Heart as well as the Commuinon of reparation on the First Saturday. She promised peace and the conversion of that nation if her request was attended to. She announced that otherwise this nation would spread her errors throughout the world, and there would be wars, persecutions of the Holy Church, martyrdom for many Christians, several persecutions and sufferings reserved for Your Holiness, and the annihilation of several nations.

Most Holy Father, this remained a secret until 1926 according to the express will of Our Lady. Then, in a revelation she asked that the Communion of reparation on the First Saturdays of the five consecutive months be propagated throughout the world, with its conditions of doing the following with the same purpose: going to Confession, meditating for a quarter of an hour on the Mysteries of the Rosary and saying the Rosary with the aim of making reparation for the insults, sacrileges, and indifferences committed against her Immaculate Heart. Our good Heavenly Mother promises to assist the persons who will practice this devotion, in the hour of their death, with all the necessary graces for their salvation. I exposed the request of Our Lady to my confessor, who tried to have it fulfilled, but only on the 13th of September, 1939, did His Excellency the Bishop of Leiria make public in Fatima this request of Our Lady.

I take this opportunity, Most Holy Father, to ask you to bless and extend this devotion to the whole world. In 1929, through another apparition, Our Lady asked for the consecration of Russia to her Immaculate heart, promising its conversion through the means and the hindering of the propagation of its errors.

Sometime afterwards I told my confessor of the request of Our Lady. he tried to fulfill it by making it known to Pius XI. In several intimate communications Our Lord has not stopped insisting on this request, promising lately to shorten the days of tribulation by which He has determined to punish the nations for their crimes, through war, famine, and several persecutions of the Holy Church and Your Holiness, if you will consecrate the world to the Immaculate Heart of Mary, with a special mention for Russia, and order that all the Bishops of the world do the same in union with Your Holiness. I truly feel your suffering, Most Holy Father!

And, as much as I can through my humble prayer and sacrifices, I try
to lessen them close to Our Lord and the Immaculate Heart of Mary.

Most Holy Father, if in the union of my soul with God I have not been
deceived, Our Lord promises a special protection to our country in this
war, due to the consecration of the nation, by the Portuguese Prelates,
to the Immaculate Heart of Mary, as proof of the graces that would have
been granted to other nations, had they also consecrated themselves to her.

Now, Most Holy Father, allow me to make one more request, which
is but an ardent wish of my humble heart, that the feast in honor of the
Immaculate Heart of Mary be extended throughout the whole world as
one of the main feasts of the Holy Church.

With deepest respect and reverence I ask for the Apostolic Blessing.
May God protect Your Holiness.

Maria Lucia de Jesus

It is to be noted that although Pope Pius XII consecrated Russia, and
then some years later, the world, to Our Lady's Immaculate Heart, and
although Pope Paul VI repeated the consecrations on November 21, 1964
in the presence of the Vatican Council Fathers, Sister Lucia did not believe
that Our Lady's request had been fulfilled at those times. Father Alonso
held the same view.

In their last official *ad limina* visit with Pope Paul VI the Polish Bishops
requested that the Pope carry out the collegial consecration of Russia to the
Immaculate Heart of Mary. The then Karol Cardinal Wojtyla, who now occupies the Chair of Peter, was among those requesting the consecration of
Russia not simply by the Pope alone as Pope Pius XII, John XXIII, and
Paul VI had all done, but rather "In union with all the Bishops of the world."
This request has now been granted, as we shall see in the last chapter. It
will then be obvious to the world that the conversion of Russia will be the
fruit of Divine intervention achieved within the Communion of Saints by
the prayers and sacrifices of Mary's children upon earth as she has interceded
with her Son in Heaven following the collegial consecration.

At the same time, both priests and lay people can spread the devotion
to the Immaculate Heart, especially through the First Saturdays, and it can
become officially propagated by Bishops, as has already happened in individual dioceses. When Heaven sees enough response to Our Lady's call,
we will see the fulfillment of her great promise: "In the end my Immaculate
Heart will triumph. The Holy Father will consecrate Russia to me, and she
will be converted, and a period of peace will be granted to the world."

16.
Portugal, Sign of Hope

Our Lady promised; "In Portugal the dogma of Faith will always be preserved." Though it is to Portugal that she extended this special protection, we can be sure that Our Mother's great desire is to see the Faith preserved and strengthened in every country of the world, and to grant her promised period of peace to the whole world as speedily as possible. However, from the very first, there was official opposition to the spread of devotion to Our Lady of Fatima. The atheistic government of Portugal spoke of "this despicable reactionary superstition." Lengthy documents could be quoted to reveal the climate of the early years in Portugal after the initial Fatima events. Only a few are related here, in order to give the reader some idea. Events of more recent years in Portugal reveal that the forces of evil, atheism itself, have never rested even in Our Lady's land.

In Lisbon about the middle of April, 1920, a strong effort to discredit Fatima erupted. It was learned that a large pilgrimage accompanying the new commemorative statue was being organized in Torres Novas for Ascension Day. People were going in hundreds by car from Lisbon; even more were traveling on horseback and on foot. Many priests were to take part in the procession, and great numbers of children were to come dressed as angels. The parade was to be the answer of the faithful to those who attempted to suppress devotion to God's Mother.

However, the government had different ideas. A letter of April 24, 1920 to Arthur Santos, the Mayor of Vila Nova de Ourem, from the Secretary of the Interior reads as follows:

> Through our mutual friend, Senhor de Sousa, it has come to our knowledge that reactionary elements in your county are preparing to canonize the deceased seer of Fatima [Jacinta, who had died on February 20] and so continue the disgusting religious exploitation of the people which has been set in motion. We beg you, therefore, to inform us as to what stage these manouevres have reached in order that we, the government, and your good self may take such precautions as seem advisable to neutralize this shameless Jesuitical trick.

The Mayor of Vila Nova de Ourem agreed. ''Not a soul shall get in there; they can't do anything against brute force!''

On May 7th, the mayor sent instructions to his regedors: ''By order of H.E. Minister Interior, Fatima repetition arranged for 13th inst. to be prevented. Kindly supply at once names, organizers and propagandists in your district in order that law may be applied in case of disobedience.'' The popularity of the pilgrimages on the 13th of the month caused the Mayor to suspect that his orders might not be fulfilled with much concern. Some of the government functionaries also believed in Fatima. Arthur Santos thought he had better ask for troops from Santarem. He received this reply from the Civil Governor: ''Armed Municipal Guard will be placed at your disposal, occupy strategic points, prevent transit Fatima procession.''

In his book entitled *Os Episódios Maravilhosos de Fátima* (1921), Dr. Formigão relates what happened as a result of these careful arrangements to keep the people from manifesting their love to God's Mother at the spot where she had chosen to appear.

> I arrived at Vila Nova de Ourem early in the morning on 13th May last. It was pouring with rain, and a thunderstorm was in progress at the same time.
>
> When I left Lisbon there were alarming rumors about Fatima, and people said that it was useless to attempt to get here because there were official orders to prevent transit through Vila Nova de Ourem. . . .
>
> Very early in the morning we heard a troop of horses passing, and ran to the window where we saw a squadron of cavalry of the Republican Guard which was proceeding at a gallop in the direction of Fatima. The rumors were not, then, without foundation. . . . A general offensive seemed to be in progress, but against what, in the name of God! No one knew.

. . . One thing was certain; from Ourem no one could go to Fatima. . . .

In Tomar, it seemed, the same prohibition was in force, also in several other districts whose authorities had forbidden the departure of vehicles. . . . People were being allowed to go as far as Fatima but no further. . . . The rain stopped and I went out into the road where I watched the passage of carts and cars, lorries, footfolk and horsemen—a regular excursion!

I wondered to what purpose all the prohibitions had been. I had expected to see nobody and yet here was this constant stream of men, women and children.

There were huge charabancs drawn by mules, filled with people roaring with laughter, laughing apparently at the Mayor whom I could see in the middle of the road looking uncomfortable in a straw hat with a forced smile on his lips. . . .

I heard Mass, lunched in great haste and set off. . . .

Coming the other way was a car traveling at speed in which I caught a glimpse of rifles, fanning out menacingly. It was the Mayor and his escort! "He's up to no good," observed a lad pedaling uphill on a bicycle. After climbing for an hour and a half we neared Fatima and the rain began to fall again. At last we entered the little square facing the church. Everywhere we saw carts, carriages and cars parked. A great crowd of people, numbering thousands, was blocking the square and the church. In the middle of the road a force of infantry and cavalry of the Republican Guard was preventing the people from passing and completing the remaining three kilometres which separate Fatima from the Cova. I asked some bystanders whether anyone had in fact passed. Until midday, I was told, everyone had gone through, but then the Mayor had arrived and forbidden it. I asked the commandant whether one might go through, but he informed me politely that he had allowed people to pass until the Mayor had given orders to the contrary. He was very sorry but he had to obey orders. . . . It was perfectly ridiculous, everyone agreed.

Many people tried to get through the fields without being seen, climbing walls and other obstacles, and managed to arrive at the place of the apparitions, counting themselves fortunate to kneel there and say the Rosary. Perhaps it was this which put the government in peril!

In addition to this government opposition, a Masonic pamphlet was circulated in Portugal addressed "To all Liberal Portuguese. Reaction let loose! The Assocation for Civil Registration and the Portuguese Federation of Free-thinkers energetically protest against the ridiculous comedy of Fatima." Among other things, the Masonic literature stated:

It is therefore our duty to demand from the public authorities the most energetic and immediate precautions against this shameless plan by which reaction seeks to plunge the people once more into medievalism. . . . Let professors in the schools and colleges educate their pupils in a rational manner, liberating them from religious preconceptions as from all others, and we shall have prepared a generation for the morrow, happier because more worthy of happiness.

Let us, then, liberate ourselves and cleanse our minds, not only from foolish beliefs in such gross and laughable tricks as Fatima but more especially from any credence in supernatural and pretended *Deus Omnipotente*, omniscient and omni-everything, instrument of subtle imaginations of rogues who wish to capture popular credulity for this purpose.

Citizens!   LONG LIVE THE REPUBLIC!
                                             DOWN WITH REACTION!
                                             LONG LIVE LIBERTY!

On May 13, 1931, all the Bishops of Portugal gathered at the Cova da Iria and consecrated their country to the Immaculate Heart of Mary. At least 300,000 Portuguese pilgrims were present on this occasion as the Cardinal Patriarch, Cardinal Cerejeira presided, assisted by the papal nuncio.

There was a strange light in the sky over Europe during the night of January 25-26 of 1938, and Sister Lucia interpreted it as the sign from God that He was about to punish the world for its sins by means of a war more terrible than the one suffered in 1914-1918. Sister Lucia had written to her confessor on February 6th, 1938, stating that she understood from God that the war was about to break out. Those who know the basic message of Fatima remember that such a terrible war was foretold by Our Lady on July 13, 1917 if mankind did not turn back to God in reparation. Sister Lucia said that God informed her that there would be a special protection of Portugal by the Immaculate Heart of Mary, due to the act of consecration made by Bishops in union with the faithful. The consecration, however, was not just the recitation of a formula but the *living* of it. The protection was also a reward for the prayers and penance of the thousands of Fatima pilgrims, many of whom walk a hundred or more miles to get to Fatima. Sister Lucia wrote in 1938:

> Our Lord also said to me: "Ask, insist again on the reparatory Communion in honor of the Immaculate Heart of Mary on the First Saturday being made public. The moment is approaching when the rigor of My justice will punish the crimes of several nations. Some will be annihilated. Finally, the rigors of My justice will fall most heavily on those who want to destroy My reign in souls."

September of 1939 saw Europe erupt into total conflict with the invasion of Poland by Nazi forces. Lucia's Bishop seemed to suffer some shock and was moved to action; the Bishop of Leiria suddenly changed from indecision to action. On the 13th of September, at the High Mass of the Fatima pilgrimage, he proclaimed and recommended the devotion of reparation requested by Our Lady of Fatima.

In a letter of December 1, 1940, Sister Lucia expressed appreciation at the consecration of all dioceses and parishes in Portugal to the Immaculate Heart of Mary, but added that many were not *living* it.

Sister Lucia also wrote to her spiritual director:

The proof that He [the Lord] gives us is the special protection of the Immaculate Heart over Portugal, due to its consecration to her. Those people whom you write to me about have a good reason to be afraid. All this would have happened to us, had our Bishops not paid attention to the requests of our good Lord, and prayed with all their heart for His mercy and the protection of the Immaculate Heart of Mary, our Blessed Heavenly Mother. But in our country there are still many crimes and sins, and since now is the hour of God's justice over the world, we need to keep on praying. For this reason I feel that it would be good to impress on people, as well as a great amount of confidence in the mercy of Our good Lord and in the protection of the Immaculate Heart of Mary, the need for prayer accompanied by sacrifice—especially that one needs to avoid sin. This request of our good Heavenly Mother since 1917 came with an inexplicable sadness and tenderness from her Immaculate heart: "Let them offend Our Lord God no more for He is already much offended."

It's a pity that we have not meditated enough on these words and measured their total reach. In the meantime don't forget, whenever you can, to take advantage of any occasions that you may have to renew our request to the Holy Father to see if we can shorten this moment. I feel sorry for the Holy Father and I pray a lot for His Holiness through my humble prayers and sacrifices.

In 1942 Sister Lucia wrote the following to the Bishop of Leiria-Fatima:

Your Lordship is not unaware of the fact that some years ago God manifested that sign which astronomers tried to describe by the name of aurora borealis. God made use of this to make me understand that His justice was ready to discharge the blow over guilty nations, for which reason I began to plead with insistence for the Communions of Reparation on the First Saturdays and for the consecration of Russia. My aim was not only to succeed in obtaining mercy and pardon for the whole world, but especially for Europe. God in His infinite mercy went on making me feel how this terrible moment was approaching, and Your Lordship is not unaware of the fact that on opportune occasions I kept pointing this out.

I say now, that the prayers and penance offered up in Portugal have not yet appeased the Divine Justice because they have not been accompanied by contrition and amendment. I hope that Jacinta will intercede for us all in Heaven.

Portugal was spared the horrors of World War II, though she had endured the sufferings of the global conflagration of 1914. Was there a connection between the Bishop's official call for First Saturday reparation and the peace which is nation enjoyed? Did his active support of Our Lady's "special" devotion and its spread in Portugal merit peace for that nation from the Queen of Peace? It is generally held by the Portuguese that their country was spared seeing World War II as a result of the bishops' consecration of their country to the Immaculate Heart of Mary. Sister Lucia has not hesitated to say so. In December of 1949, the foundation stone of the monument of the Sacred Heart which now towers on the bank of the Tagus, opposite Lisbon, was laid as a thanksgiving memorial for Portugal being preserved from World War II.

When I visited Portugal in 1974, the Communists had made great inroads in that country. Rumors had been spread all over Portugal that the Cova would be bombed that October 13th, and people had been warned to stay away. I noticed that the nearer we came to Fatima, the more posters there were of the hammer and sickle. Communist demonstrations with their red flags were obvious in Lisbon, and Communist-dominated soldiers stopped our buses, even aiming guns at some pilgrims. The evening of the 12th and 13th, I saw some of these very same uniformed soldiers crawling in penance on the penitential path in the Cova; they were in their late teens or early twenties.

In 1974-75, Portugal was very much in the news, as the Communists struggled to take over. Even at the time of the Fatima apparitions in 1917, it was already hoped that Lisbon would become a Communist capital for the world outside Moscow. During the years after the Fatima events, Communist cells worked undercover in Portugal—and they have not given up there yet. The vast farm lands of southern Portugal were collectivized during the 1974-75 revolution by the communists, throwing the country into greater economic disaster, for the collective farms produced poorly. Russia dumped millions of dollars into this revolution. The Communists temporarily took over the government of Portugal, seizing all public communications media. I am convinced that it was the renewed penance of the Portuguese people, who after the near-takeover again came to Fatima by the hundreds of thousands, which saved the country from a complete Communist victory. Miraculously, the communists seemed to lose complete domination shortly after the Bishops of Portugal renewed the consecration of their country at Fatima on May 13, 1975. Over a million people were present.

On September 18, 1977, the Patriarch of Lisbon Cardinal Cerejeira, spoke to the 8th Fatima Congress in the Sanctuary of Our Lady of Kevelaer:

> Actually, there is no real motive for discouragement or fear. In our most difficult moments, we have with us the certainty of victory, for "this is the victory which overcomes the world, our faith" (1 John 5:4). We have unshakeable confidence in the efficacious intercession of Mary Most Holy, demonstrated so clearly on countless occasions, to such a point that Christian piety could exclaim: "Never was it known that anyone who fled to thy protection, implored thy help, or sought thy intercession was left unaided."
>
> Of this there is the witness not only of the history of persons, but also the history of peoples. And here I could cite the concrete example of my own country. The protecting presence of the Mother of God has more than once been manifest in the destiny of Portugal. Only to allude to recent facts, I can say that it was the consecration made in Fatima to the Immaculate Heart of Mary by Portuguese Bishops in 1931 and in 1938, that defended Portugal from the Communist peril, then so close to her borders. It was the same consecration, renewed in 1940, that saved Portugal from the horror of the last world war, at a time when it was spreading death and destruction throughout so many countries in Europe. And, certainly, it was the great devotion of the Portuguese people to the Virgin Mary, ratified anew by the consecration effected by the Bishops in 1975, which halted the advance of atheistic Communism among us, when it had already seized control of many departments of our government and threatened to submerge the whole of the public and private life of the Portuguese people.

What the Cardinal Patriarch of Lisbon did not mention was the following curious fact: As the Bishops of Portugal renewed the consecration of Portugal on May 13, 1975, from the speakers booming out over the Cova da Iria a woman's voice was also heard, speaking the same words of consecration. No woman was near the microphones, but all clearly heard the feminine voice raised in union with Portugal's Bishops in that country which has experience what Cardinal Cerejeira in 1942 called "the foreshadowing of what the Immaculate Heart of Mary is preparing for the world!"

17.
Jacinta and Francisco Today
Including an Interview with Canon Galamba

Many Catholics today are hoping and praying that Jacinta and Francisco Marto will soon be beatified, and eventually canonized, as an example to the entire Church. God has already given many extraordinary graces through Jacinta's intercession. The Process for the Beatification of the Servant of God, Jacinta Marto, was sent to the Sacred Congregation in Rome on July 2, 1979. It was my privilege, just twenty-four days after the Diocese of Leiria-Fatima sent the Process to Rome, to meet and speak for a short time with Pope John Paul II and present to him a large picture of Jacinta. Later from the Vatican came a thank you letter as directed by the Holy Father.

If the Pope sees fit to beatify Jacinta, together with her brother, Francisco, this would not only be a consoling stimulus to holiness for the children of the whole world, but the message of Fatima would doubtlessly be reviewed in sharper focus. Then most Catholics who have heard of Fatima only superficially, as a story to entertain, would be challenged to meditate on the message, comprehending that the sad state of the present world was all foretold by Our Lady. Hopefully this would lead to a *living* of the message, for most do not yet *live* the message.

Francisco Marto was nearly eleven years old when he died on April 4, 1919. At his third appearance, the Angel had said to the three young shepherds: "Console your God." These words impressed Francisco deeply and thereafter guided his whole life. He wanted to be the "Consoler of Jesus." Francisco wanted to avoid sin and to influence others to avoid sin, so as to stop the sadness he saw it caused Jesus.

To console Jesus, as we have seen, Francisco would stay alone for long hours in church before the Most Blessed Sacrament, or hide himself in some lonely place while the children were herding sheep. Then he would pray. He fulfilled Our Lady's request that he say "many Rosaries." Shortly before he died, Francisco said, "In Heaven I shall give much consolation to Our Lord and Our Lady." God has already granted many graces through his intercession. The canonical Process for his Beatification was sent to the Holy See in Rome on August 3, 1979.

On July 31st of 1978, the Feast of St. Ignatius of Loyola, I was privileged to interview the Reverend (Canon Doctor) Joseph Galamba De Oliveira at the Seminary in Leiria, Portugal. This priest is sometimes called "Canon Galamba"; a *canon* theologian is an official of a diocesan chapter who helps the Bishop as the authority on dogmatic and moral theological problems and also helps in the administrative and pastoral fields. Those who have studied the *Memoirs* of Sister Lucia may remember her repeated mention of Canon Galamba, especially in the *Fourth Memoir*. Perhaps few have penetrated the message better than this good priest scholar, whose humility is seen in the preface to this book.

Canon Galamba, who was seventy-five years old at the time of the interview, remains very active in the field of Catholic education. In the following interview, the reader will note that the words in brackets have been added to complete certain sentences. Readers will also be mindful that although Canon Galamba speaks English well, it is not his native language.

Fox Canon Galamba, would you tell me what is your position on the Commission for the canonization of Jacinta?

G. Well, we are the front people in this commission, called the "Tribunal for the Beatification and Canonization of Jacinta." I was appointed as the President Judge for this tribunal. We have finished all the [diocesan] Process and we are now waiting for the opportunity to close the Process and to publish everything.

Fox Is the Process officially opened as far as the Holy See is concerned?

G. Yes! Yes, with all the directions of the Holy See and after it is closed [in the diocese], it will be sent to the Holy See in order to have the *Apostolic* Process.

Fox Have you gone to Rome recently in this regard?

G.   No. I had the intention of going just last month [June, 1978] for the first time in order to contact some people, but I could not because of the illness of Father Louis Kondor, the diocesan Postulator of the Process. We will go before December of 1978. [Fr. Kondor was later named international Vice Postulator.]

Fox   *Do you anticipate after your visit to the Vatican, that Jacinta will be declared Venerable?*

G.   Well, not the title "Venerable." Now the title is "Servant of God."

Fox   *Is that her official title now—"Servant of God?"*

G.   Yes, "Servant of God."

Fox   *Who gave Jacinta that title?*

G.   That's the regular title of people whose Process is made under the permit of the Holy See.

Fox   *And that title with the permit of the Holy See, "Servant of God"— that means that the Church has officially opened her cause and recognizes possibilities?*

G.   Yes. Yes, because if the Holy See doesn't recognize the possibility, she doesn't give the permit to open the Process—the diocesan Process.

Fox   *Do you anticipate Jacinta being beatified within a few years?*

G.   We don't know. You know that some saints, very big saints, must wait centuries to be canonized. You know, for instance, St. Robert Bellarmine and some others. We now have also some Processes that wait. We don't know why. When all of the Process will be in the hands of the people of the [Roman] Congregation, no difficulties should be encountered when they contact the real sanctity of Jacinta and Francisco, her brother. It is just not in our hands but in the hands of the congregation [of Rome].

Fox   *You are working for the beatification first of Jacinta not of Francisco?*

G.   No. No, we introduced the Processes together. "Together" means at the same time. But both [diocesan] Processes are finished now. When the Process of beatification will go to Rome, the Process of Francisco will go at the same time.

Fox   *Has Francisco been declared a Servant of God?*

G.   Yes, both of them. Both of them by the same reason because the Process of beatification could be introduced here by the permit of the Holy See, the diocesan Process, you know. It is now only the first time that the Process of their lives and their virtues has been made.

Fox   *Is Jacinta's cause progressing better than Francisco's?*

G.   I don't think so. We have all the testimonies presented by the Postulator. Then we have had the intention of going ahead with one, and the second one of Francisco's Process just as with Jacinta's Process. Both were finished at the same time.

Fox   *Could you summarize your thoughts when you saw that Jacinta's body was incorrupt the first time her body was exhumed in 1935 and later when you read the reply that Sister Lucia wrote in thanking the Bishop of Leiria, José Alves Correia da Silva, for the picture he had sent her of Jacinta's incorrupt body.*

G.   You know that not every incorruption of a body is a sign of sanctity. We have some bodies, incorrupt bodies, that belong to common people.

Fox   *Well yes, natural causes.*

G.   But as we could know the life of Jacinta, it was our impression that the cause of incorruption adds some sign of the supernatural. Do you understand me? But we must not give a big importance to this fact because Francisco, the brother, was perhaps a boy of as high virtues in the spirit of prayer and reparation as was Jacinta, but the body of Francisco was absolutely corrupt.

Fox   *But didn't Sister Lucia in her Memoirs indicate that Heaven had given Jacinta very special insights and she had a high decreee of virtue? Francisco too, of course, but does not Sister Lucia indicate that there was something very, very special about Jacinta?*

G.   Well, they were brother and sister but perhaps the vocation of each was not the same. Francisco had a special way of sanctity that was not the way of sanctity of Jacinta.

Fox   *You admit that there can be natural causes for incorruption, yet you seem to think that in Jacinta's case it was supernatural. Why do you think it was supernatural?*

G.   Well, it is my impression because of the knowledge we had before this of the virtues and sanctity of Jacinta. It was general knowledge before the manuscript of Sister Lucia, you know, because all the letters she wrote were after this. It was just a matter of a general impression of the sanctity of two people, Jacinta and Francisco, and their place in the apparitions.

Fox   *Would this indicate then that Jacinta had a greater degree of sanctity than Francisco because his body was corrupt while hers was not?*

G.   Not at all. No. The corruption of the body of Jacinta and Francisco is no influence in the sanctity, you know.

Fox   *After they exhumed her body in 1935 they showed only her face. Then it was exhumed again in 1951. They had relimed the body in 1935. In 1951 was the body still incorrupt?*

G.   The face was incorrupt as in the first time. One couldn't see the fingers the first time. The second time we could recognize that one finger was corrupt.

Fox   *The index finger?*

G.   I don't remember.

Fox   *You examined the body down to the waist.*

G.   Oh! No. No.

Fox   *How much?*

G.   No, because it was just to recognize that it was the body of Jacinta. That's the regular action we must make in the Process in the cause of identification. So after seeing that it was that, the body of Jacinta, we closed everything and we brought it to the Basilica where it is now.

Fox   *How much of the body did you look at? Just the head and hands?*

G.   Because the other parts of the body were with clothes.

Fox   *Will you open her coffin again? Will you be looking at her body in the future?*

G.   Now the Process is being sent to Rome and if the Congregation agrees, it will write to the Bishop to make the Apostolic Process. At that time we must recognize a second time officially the body of Jacinta and Francisco. We have the bones of Francisco in a special little box.

Fox   *Do you anticipate opening Jacinta's grave again then in the next year?*

G.   Not within the next year. We do not know when. Sometime, yes. Perhaps it will not be in my lifetime.

Fox   *Francisco's grave too?*

G.   Yes.

Fox   *But the causes of Jacinta and Francisco are separated?*

G.   Two [different] causes. yes.

Fox   *And you work at them individually?*

G.   Yes. We sit down to hear all the testimonies for one and then another. Everything is separated. For convenience sake we went ahead with both Processes at the same time. Rather than come twice, once for Jacinta and once for Francisco, it was easier to give your testimony on the same day or on the following day, than to come from your village or your city once for one and another time for the second one.

Fox   *If people are praying or beseeching the intercession of Jacinta or Francisco, it would seem for the sake of the causes, it is better to make their choice which one they are praying to. For instance, if one prays to both Jacinta and Francisco at the same time, and say, a miraculous cure takes place, then you don't know which one to attribute it to.*

G.   Well, I think that there is more devotion for Jacinta than for Francisco.

Fox   *Did you say that you have more devotion.*

G.   No, not myself but I think some people are at least praying more to Jacinta's than to Francisco's intercession. Can you understand?

Fox   *Yes, but I don't know why. Why?*

G.   Why? It is a special sympathy in devotion. For instance, I myself, I have more devotion for some canonized saints than for some others. There are many, many saints whose intercession I have never sought in my life.

Fox   *To change the subject, in 1938 Hitler was ready to conquer Spain and Portugal. At the same time the Bishops of Portugal were meeting here at Fatima. Do you recall what the Bishops' reactions were upon reading the first type-written manuscript which you wrote about Jacinta?*

G.   I think so. I think that the knowledge of special things about the apparitions and about the lives of Jacinta and Francisco was the reason why the Bishops sought the intercession fo the Immaculate Heart of Mary and made the consecration of Portugal in order to avoid the war and the dangers to our country here.

Fox   *Do you think that the Cardinals and the bishops of Portugal would have made the consecration of Portugal to the Immaculate Heart of Mary if the manuscript [on Jacinta] had not been read at their meeting and they had not known the details of the apparitions?*

G.   I think you are right. Really, if they were without this knowledge they perhaps would not have made the consecartion because my Bishop was in knowledge of some of the titles and petitions of Sister Lucia to the Holy Father for the consecration of the world to the Immaculate Heart of Mary, but not all the Bishops [had this knowledge]. It was just the knowledge of *my* Bishop because of the letters and the talks between him and Sister Lucia, and perhaps the consecration would not have been made in these conditions if they had not [had access to the manuscript about Jacinta].

Fox   *In other words, when you learned how Sister Lucia reacted to the picture taken of Jacinta's incorrupt face in 1935, you urged the first Bishop of Fatima to ask Sister Lucia to tell us more, to write more about Jacinta.*

G.   To tell "everything" she knows about Jacinta's life and sanctity.

Fox   *What moved you to do that?*

G.   Because of the words she [Sister Lucia] wrote in her letter to the Bishop telling him [what little she did] because of the picture he had sent to Sister Lucia. This made it known that many things of much impor-

tance were behind this knowledge [indicated by her brief remarks made
on the occasion of seeing the picture of the incorrupt face of Jacinta].
[It is the reason why] we are in touch in doing everything and it is
the reason why all the former manuscripts were asked by myself, you
know, and I asked the Bishop to tell Sister Lucia to write about this.

It [Sister Lucia's reaction to the picture] was the origin of all the
former manuscripts she wrote when all the story of the apparitions
[was told] and she wrote another about the life of Francisco too.

I think that Sister Lucia is not dreaming. She is very strict in things
she is writing and she wrote not very well and always when she is
writing [it is] just to obey. To the Bishop she tells us that it is very
difficult for her and she would like not to write about the apparitions.

Fox   *She wrote only under obedience. It was you who* pressured *the Bishop
to* command *Sister Lucia to always write more and more times. Why
do you think Sister Lucia was so reluctant to write? Why did Sister
Lucia find is so distasteful to write?*

G.   Well, in the mind of Sister Lucia was always the secret that they have
brought [received] from Our Lady. [It was] just between them [Our
Lady and the children] and you know a part of the secret was supernatural and [the secrecy was] asked by Our Lady but some other [parts]
just by the conversations between the three people [children]. Perhaps
[they thought] it's better not to tell anyone about the apparitions. It
was Jacinta who gave the knowledge of the apparitions but in the mind
of Lucia it was always these loving ways of having the secret about
everything.

Fox   *But as you indicated, Heaven first used Jacinta as the instrument
because she could not keep her mouth shut. That is how it got out
to the world. And then Jacinta said to Lucia before she died, "When
the time comes to make known about the devotion to the Immaculate
Heart of Mary, tell all the world." So it would seem that years after
Jacinta was dead, Heaven was still using Jacinta as an instrument
to get the message of these first two parts of the secret to the world,
because if her body had not been exhumed and the face found incorrupt and the picture sent to Lucia, there would not have been the demand that she write more ("everything"). So Jacinta was still doing
her work as an instrument of Heaven long after she was dead.*

G.   I understand and I agree with you that it was very small things in the
hands of God. [It was] just the way of making [known] all these revelations made by Sister Lucia to the world.

In 1980 a message came from Father Louis Kondor, S.V.D., presently the international Vice-Postulator of the Causes of Jacinta and Francisco stating:

> The Servants of God, Francisco and Jacinta Marto, the little seers of Fatima, have become ever more known, admired and invoked throughout the whole world for their exemplary practice of virtue, their deep interior lives, surrounded by the innocence and candour of their tender age.
>
> Faithfully fulfilling the message of Our Lady of the Rosary, the humble little shepherds of the Cova da Iria possess a charm and attraction for souls, and are more and more regarded as authentic models fo holiness. The Processes for their beatification were taken to Rome in 1979, and the Sacred Congregation is now more closely involved with the lives of Francisco and Jacinta.
>
> The faithful are requested to manifest their ardent desire of seeing the little shepherds of Fatima beatified, by requesting their enrollment in the League of Prayer and Sacrifice founded in 1963 for this purpose. The members' names, with complete address, will be registered in special books in the Vice-Postulation at Fatima, and forwarded in due time to Rome.
>
> The Vice-Postulation publishes a bulletin every two months, giving information regarding the Process of beatificaton of the little seers, and all that would promote particular veneration among the faithful towards the Servants of God. This bulletin is published in seven languages.
>
> Enrollment cards will be sent gratis to all those who request them. These cards are to be filled in simply by making a cross (X) in the respective places, together with full name and address, and then returned to:

> Vice Postulation of the Seers
> Apartado 6, P-2496
> Fatima, Portugal

18.
Collegial Consecration Takes Place

The Pope Speaks at Fatima, May 13, 1982

On May 13, 1982 the Collegial Consecration of Russia to the Immaculate Heart of Mary took place. Before leaving for Fatima, Pope John Paul II sent a letter to the Bishops of the world inviting them to join him in the act of consecration. Many conferences of Bishops throughout the world had requested the collegial consecration which pleased the Pope. Sister Lucia had waited for years for the collegial consecration. It was a condition required before Our Lady could keep her promise: "Russia will be converted and there will be peace." (July 13, 1917).

At first there was speculation whether in fact all the conditions of collegial consecration to include "especially Russia" had in fact taken place. A study of documents, including the Pope's letter to the world's bishops and the words of the Pope spoken in the Cova verify that the conditions were indeed met. Pope John Paul II in inviting the world's bishops to join him in his consecration at Fatima, May 13, 1982, made reference to the consecration of the world by Pius XII in 1942 and then of Russia in 1952.

The Pope called for a *collegial* consecration this time in reaffirming the acts of Pius XII. [At the publication of this book some have continued to question whether the conditions for the collegial consecration were in fact fulfilled. Cardinal Carberry and others influential in the Fatima Apostolate have continued to maintain that the conditions were fulfilled.]

In speaking in the Cova da Iria at Fatima the Pope said: "I am here, united with all the pastors of the Church in that particular bond where by we constitute a body and a college, just as Christ desired the Apostles to be in union with Peter. In the bond of this union, I utter the words of the present act, in which I wish to include, once more, the hopes and anxieties of the Church in the modern world."

In the 1917 apparitions Our Lady referred to Russia by name. Pope John Paul II on one occasion used the word "Russia" in the Cova. Cheers were heard arising from the people at the mention of "Russia."

In stating that he wished to renew the consecrations made by Pius XII, only now in a collegial manner, the Pope said: "The appeal of the Lady of the message of Fatima is so deeply rooted in the Gospel and the whole of Tradition that the Church feels that the message imposes a commitment on her. She has responded through the Servant of God, Pius XII (whose episcopal ordination took place precisely on 13 May 1917): he consecrated the human race and especially the peoples of Russia to the Immaculate Heart of Mary. Was not that consecration his response to the evangelical eloquence of the call of Fatima?"

I contacted John Cardinal Carberry on May 17, 1982 to discover his opinion as to whether the long-awaited collegial consecration had in fact taken place. Cardinal Carberry is the same well known Marian Bishop and Cardinal who at the 1981 November meeting of the Bishops of the United States proposed petitioning the Pope for the collegial consecration of Russia to the Immaculate Heart of Mary if the Pope deemed it proper. Cardinal Carberry said: "In my humble opinion the collegial consecration has now taken place."

John M. Haffert, who for many years has worked in the world-wide Fatima apostolate for the collegial consecration of Russia, after May 13, 1982, went to Coimbra to ask Sister Lucia herself if she felt the collegial consecration had now in fact been fulfilled. John was able to communicate with Sister Lucia through her superior. Sister Lucia answered "Yes," the collegial consecration had taken place. At the same time Sister Lucia mentioned that it was, however, late and by now communism had spread throughout the world. It would now be necessary for peoples to implement the consecration in their lives.

These words of reaction from Sister Lucia coincide with what she had written many years previously: "They will repent and do it, but it will be late. Russia will have already spread her errors throughout the world, provoking wars, and persecutions of the Church; the Holy Father will have much to suffer." It is significant that the Pope's pilgrimage to Fatima, May 13, 1982 coincided with a meeting in Moscow of about 480 leaders of various religions of the world for a religious peace conference in an appeal against nuclear arms. The fact that Communist Russia permitted religious leaders, including U.S. evangelist Billy Graham, to meet in its country, was in itself significant. Billy Graham who left Russia on May 13th as the Pope was in Fatima, found himself criticized for saying he found Soviet churches to be well-attended, and he saw more religious freedom than he expected. The country had been officially atheist for 65 years even though in its past history the most eloquent voices of Russian history have rung with a powerful note of faith and Russia was once known as "Holy Russia."

It was significant that on May 14, 1982, just two days after the collegial consecration, the AP Religious Writer, George W. Cornell, wrote for papers across the United States the following:

> While evidence has indicated Soviet government attempts to manipulate Russian church leaders, they nevertheless remain public symbols of a persisting faith among the people.
>
> It is a deep-rooted thing, a part of an engrained memory, of a Russian 'soul' that has pulsed through the works of Russian literary greats, of the 19th century Dostoevski and Tolstoy, of the contemporary Alexander Solzhenitsyn.
>
> He himself, now in U.S. exile, has maintained that Christianity's greatest strength, forged in fires of opposition, will eventually emerge in Russia when it is free. Even under present circumstances, recurrent reports indicate an increased turning faith.
>
> "Religious belief is growing amazingly, despite intensified atheist propaganda." says the Rev. Blahoslave Hruby, editor of a documentary journal, Religion in Communist Dominated Areas.
>
> Some experts on the situation have said that believing Christians in Russia outnumber Marxists.

The Russian Revolution that took place in 1917 put the communists in power. In May of that year Czar Nicholas II had abdicated under pressure from members of the national legislature and a provisional government was established. On November 7, the provisional government was overthrown and a communist government headed by Vladimir Ilyich Lenin took power, forming what remains to the present day the modern state of the Soviet Union.

Pope Paul VI had called Sister Lucia from her convent in Coimbra to the Cova da Iria when he went on pilgrimage to Fatima in 1967. Now again, in 1982 Sister Lucia came to Fatima to be present at the Mass with the Pope. It was reported that tears of joy were seen to run down Sister Lucia's face as Pope John Paul finished the consecration at the end of the three-hour Mass. Photos revealed Sister Lucia smiling "bright as the sun" as she stood with the Pope after her private meeting with him. Sister Lucia had waited long for the collegial consecration and while millions of petitions had gone to the popes over the years, it now was officially conducted by the Pope right at Fatima itself, 65 years after the first apparition of Our Lady.

Before the papal pilgrimage, speculation was carried in the papers as journalists again made statements to the effect: "The four-day visit may shed some light on the third secret of Fatima." However, the Pope had much greater things on his mind. The Pope spoke:

> And so I come here today because on this very day last year, in Saint Peter's Square in Rome, the attempt on the Pope's life was made, in mysterious coincidence with the anniversary of the first apparition at Fatima, which occurred on 13 May 1917.
>
> I seemed to recognize in the coincidence of the dates a special call to come to this place. And so, today I am here. I have come in order to thank Divine Providence in this place which the Mother of God seems to have chosen in a particular way. *Misericordiae Domini, quia non sumus consumpti* (Through God's mercy we were spared—Lam. 3:22). . . .
>
> The Church has always taught and continues to proclaim that God's revelation was brought to completion in Jesus Christ, who is the fullness of that revelation, and that "no new public revelation is to be expected before the glorious manifestation of our Lord." (*Dei Verbum*, 4). The Church evaluates and judges private revelations by the criterion of conformity with the single public Revelation.
>
> If the Church has accepted the message of Fatima, it is above all because that message contains a truth and a call whose basic content is the truth and the call of the Gospel itself.
>
> "Repent, and believe in the gospel" (Mk. 1:15): these are the first words that the Messiah addressed to humanity. The message of Fatima is, in its basic nucleus, a call to conversion and repentance, as in the Gospel.
> . . .
>
> When Jesus on the Cross said: 'Woman, behold, your son' (Jn. 19:26), in a new way he opened his Mother's Heart, the Immaculate Heart, and revealed to it the new dimensions and extent of the love to which she was called in the Holy Spirit by the power of the sacrifice of the Cross.
>
> In the words of Fatima we seem to find this dimension of motherly love, whose range covers the whole of man's path towards God; the path

that leads through this world and that goes, through Purgatory, beyond this world. The solicitude of the Mother of the Saviour, is solicitude for the work of salvation: the work of her Son. It is solicitude for the salvation, the eternal salvation, of all. Now that sixty-five years have passed since that 13 May 1917, it is difficult to fail to notice how the range of this salvific love of the Mother embraces, in a particular way, our century.

In the light of a mother's love we understand the whole message of the Lady of Fatima. The greatest obstacle to man's journey toward God is sin, perseverance in sin, and finally, denial of God. The deliberate blotting out of God from the world of human thought. The detachment from him of the whole of man's earthly activity. The rejection of God by man.

In reality, the eternal salvation of man is only in God. Man's rejection of God, if it becomes definitive, leads logically to God's rejection of man (cf. Mt. 7:23, 10:33), to damnation.

And so, while the message of Our Lady of Fatima is a motherly one, it is also strong and decisive. It sounds severe. It sounds like John the Baptist speaking on the banks of the Jordan. It invites to repentance. It gives a warning. It calls to prayer. It recommends the Rosary.

The message is addressed to every human being. The love of the Saviour's Mother reaches every place touched by the work of salvation. Her care extends to every individual of our time, and to all the societies, nations and peoples. Societies menaced by apostasy, threatened by moral degradation. The collapse of morality involves the collapse of societies.

The Pope went on to speak of the meaning of consecration: "Consecrating the world to the Immaculate Heart of Mary means drawing near, through the Mother's intercession, to the very Fountain of life that sprang from Golgotha. This Fountain pours forth unceasingly redemption and grace. In it reparation is made continually for the sins of the world. It is a ceaseless source of new life and holiness."

Consecrating ourselves to Mary means accepting her help to offer ourselves and the whole of mankind to Him who is Holy, infinitely Holy; it means accepting her help—by having recourse to her motherly Heart, which beneath the Cross was opened to love for every human being, for the whole world—in order to offer the world, the individual human being, mankind as a whole, and all the nations to Him who is infinitely Holy. God's holiness showed itself in the redemption of man, of the world, of the whole of mankind, and of the nations: a redemption brought about through the Sacrifice of the Cross. "For their sake I consecrate myself," Jesus had said (Jn. 17:19).

By the power of the redemption the world and man have been consecrated. They have been consecrated to Him who is infinitely Holy. They have been offered and entrusted to Love itself, merciful love.

The Mother of Christ calls us, invites us to join with the Church of the living God in the consecration of the world, in this act of confiding by which the world, mankind as a whole, the nations, and each individual person are presented to the Eternal Father with the power of the Redemption won by Christ. They are offered in the Heart of the Redeemer which was pierced on the Cross.

In its Dogmatic Constitution on the Church (*Lumen Gentium* and its Pastoral Constitution on the Church in the Modern World *Gaudium et Spes*) the Second Vatican Council amply illustrated the reasons for the link betwen *the Church and the world of today*. Furthermore, its teaching on Mary's special place in the mystery of Christ and the Church bore mature fruit in Paul VI's action in calling Mary *Mother of the Church* and thus indicating more profoundly the nature of her union with the Church and of her care for the world, for mankind, for each human being, and for all the nations: what characterizes them is her motherhood.

This brought a further deepening of *understanding of the meaning of the act of consecrating* that the Church is called upon to perform with the help of the Heart of Christ's Mother and ours.

Today John Paul II, successor of Peter, continuer of the work of Pius, John, and Paul, and particular *heir of the Second Vatican Council*, presents himself before the Mother of the Son of God in her Shrine at Fatima. In what way does he come?

He presents himself, reading again with trepidation the motherly call to penance, to conversion, the ardent appeal of the heart of Mary that resounded at Fatima sixty-five years ago. Yes, he reads again with *trepidation in his heart*, because he sees how many people and societies—how many Christians—have gone in *the opposite direction* to the one indicated in the message of Fatima. Sin has thus made itself firmly at home in the world, and denial of God has become widespread in the ideologies, ideas and plans of human beings.

But for this very reason the evangelical call to repentance and conversion, uttered in the Mother's message, remains ever relevant. It is still more relevant than it was sixty-five years ago. It is still more urgent. And so it is to be the subject of next year's *Synod of Bishops* which we are already preparing for.

The successor of Peter presents himself here also as *a witness to the immensity of human suffering*, a witness to the almost apocalyptic menaces looking over the nations and mankind as a whole. He is trying to embrace these sufferings with his own weak human heart, as he places himself before the mystery of the Heart of the Mother, the Immaculate Heart of Mary.

In the name of these sufferings and with awareness of the evil that is spreading throughout the world and menacing the individual human being, the nations, and mankind as a whole, Peter's successor presents himself

here with greater *faith in the redemption of the world*, in the saving Love
that is always stronger, always more powerful than any evil.

My heart is oppressed when I see the sin of the world and the whole
range of menaces gathering like a dark cloud over mankind, but it also
rejoices with hope as I once more do what has been done by my
Predecessors, when they consecrated the world to the Heart of the Mother,
when they consecrated especially to that Heart those peoples which particularly need to be consecrated. Doing this means consecrating the world
to Him who is infinite Holiness. This Holiness means redemption. It means
a love more powerful than evil. No "sin of the world" can ever overcome this Love.

Once more this act is being done. *Mary's appeal is not for just once*.
Her appeal must be taken up by generation after generation, in accordance with the ever new "signs of the times." It must be unceasingly
returned to. It must ever be taken up *anew*.

The author of the Apocalypse wrote: "And I saw the holy city, new
Jerusalem, coming down out of heaven from God, prepared as a bride
adorned for her husband; and I heard a loud voice from the throne saying, 'Behold, the dwelling of God is with men. He will dwell with them,
and they shall be his people, and God himself will be with them' " (Rev
21:2-3).

This is the faith by which the Church lives.

This is the faith with which the People of God makes its journey.

The dwelling of God is with men on earth even now.

In that dwelling is the Heart of the Bride and Mother, Mary, a Heart
adorned with the jewel of her Immaculate Conception. *The heart of the
Bride and Mother* which was opened beneath the Cross by the word of
her Son to a great new love for man and the world. The Heart of the Bride
and Mother which is *aware of all the sufferings* of individuals and societies
on earth.

The People of God is a pilgrim along the ways of this world *in an
eschatological direction*. It is making its pilgrimage towards the eternal
Jerusalem, towards "the dwelling of God with men." God will there "*wipe
away ever tear* from their eyes, and death shall be no more, neither shall
there be mourning nor crying nor pain any more, for the former things
have passed away."

But at present "the former things" *are still in existence*. They it is that
constitute the temporal setting of our pilgrimage.

For that reason we look towards "him who sits upon the throne and
says, 'Behold, I make all things new' " (cf. Rev 21:5).

And together with the Evangelist and Apostle we try to see with the
eyes of faith "the new heaven and the new earth"; for the first heaven
and the first earth have passed away.

But "*the first heaven and the first earth*" still exist about us and within *us. We cannot ignore it. But this enables us to recognize what an immense grace* was granted to us human beings when, in the midst of our pilgrimage, there shone forth on the horizon of the faith of our times this "great portent, a woman" (cf. Rev. 12:1).

Yes, truly we can repeat: "O daughter, you are blessed by the Most High God above all women on earth . . . walking in the straight path before our God . . . *you have avenged our ruin.*"

Truly indeed, you are blessed.

Yes, here and throughout the Church in the heart of every individual and in the world as a whole, may you be blessed, O Mary, our sweet Mother.

The news media, while the Pope was in Fatima, became obsessed with the attempt on the Pope's life. While it was significant that just one year earlier there was a near successful attempt on the Pope's life, leaving him within minutes of death, this time at Fatima another attacker did *not* succeed in touching the Pope. While the attacker at Fatima came within four or five feet of the Pope, Our Lady was not to permit any physical harm to her favorite son on earth, the Vicar of Jesus Christ, not while he was on her hallowed grounds in the Cova da Iria at Fatima.

What the news media did not address was the most significant act of all which took place at Fatima at May 13, 1982, *the collegial consecration of Russia to the Immacualte Heart of Mary.*

Forty years ago and again ten years later, your servant Pope Pius XII, having before his eyes the painful experience of the human family, *entrusted and consecrated to your Immaculate Heart* the whole world, especially the peoples for which you have particular love and solicitude.

This *world of individuals and nations* I too have before my eyes today, as I renew the entrusting and consecration carried out by my Predecessor in the See of Peter: the world of the second millennium that is drawing to a close, the modern world, our world today!

The Church, mindful of the Lord's words: "Go . . . and make disciples of all nations . . . and lo, I am with you always, to the close of the age" (Matt. 28:19-20), renewed, at the Second Vatican Council, her awareness of *her mission in this world.*

And therefore, *O Mother of individuals and peoples*, you who "know all their sufferings and their hopes," you who have a mother's awareness of all the struggles between good and evil, between light and darkness, which afflict the modern world, accept the cry which we, as though moved by the Holy Spirit, address directly to your Heart. *Embrace* with the *love* of the Mother and Handmaid, this human world of ours, which we entrust and consecrate to you, for we are full of disquiet for the earthly and eternal destiny of individuals and peoples.

In a special way we entrust and consecrate to you those individuals *and nations* which particularly need to be entrusted and consecrated.

"We have recourse to your protection, holy Mother of God: *reject not the prayers we send up to you in our necessities.*"

Reject them not!

Accept our humble trust—and our act of entrusting!

"For God so loved the world that He gave His only Son, that whoever believes in Him should not perish but have eternal life" (John 3:16).

It was precisely by reason of this love that the Son of God consecrated Himself for all mankind: "And for their sake I consecrate myself that they also may be consecrated in truth" (*John 17:19*).

By reason of that consecration the disciples of all ages are called to spend themselves for the salvation of the world, and to supplement Christ's afflictions for the sake of His Body, that is the Church (cf. II *Cor. 12:14; Col 1:24*).

Before you, Mother of Christ, before your Immacualte Heart, I today, together with the whole Church, unite myself with our Redeemer in this His consecration for the world and for people, which only in His Divine Heart has the power to obtain pardon and to secure reparation.

The power of this consecration lasts for all time and embraces all individuals, peoples, and nations. It overcomes every evil that the spirit of darkness is able to awaken, and has in fact awakened in our times, in the heart of man and in his history.

The Church, the Mystical Body of Christ, unites herself, through the service of Peter's successor, to this consecration by our Redeemer.

Oh, how deeply we feel the need for consecration on the part of humanity and of the world—our modern world— in union with Christ Himself! The redeeming work of Christ, in fact, must be *shared in by the world by means of the Church*.

Oh, how pained we are by all the things in the Church and in each one of us that are *opposed to holiness and consecration*! How pained we are that the invitation to repentance, to conversion, to prayer, has not met with the acceptance that it should have received!

How pained we are that many share so coldly *in Christ's work of redemptiont* That "what is lacking in Christ's afflictions" is so insufficiently completed in our flesh.

And so, blessed be all those souls that obey the call of eternal love! Blessed be all those who, day after day, with undiminished generosity accept your invitation, O Mother, to do what your Jesus tells them (cf. *John 2:5*) and give the Church and the world a serene testimony of lives inspired by the Gosepl.

Above all blessed be you, the Handmaid of the Lord, who in the fullest way obey the divine call!

Hail to you, who *are wholly united* to the redeeming consecration of your Son!

Mother of the Church! Enlighten the People of God along the paths of faith, of hope, and love! Help us to live with the whole truth of the consecartion of Christ for the entire human family of the modern world.

In entrusting to you, O Mother, the world, all individuals and peoples, *we* also entrust to you the consecration itself, for the world's sake, placing it in your motherly Heart.

Oh, Immaculate Heart! Help us to conquer the menace of evil, which so easily takes root in the hearts of the people of today, and whose immeasurable effects alreay weigh down upon our modern world and seem to block the paths towards the future!

From famine and war deliver us.

From nuclear war, from incalculable self-destruction, from every kind of war, *deliver us*.

From sins against the life of man from its very beginning, *deliver us*.

From hatred and from the demeaning of the dignity of the children of God, *deliver us*.

From every kind of injustice in the life of society, both national and international, *deliver us*.

From readiness to trample on the Commandments of God, *deliver us*.

From attempts to stifle in human hearts the very truth of God, *deliver us*.

From sins against the Holy Spirit, *deliver us, deliver us*.

Accept, O Mother of Christ, this cry laden with the sufferings of all individual human beings, *laden with the sufferings* of whole societies.

Let there be revealed, once more, in the history of the world the infinite power *of merciful love*. May it put a stop to evil. May it transform consciences. May your Immaculate Heart reveal for all the *light of hope*.

The following is the letter which the Cardinal Secretary of State sent, on behalf of the Holy Father, to the Bishops of the world before going to Fatima May 13, 1982.

From many Bishops and also from a number of Episcopal Conferences, the Holy Father has received letters recalling the Message of Fatima and asking him to renew, by a collegial act, the consecration to the Immaculate Heart of Mary made by Pope Pius XII on 31 October 1942 and 7 July 1952 (cf. *AAS* 34 (1942), p. 318 and *AAS* 44 (1952), p. 511 copies of which are enclosed).

As is well known, Pope Paul VI made a reference to the 1942 act on 21 November 1964, on the occasion of the closing of the Third Session of the Second Vatican Ecumenical Council (cf. *AAS* 56 (1964), p. 1017), and His Holiness Pope John Paul II, on the Solemnities of Pentecost and of the Immaculate Conception last year, explicitly referred to both the above-mentioned acts.

I now fulfill the honoured task of informing you that in the course of his visit to Fatima on 13 May next, when he intends to thank the Blessed Virgin for having saved his life on the occasion of the attack of 13 May last year, the Holy Father also intends, in spiritual union with all the bishops of the world, to renew the two acts whereby Pope Pius XII entrusted the world to the Immaculate Heart of Mary.

As he asks you to begin now to accompany with your prayer his pilgrimage to Fatima, in order that it may serve to increase in the Church devotion to the Blessed Virign and be to the glory of the Most Holy Trinty, His Holiness cordially sends you his special Apostolic Blessing, which he willingly extends to all in your pastoral care.

An eminent Marian theologian in Europe once told me that the Holy Spirit is speaking in the Church today through Our Lady of Fatima. The words of Pope John Paul at Fatima were especially meaningful in light of this: "Mary's spiritual motherhood is therefore a sharing in the power of the Holy Spirit, of 'the giver of life.' " Just five months later at Rome the Pope was to canonize the geat Marian Saint of these times, Saint Maximilian Kolbe who wrote boldly of Mary and the Holy Spirit:

> The Most Blessed Virgin is the one in whom we venerate the Holy Spirit, for she is his spouse. The third Person of the Blessed Trinity never took flesh; still, our human word 'spouse' is far too weak to express the reality of the relationship between the Immaculata and the Holy Spirit. We can affirm that she is, *in a certain sense*, the 'incarnation' of the Holy Spirit. It is the Holy Spirit that we love in her; and through her we love the Son.

Father Kolbe was careful to qualify his strong statement with *"in a certain sense."* In the last of his writings he wrote: "The Son is incarnate: Jesus Christ. The Holy Sirit is quasi-incarnate; the Immaculata." Father Kolbe developed his theology of the Holy Spirit as the Immaculate Conception of God the Father and God the Son within the Holy Trinity, the Person of Love which they conceive together and he was thus astonished at Mary saying at Lourdes, "I am the Immaculate Conception." There was such a profound union of wills between Mary, the Immaculata, and the Holy Spirit, as Mary surrendered totally to the Holy Spirit that Mary's will is absolutely conformed to that of the Holy Spirit as a dutiful and good spouse would be. The Holy Spirit dwelling in Mary finds Her a choicest temple, a temple of Light.

When God calls us to devotion and consecration to the Immaculate Heart of His Mother, in light of these meditated truths, we see in it a call to con-form our will to that of the Holy spirit as Mary did, who, under the action of the Holy Spirit pondered and responded perfectly to the Word of God. Pope John Paul II at Fatima in 1982 re-echoed Pius XII who had said: "Fatima is a reaffirmation of the Gospels." Pope John Paul put it this way: "that message contains a truth and a call whose basic content is the truth and the call of the Gospel itself." At Fatima Pope John Paul reminded us that entrusting the world and ourselves "the Immaculate Heart of Mary means drawing near, through the Mother's intercession, to the very Fountain of life that sprang from Golgotha. . . . Entrusting the world (and ourselves) to the Immaculate Heart of the Mother means returning beneath the Cross of the Son."

The words of the Pope are a call to Eucharistic Reparation, for does not the Sacrifice of the Mass perpetuate the infinite act of reparation, Calvary, since "entrusting" ourselves to the Immaculate Hearts "means returning beneath the Cross of the Son?"

On July 13, 1917 Mary announced: "God wishes to establish in the world devotion to my Immaculate Heart." On May 13, 1982 the Vicar of Christ came to Fatima to call the world to entrust itself to the Immaculate Heart. Sister Lucia has said that we must now respond to that consecration. We must live the consecration.

In what has been called the "Last Vision," Sister Lucia (June 1929) had revealed to her the Mystery of the Most Holy Trinity "which I am not permitted to reveal." At Fatima Pope John Paul II called Mary the "dwelling-place of the Most Holy Trinity." As Sister Lucia saw representations of the Most Holy Trinity, under the left arm of the cross were large letters, as of crystal clear water which ran down over the altar, and formed these words: "Graces and Mercy."

Pope John Paul II at Fatima called the world back to what Lucia says was revealed in the "Last Vision." Speaking of sufferings and evil in the world and which menaces the individual human bineg, "Peter's successor presents himself here with greater faith in the redemption of the world, in the saving Love that is always more powerful than any evil." In the words of consecration, the Pope asked that there be revealed, once more, "in the history of the world the infinite power of merciful love."

Consecration to Mary makes living realities for each of us of the rela-tionships established at our baptism. Jesus became Lord of our lives. The Holy Spirit Who filled Jesus from His conception entered us too. Christ's Father became our Father. His mother became our mother. Consecration to Mary then is really living our baptism. The message is clear to those "pure of heart." If we do not understand the message, it is because we are not disposed to understand in love the Mother of God, the Mother of the Church, the "Lady of the Message." To understand the message we must undertand the Mother who brings it.

Devotion to the Immaculate Heart of Mary will require an openness, a surrender to the Holy Spirit in faith, reparation, prayer, and love, with Mary, Spouse of the Holy Spirit, as Model. At every Sacrifice of the Mass, where we return to our place beneath the Cross, we also re-consecrate ourselves to Mary's Immaculate Heart. Devotion to the Immaculate Heart of Mary gives cause to look to the message of Fatima, to her whom Pope Paul II called our "Lady of the Message" as the Hope of the World.

Appendix
Prayers Taught at Fatima

Eucharistic Prayer

Most Holy Trinity, I adore You! My God, My God, I love You in the Most Blessed Sacrament.

Sacrifice Prayer

O my Jesus, it is for love of You, in reparation for the offenses committed against the Immaculate Heart of Mary, and for the conversion of poor sinners.

Angel's Prayer

O Most Holy Trinity, Father, Son and Holy Spirit, I adore Thee profoundly. I offer Thee the Most Precious Body, Blood, Soul and Divinity of Jesus Christ, present in all the Tabernacles of the world, in reparation for the outrages, sacrileges and indifference by which He is offended. By the infinite merits of the Sacred Heart of Jesus, and the Immaculate Heart of Mary, I beg the conversion of poor sinners.

Pardon Prayer

My God, I believe, I adore, I trust and I love Thee! I beg pardon for those who do not believe, do not adore, do not trust, and do not love Thee.

Decade Prayer

O my Jesus, forgive us; save us from the fire of Hell; take all souls to Heaven, especially those most in need.

Novena Prayer

(For private recitation. With ecclesiastical approval of the Bishop of Leiria-Fatima, December 17, 1974.)

My God, I love You in thanksgiving for the graces which You have granted to me.

Oh my Jesus, I love You! Sweet Heart of Mary, be my Salvation.

Most Holy Trinity, Father, Son and Holy Spirit, I adore Thee profoundly with all the powers of my soul, and I thank Thee for the apparitions of the Most Holy Virgin in Fatima which have made manifest to the world the treasures of her Immaculate Heart.

By the infinite merits of the Sacred Heart of Jesus and through the intercession of the Immaculate Heart of Mary, I implore Thee—if it should be for Thy greater glory and the good of souls—to glorify in the sight of Thy Holy Church, Jacinta the shepherdess of Fatima, granting us through her intercession the grace which we implore. Amen. (Our Father, Hail Mary, Glory Be.)

Pledge To Our Lady

Dear Queen and Mother, who promised at Fatima to convert Russia and bring peace to all mankind, in reparation to your Immaculate heart for my sins and the sins of the whole world, I solemnly promise: 1) To offer up every day the sacrifices demanded by my daily duty; 2) To say part of the Rosary (five decades) daily while meditating on the Mysteries; 3) To wear the Scapular of Mt. Carmel as profession of this promise and as an act of consecration to you. I shall renew this promise often, especially in moments of temptation.

Signature_____

(Note: This pledge is not a vow and does not bind under pain of sin. Nevertheless, it is a promise, your word given to your Heavenly Mother. You may care to make a copy of it and mail it to Ave Maria Institute ; Washington, N.J. 07882.

Those who desire continued information on the worldwide Fatima apostolate should subscribe to *Soul Magazine*, available from the same address. The last eight pages of each issue are dedicated to the Cadets of Our Lady of Fatma, a Fatima youth apostolate of which Father Fox is the national spiritual director.)

Additional Sources of Information About Fatima

Fatima, In Lucia's Own Words (Memoirs ordered by her Bishop) Stella Maris Books, P.O. Box 11483 Fort Worth, Texas 76110

*Catholic Truth for Youth by Father Robert J. Fox. (This book is based on statement of Pope Pius XII, "Fatima is a reaffirmation of the Gospel.") Ave Maria Press, Washington, N.J. 07882

*The Marian Catechism by Fr. Robert J. Fox. Our Sunday Visitor Press, 200 Noll Plaza, Huntington, Indiana 46750

*The Call of Heaven, Br. Gino, Stigmatist by Father Robert J. Fox. This book relates the Fatima message as lived in the life of a Stigmatist still living. Christendom Publications; Route 3, Box 87, Front Royal, Va. 22630.

Fatima The Great Sign by Francis Johnston. Ave Maria Press, Washington, N.J. 07882

The Secret of Fatima by Fr. Joaquin Maria Alonso, C.M.F. The Ravengate Press, Cambridge, Mass. 02138

1917: Red Banners, White Mantle by Warren H. Carroll. Christendom Publications, Route 3, Box 87, Front Royal, Va. 22630

Fatima From the Beginning by Fr. John De Marchi, I.M.C. Edocoes: Missoes Consolata—Fatima, Portugal.

Our Lady of Light by Barthas and Fonseca, S.J. Bruce Publishing Co. (1947).

The Finger of God is Here by G.L. Baker. Society of St. Paul, Middle Green, Langley, Bucks.

Dear Bishop by John M. Haffert (History of the Blue Army) AMI International Press, Washington, N.J. 07882.

Soul—bi-monthly Fatima Publication. Ave Maria Institute, Washington, NJ 07882. Fr. Fox writes in each issue for the national Fatima Youth Apostolate ($2.00 per year)

More About Fatima by Fr. V. Montes De Oca, C.S.Sp. Marian Centre, Big Bear Plaza, Neutral Bay, Sydney, N.S.W. 2089

*10 Sermons on the Mother of God (based on Fatima and Vatican II) by Fr. Robert J. Fox, Ave Maria Press, Washington, NJ 07882

*Saints & Heroes Speak by Fr. R.J. Fox. Ave Maria Press, Washington, NJ 07882 (This book tells the life story not only of the three Fatima children, but of other saints who have lived the Fatima message).

*Prayerbook for Young Catholics by Fr. Robert J. Fox. Our Sunday Visitor Press, 200 Noll Plaza, Hungtington, Indiana 46750. (This prayerbook incorporates the spirituality of Fatima into balanced prayers for young

Catholics).
Rediscovering Fatima by Fr. Robert J. Fox. Our Sunday Visitor Press,
200 Noll Plaza, Huntington, Indiana 46750

*These titles are by Fr. Fox.

The publication of this book was made possible in part through the support of the Christendom Publishing Group. Members are listed below:

Mr. Wil Van Achthoven
All Saints Religious Art and Books
Anonymous
Anonymous
Mr. & Mrs. Edward Baryla
Mr. & Mrs. John and Opal Baye
Mr. Joseph C. Berzanskis
Mr. John F. Bradley
Mr. George Bridgman
Mr. & Mrs. Robert Brindle
Mrs. Martha Brown
Mrs. Robert C. Bryant
Paul A. Busam, M.D.
Mr. Robert M. Caley
Mr. Thomas Calvo
Mr. Charles M. Campbell
Miss Priscilla Carmody
Mr. Herb Cary
Joseph C. Cascarelli, Esq.
Mrs. Virginia J. Chipp
Mrs. S. J. Conner
Rev. Edward J. Connolly
Mr. John W. W. Cooper
Mr. & Mrs. Chris N. Cuddeback
Msgr. Cusack, St. Richard Parish
Mr. Robert J. Cynkar
Mrs. Ellen L. Dalby
Sr. M. Damian
The Dateno Family
Mr. B. P. Davidson
Mrs. Jack Deardurff
Rev. Herman J. Deimel
Mrs. George de Lorimier
Rev. Robert J. Dempsey
Mr. Joseph L. DeStefano
Rev. Daniel B. Dixon
Mr. Thomas C. Domeika
Mr. Francis Donahue
Mr. & Mrs. Leon W. Doty
Mr. Thomas J. Dowdall
Mr. Edward A. Dreis
Mr. John H. Duffy
Rev. J. A. Duraczynski
Mrs. Clarence Ebert

Mr. D. N. Ehart
Mr. Clinton M. Elges
Sister Ellen, S.J.W.
Mr. William W. Elliott
Rev. George S. Endal, S. J.
Mr. Francis G. Fanning
Mr. & Mrs. Victor Fernandez
Mrs. Gilda Fidell
Miss Margaret C. Fitzgerald
Mr. Eugene P. Foeckler, Sr.
Mr. John F. Foell
Mrs. Donald B. Fox, M.D.
Mr. J. P. Frank, Jr.
Mrs. Claudette Fredricksen
Mrs. Adele Fricke
Mr. Edward Patrick Garrigan
Mr. Richard L. Gerhards
Gysgt. R. P. Gideon
Mr. Patrick Guinan
Mrs. Paula Haigh
Rev. A. A. Halbach
Mr. Robert E. Hanna
Mrs. Mary J. Hart
Mr. Frank E. Hauck
Mr. David Havlicek
Rev. Brian J. Hawker
Mrs. Francis Heaverlo
Rev. Herman L. Heide
Rev. Hugh P. Henneberry, S.S.J.
Rev. Albert J. Herbert, S.M.
Mrs. W. Herbert
Mr. E. P. Holcombe
Arthur Hopkins, M.D.
Mr. & Mrs. André Huck
Mrs. Doris L. Huff
Edgar Hull, M.D.
Rev. Jeffrey A. Ingham
Mr. Herman Jadloski
Mr. & Mrs. Dave Jaszkowiak
Mr. Marley Francis Jones
Mr. Daniel P. Judge
Mr. Edward E. Judge
Mr. & Mrs. Albert Kais
Mrs. Betty Kelly

Rev. Michael J. Kelly
Mr. & Mrs. Frank Knoell
Mr. John R. Knoll
Mr. William C. Koneazny
James W. Lassiter, M.D.
Miss Thérèse Lawrence
Rev. Harry J. Lewis
Very Rev. Victor O. Lorenz
Mrs. Carolyn C. MacDonald
Mrs. Katherine I. MacDonald
Mr. George F. Manhardt
Mr. Thomas Manning
Mrs. Jeanette Maschmann
N. Anthony Mastropietro, M.D.
Mr. Thomas J. May
Rev. Mark G. Mazza
Mrs. W. C. McCarthy
Rev. William R. McCarthy
John A. McCarty, Esq.
Mr. James McConnell
Mr. Robert McConville
Mrs. Miriam McCue
Robert E. McCullough, M.D.
Mr. Joseph D. McDaid
Mr. & Mrs. Dennis P. McEneany
Rev. P. J. McHugh
Mr. Thomas A. McLaughlin
Mr. J. R. McMahon
Mr. Robert Cruise McManus
Mrs. Kenneth McNichol
Rev. Edward J. Melvin, C.M.
Mr. Larry G. Miezio
Mr. Larry Miggins
Mr. Michael P. Millner
Mr. Joseph Monahan
Rev. Hugh Monmonier
Mr. James B. Mooney (St. Gerard
  Foundation)
Mrs. Gertrude G. Moore
Miss A. Morelli
Col. Chester H. Morneau
Mrs. Stella Morrison
Mr. Nicholas J. Mulhall
Mr. Frank Newlin
Mr. Joseph F. O'Brien
Rev. Philip O'Donnell
Mr. & Mrs. Tim O'Donnell
Mr. John F. O'Shaughnessy, Jr.
Mr. Lawrence P. O'Shaughnessy
Mrs. Veronica M. Oravec

Mrs. John F. Parker
Mr. Ernest Patry
Rev. Laszlo Pavel
Mr. & Mrs. Bill Peffley, The Catholic
  Shop
Robert N. Pelaez, M.D.
Mr. & Mrs. Joseph and Mary Peek
Mr. Alfred H. Pekarek
Robert N. Palaez, M.D.
Mr. & Mrs. William H. Power, Jr.
Mr. Stuart Quinlan
Mrs. Mary F. Quinn
Dr. William E. Rabil
Rev. T. A. Rattler, O.S.A.
Mr. & Mrs. Joseph E. Rau
Rev. Robert A. Reed
Mrs. John F. Reid
Mr. & Mrs. John J. Reuter
Mrs. John B. Reynolds
Dr. Charles E. Rice
Bro. Philip Romano, O.F.M. Cap.
Mr. Bernard J. Ruby
Mr. G. Salazar
Mr. Richard W. Sassman
Mr. & Mrs. George Scanlon
Mrs. Marian C. Schatzman
Miss Constance M. Scheetz
Mrs. Margaret Scheetz
Mrs. Francis R. Schirra
Mrs. Clargene Schmidt
Mrs. Job A. Schumacher
Mr. & Mrs. Ralph Schutzman
Mr. Frank P. Scrivener
Dr. John B. Shea
John R. Sheehan, M.D.
Mrs. Anne Sherman
Mr. W. R. Sherwin
Mrs. Bernice Simon
Mr. Richard M. Sinclair, Jr.
Capt. Arthur Sippo
Mrs. Walter Skorupski
Mr. S. C. Sloane
Mrs. Mary Smerski
Mr. Vincent C. Smith
Mrs. William Smith
Mrs. Ann Spalding
Miss Anne M. Stinnett
Mr. Edward S. Szymanski
Mr. Raymond F. Tesi
Rev. Clyde Tillman

Mr. Dominic Torlone
Mr. Clifford Towle
Mr. Christ Twohig
Mr. & Mrs. Albert Vallone
Rev. Frederick J. Vaughn
Mr. William C. Vinet, Jr.
Mrs. Margaret Vogenbeck
Rev. George T. Voiland
Mr. & Mrs. David and Marie Walkey
Honorable Vernon A. Walters

Mr. Fulton John Waterloo
Mr. Ralph A. Wellings
Mr. Alfred L. White
Mr. John R. Wilhelmy
Mrs. Mary Williams
Mrs. Mary Wimmenauer
Mr. Michael C. Winn
Mr. Walter D. Young
James F. Zimmer, M.D.